CW01648880

THE PINK BOOK: Legislation

for tourist accommodation and attractions

13TH EDITION

Published by VisitEngland,
Victoria Square House,
Victoria Square,
Birmingham B2 4AJ.
Publishing Manager: Hannah Lowe

Disclaimer

No advice
This Pink Book contains general information about laws applicable to your business. The information is not advice, and should not be treated as such.

Limitation of warranties
The legal information on the Pink Book is provided "as is" without any representations or warranties, express or implied. VisitBritain/VisitEngland makes no representations or warranties in relation to the information in the Pink Book.
Without prejudice to the generality of the foregoing paragraph, VisitBritain/VisitEngland does not warrant that:

- the information in this Pink Book will be constantly available, or available at all; or
- the information in this Pink Book is complete, true, accurate, up-to-date, or non-misleading

Professional assistance
You must not rely on the information in this Pink Book as an alternative to legal advice from your attorney or other professional services provider.
If you have any specific questions about any legal matter you should consult your attorney or other professional services provider.
You should never delay seeking legal advice, disregard legal advice, or commence or discontinue any legal action because of information in this Pink Book.

Liability
Nothing in this disclaimer will limit any of our liabilities in any way that is not permitted under applicable law, or exclude any of our liabilities that may not be excluded under applicable law.

ISBN: 978-0-7095-8415-5
Printed in England

Legislation for tourist accommodation and attractions

Welcome to the thirteenth edition of VisitEngland's *Pink Book: Legislation for tourist accommodation and attractions*.

The Pink Book has always been recognised as providing significant support to the tourism sector. It provides a common sense approach to helping tourism businesses understand their legal obligations.

The guidance contained here is also available online at **visitengland.org/pinkbookonline** – this is updated as legislation changes.

Keeping up to date with legislation

If you run a tourist accommodation business or visitor attraction, or are involved with running or advising tourism businesses, you need to be aware of the legislation that applies. There is a wide range of applicable legislation. Customers are increasingly demanding higher quality and are becoming more aware of their rights. Complying with legislative requirements helps you to meet these expectations and avoid claims, prosecution and fines.

This book provides practical guidance on the legislation relevant to accommodation and visitor attraction providers in England. For legislation relevant to those outside England, please contact the relevant National Tourist Board.

Using the book

This book is arranged into nine main sections, as follows, each of which contains a number of topics. Page tabs have been provided to help you quickly reach the section you need:

- Licences & Consents
- Marketing
- Customers
- Food & Drink

- Environmental Protection
- Health & Safety
- Staff
- Business Management & Tax
- Further Information

The final section, Further Information, provides details of where to go for further help and a list of useful websites and definitions.

See the Contents page or **visitengland.org/pinkbookonline** for an immediate pointer to these main sections and topics or go to the Index at the back of the book for an alphabetical listing of the subjects and legislation covered.

Legislation which has been updated since the 12th edition of the Pink Book (published 2023) is identified by an 'Updated' tab in the margin. New information is identified by a 'New' tab in the margin. All content is correct as of January 2025.

Disclaimer

No advice

This Pink Book contains general information about laws applicable to your business. The information is not advice, and should not be treated as such.

Limitation of warranties

The legal information on the Pink Book is provided "as is" without any representations or warranties, express or implied. VisitBritain/VisitEngland makes no representations or warranties in relation to the information in the Pink Book.

Without prejudice to the generality of the foregoing paragraph, VisitBritain/VisitEngland does not warrant that:

- the information in this Pink Book will be constantly available, or available at all; or
- the information in this Pink Book is complete, true, accurate, up-to-date, or non-misleading

Professional assistance

You must not rely on the information in this Pink Book as an alternative to legal advice from your attorney or other professional services provider.

If you have any specific questions about any legal matter you should consult your attorney or other professional services provider.

You should never delay seeking legal advice, disregard legal advice, or commence or discontinue any legal action because of information in this Pink Book.

Liability

Nothing in this disclaimer will limit any of our liabilities in any way that is not permitted under applicable law, or exclude any of our liabilities that may not be excluded under applicable law.

Welcome to the 13th Edition of the *Pink Book*

The Pink Book is an important tool for England's tourism businesses, providing a repository of easy to use, practical guidance on legislation. It is vital in supporting the industry to maintain its high standards and assisting hard-working businesses in meeting their regulatory obligations.

We are committed to working with our stakeholders to support tourism businesses and grow the visitor economy in an inclusive, accessible and sustainable way, ensuring that all corners of England continue to be a fantastic place to visit.

The content provided here can also be found digitally as the Pink Book Online in VisitEngland's Business Advice Hub, which is kept up to date as legislation changes.

Tourism is one of England's largest and most valuable industries, supporting hundreds of thousands of small-to-medium sized businesses, employing 2.6 million people and generating about £71.6 billion annually for the economy in domestic visitor spending.

We wish your business every success as we all do our bit to allow English tourism to flourish long into the future.

Andrew Stokes OBE, VisitEngland Director

Contents

HEALTH & SAFETY

STAFF

BUSINESS MANAGEMENT & TAX

FURTHER INFORMATION

Alcohol, entertainment and gaming licensing

KEY FACTS

- If you wish to sell alcoholic drinks you will need a licence. This includes providing 'free' alcohol to customers.
- There are two types of licence: premises licences and personal licences.
- It is illegal to buy alcohol from a wholesaler who is not registered.
- For gaming machines, other than skills with prizes (SWP) machines, you will need a licence or permit from your local licensing authority and possibly from the Gambling Commission.

Does the legislation apply to me?

If you wish to sell alcoholic drinks you will need an alcohol licence. It is an offence to sell intoxicating liquor without one.

Providing 'free' alcohol to guests

You need a licence to sell alcohol – this includes providing 'free' alcohol because it is an incentive to purchase and/or is included in your pricing structure. If you charge the customer to enter or stay at your premises, or for some other product that must be purchased in order to receive the free alcohol, this means that they are essentially paying for the alcohol that is provided. In other words, the customer has effectively paid a 'consideration' for that service. It is not free.

The Licensing Act 2003

The **Licensing Act 2003** rationalised the previous licensing systems (in England and Wales) to produce a simpler system that is easier for all involved to understand.

Local authorities are required to consult on their statement of licensing policy every three years. Before applying for a licence, it is therefore important for you to read this policy. This will enable you to tailor your application to the local authority's policy and thereby reduce the risk of your application being rejected.

Administration and enforcement

Administration and enforcement of the Licensing Act 2003 lies with local authorities (and other agencies where appropriate), for example fire safety, police, licensing officers, and environmental health. Each local authority has a licensing committee of 10 to 15 locally elected councillors who decide on licensing applications.

In practice, their responsibilities are devolved to a licensing manager and staff who deal with the administrative functions. All contested applications will be heard before a sub-committee of at least three members of that committee.

Licensing objectives

There are four principles which underpin the Licensing Act 2003 and impact everyone. They are:

- The prevention of crime and disorder;
- Public safety;
- The prevention of public nuisance;
- The protection of children from harm (including sexual exploitation).

These principles are the key elements to be addressed by applicants, local authorities, police and other statutory authorities, and objectors to your licence.

Licensable activities

Activities regulated by the **Licensing Act 2003** fall into one of the following four categories:

- The sale of alcohol;
- The supply of alcohol by or on behalf of a club;
- Provision of regulated entertainment;
- Provision of late-night refreshments.

The activities that tourism businesses should be familiar with are as follows:

Provision of regulated entertainment

Regulated entertainment includes many of the activities offered for the benefit of customers in, for example, attractions, public houses, hotels, guesthouses or club rooms at caravan parks. These may include:

- Dancing, either as a show for customers or as an activity for

them to take part in;
- Films (defined as any showing of moving pictures) not being shown in a community premises;
- Plays;
- All indoor sporting events (physical skills must be a factor);
- Music, such as the public playing of recorded music (for example DJs) as an accompaniment to dancing. (See *Live Music Act 2012* below).

Provision of late-night refreshment

Provision of late-night refreshment covers the supply of hot food or drinks from premises for consumption on or off premises between 11pm and 5am. This aspect is mainly focused on late-night takeaway premises, so an exception is made for the provision of refreshments by hotels, guesthouses, hostels and caravan sites.

However, if you have a restaurant which serves hot food and drinks to members of the public after 11pm, or are staging an event at an attraction where hot food and drink will be provided to customers such as a midnight movie, you will need to nominate this as one of your licensable activities. Should you have any doubts about what should be included as licensable activities, your local licensing authority will be able to give advice.

Temporary Event Notices (TENs)

UPDATED

A Temporary Event Notice (TEN) is a licence to hold one-off licensable activities in unlicensed premises, and is particularly useful for attractions that want to stage a limited number of licensable events during the year. A single event can last up to seven days, and you are limited to a maximum of five per year if you do not hold a personal licence or 50 if you do. No more than 15 TENs can be given to a single premises in any calendar year, and the total length of the events cannot exceed 21 days. Events covered by a TEN can only be attended by a maximum of 499 people, and there must be a minimum of 24 hours between consecutive events.

The *Temporary Event Notice* section of Gov.uk gives more information related to TENs and how to apply for one.

Types of licences

There are two types of licence:
- **Premises licence:** required for any premises that offer any of the licensable activities previously described.
- **Personal licence:** a separate, portable system of personal licences that provides authority to sell alcohol. Personal licences are valid indefinitely and do not need to be renewed.

A designated premises supervisor, who must be a personal licence holder, must be nominated for any premises where the licence includes permission to sell alcohol. In order to obtain a personal licence the applicant must be:

- Aged 18 or over;
- Possess an accredited licensing qualification;
- Not have forfeited a personal licence within five years of the application;
- Not have been convicted of any relevant offence.

To sell alcohol on your premises, you are required to have a premises licence and for at least one person to have a personal licence. That person does not have to be present on the premises to oversee the sale of alcohol, but is responsible for any sales made by other members of your staff.

Applying for a premises licence

Your application must embrace the four licensing objectives and you will need to assess any risks associated with each activity you propose to offer.

Advice can be obtained from the relevant statutory authority to achieve this, for example consulting a Fire Safety Officer about the means of escape under the public safety objective. The police may require CCTV or door supervisors (usually for premises which stay open until the early hours) under the prevention of crime and disorder objective. Environmental Health Officers may offer advice on noise arising from any associated music under the prevention of public nuisance objective.

All statutory authorities and your neighbours/local businesses must also confine themselves to the four licensing objectives if they make any representation or objections.

Application process

Applications are made to the local licensing authority where the premises are located. The forms will be available from the local authority's website and can be downloaded for completion together with guidance notes.

While the forms are relatively straightforward, you may wish to engage the services of a specialist licensing solicitor or consultant to assist you. The application can be made by anyone who undertakes, or proposes to undertake, any business involving licensable activities. It includes limited companies or partnerships. If the application is made by an individual, that person must be at least 18 years of age.

You can apply for any of the licensable activities which are applicable to your business. Be mindful, however, that you also have to serve a copy to the following statutory authorities:

- The Chief Officer of Police;
- The body recognised as responsible for the protection of children;
- Trading Standards officers;
- Local planning authority;
- Environmental health authority;
- Health and safety authority;
- Fire and rescue authority.

They will all wish to see that your premises and the activities you ask for are compatible.

For details of the responsible authorities in your area, contact your local licensing team. Details may also be available on your local authority's website.

Consultation

You are required to consult with your neighbours and local businesses in the area when seeking to gain a licence or to vary an existing licence. This can be done by placing an advert in a local newspaper, setting out the brief details of your application, and displaying a notice on your premises that advertises details to passers-by. The guidance notes will give advice on these procedures.

The consultation process lasts for 28 days, commencing on the day you submit the application to the local authority. Copies to the other statutory authorities (mentioned above) must be served at the same time.

Provided that there are no unresolved objections or representations, the licensing authority will automatically issue your premises licence without you having to attend any meetings. Should there be any representations or objections which cannot be resolved by negotiation, the licensing authority will hold a hearing within 20 working days (from the end of the consultation period) to determine the application.

Fees

There are two sets of fees when applying for a premises licence. Both are based on rating bands, and whether the primary or main purpose of the premises is to sell alcohol.

- The first fee is the cost to apply or to vary a licence.
- The second fee is the annual charge once the licence has been granted.

Once issued, the licence effectively lasts for as long as your business operates. The licence can be transferred from one licence holder to another. Again, the forms and guidance notes can be accessed on the local authority's website.

The *Alcohol Licensing* section of Gov.uk offers information related to the Licensing Act 2003 and the application process.

Variations to licences

Once a licence has been granted, licensees are required to operate within the conditions of the licence. If you would like a minor variation to these conditions, a simplified application process exists for this purpose. This process can only be used for variations that could have no adverse impact on any of the four licensing objectives.

For example, a Minor Variation Application could not be used in the following situations:

- To extend the period for which the licence or certificate has effect;
- To transfer the licence to other premises;
- To specify, in a premises licence, an individual as the premises' supervisor;
- To add the sale by retail or supply of alcohol as an activity;
- To authorise the sale of alcohol at any time between 11pm and 7am;
- To authorise an increase in the amount of time on any day during which alcohol may be sold.

The cost of applying for a Minor Variation Application has been set at £89, and the maximum time that licensing authorities are able to take to process the application has been set at 15 days. Unlike a major variation to a licence, there is no requirement to advertise or make other 'responsible authorities', such as the police, aware of your intention to seek a minor variation.

Mandatory Code for the sale of alcohol

In addition to the provisions of the Licensing Act, if you sell alcohol you are also required to comply with a Mandatory Code. This code:

- Bans businesses from undertaking irresponsible promotions that encourage people to drink quickly, or to drink more than they otherwise would. Examples include 'all you can drink for £10' or 'free drinks when a football team scores';
- Bans drinks being poured directly into customers' mouths, known as a 'dentist's chair';
- Requires operators to supply free tap water to customers;
- Requires businesses that sell alcohol to have an age-verification policy in place, and to check the ID of anyone who looks under 18;

- Requires businesses to sell alcohol in small measures (a half pint for beer and cider, 25ml or 35ml for spirits and 125ml for wine) as well as larger measures;
- Bans the sale of alcohol below the 'permitted price', which is defined as alcohol duty plus VAT. The Home Office has published the guide *Guidance on banning the sale of alcohol below the cost of duty plus VAT* to help businesses calculate the cost of duty and VAT for a range of products.

How long can I stay open?

While the Licensing Act created the opportunity to stay open 24 hours, very few premises (with the exception of supermarkets) actually operate these hours. You can apply to have any of the licensable activities on your premises starting and finishing at any time to suit you and/or your customers.

Bear in mind that the statutory authorities and your neighbours have to be notified and may not agree with your proposals. Common sense usually applies, and many establishments have extended their operating hours by perhaps one or two hours.

Who can I sell alcohol to?

Children aged 16 and 17 can consume alcohol as long as it is beer, cider or wine, it has been purchased for them by an adult, and it is consumed with a table meal. The adult must be with the child at all times.

You can also decide at what age children are allowed into the licensed areas of your premises. Therefore babies and very young children can be in your bar/restaurant, on the condition that they are accompanied by an adult.

Alcohol Wholesaler Registration Scheme

In response to the growing problem of counterfeit alcohol, the Government introduced the Alcohol Wholesaler Registration Scheme. All wholesale sellers of alcohol are required to register with HMRC. On registration, wholesalers receive a Unique Reference Number (URN) as proof that they are legally able to sell alcohol to businesses.

It is illegal to buy alcohol from a wholesaler who is not registered and able to provide you with their URN (you can check online whether a wholesaler is approved). If you buy your alcohol from an unregistered business, then you may be liable for a criminal or civil penalty and your alcohol may be seized. You must keep records to prove you have checked that your supplier is registered with HMRC.

Note: there is one important exemption to this scheme. Retailers who make occasional trade sales of alcohol are excluded, meaning that if you buy your alcohol from a supermarket or off-licence, then they will not be registered and you don't have to check their URN registration.

UPDATED

Pavement licences

A pavement licence is granted by the local authority and allows businesses in England such as cafés, restaurants and bars to place furniture on the pavement adjacent to their licenced premises. During the COVID-19 pandemic, the Government introduced a temporary streamlined process for businesses to apply for a pavement licence. On 31 March 2024, this was replaced by a permanent pavement licensing regime through the **Levelling Up and Regeneration Act**.

For a fixed fee of £500 for new applications (£350 for renewals), subject to a 14-day consultation period, businesses may use this licence to place the following furniture on the pavement outside their premises:

- Counters or stalls for selling or serving food or drink;
- Tables, counters or shelves on which food or drink can be placed;
- Chairs, benches or other forms of seating, and;
- Umbrellas, barriers, heaters and other articles used in connection with the outdoor consumption of food or drink.

Local authorities can specify the duration of the licence, although the Government's expectation is that licences will be valid for two years, unless there are good reasons for granting a licence for a shorter period such as plans for future changes in use of road space.

Guidance on the new pavement licencing regime is available on Gov.uk.

Note: temporary amendments to the Licensing Act 2003 allow premises with a licence for the sale of alcohol on the premises to sell alcohol for consumption off the premises without needing to apply for a variation of their licence. These temporary amendments apply if the premises had a licence for on-site consumption on 22 July 2020, and the premises still retain that licence. This temporary amendment will end on 31 March 2025.

Live Music Act 2012

The **Live Music Act 2012** exempts small licenced venues with audiences of up to 200 (including attractions, accommodation establishments, pubs, restaurants and community halls) from requiring a separate special licence to hold live shows with amplified music between 8am and 11pm. It also removes the need for a licence for unamplified live performances between 8am and 11pm in all venues.

However, operators will still have to gain a licence for any alcohol sales at such an event, and comply with any restrictions on the performances that are imposed by the licensing authority.

Gaming machines

The installation and use of gaming machines is covered by the **Gambling Act 2005**. Under this Act, 'gaming' means 'playing a game of chance for a prize'.

Skill With Prize machines (SWPs)

There are some machines that fall outside the Gambling Act 2005. Skill With Prize machines (SWPs) are not classified as gaming machines because they are deemed to be a game of skill, rather than a game controlled by chance.

These are machines where the customer displays a skill in order to win, rather than there being a large element of chance. An example of an SWP is a quiz machine found in pubs that tests the customer's knowledge. Some crane grab machines can also operate on a skill only basis, but must utilise a 'compensator' to regulate the number of prizes and are therefore games of chance and rules apply to their location, maximum permitted stake and prize (see below).

The vast majority of skill-based games, such as basketball-type games, are found in Family Entertainment Centres (more commonly known as seaside amusement arcades) but can be sited anywhere.

Gaming machine classification

The legislation regarding gaming machines is complex and there are a wide range of categories for gaming machines.

Category A, B1, B2, B3, B3A and B4 machines

Machines in categories A to B4 can only be used in a limited range of premises, such as casinos, betting shops, some membership clubs and Adult Gaming Centres (B4 machines).

Category C and D machines

This section relates to Category C and D gaming machines, which are mainly found in Family Entertainment Centres and pubs.

LICENCES & CONSENTS

The following table shows the range of Category C and D machines and the maximum stake and prizes for each type of machine.

Category	Maximum stake	Maximum prize
C	£1	£100
D money prize	10p	£5
D non-money prize (other than crane grab machine)	30p	£8
D non-money prize (crane grab machine)	£1	£50
D combined money and non-money prize (other than coin pusher or penny falls machines)	10p	£8 (of which no more than £5 may be a money prize)
D combined money and non-money prize (coin pusher or penny falls machines)	20p	£20 (of which no more than £10 may be a money prize)

Category C machines must be restricted to people aged 18 and over. There is no age restriction related to the use of category D machines.

Return To Player (RTP)

Category C and D machines must display the 'theoretical target percentage return to player' as well as a declaration of their category. Return To Player (RTP) is an average measured over a large number of games, and will vary over a typical session due to normal game volatility. It is up to the manufacturer to decide upon the game RTP and there is no minimum requirement, but the minimum average return must be displayed to the player for the game.

Gaming licensing

Family Entertainment Centre operating licence

Premises which are entirely or mainly used for making gaming machines available for use, such as small arcades (whether they be stand-alone arcades or arcades incorporated into larger premises such as a holiday park or attraction) are known as Family Entertainment Centres (FEC).

If you want to install any category C machines, you will need a Family Entertainment Centre operating licence (FEC licence), which is issued by the Gambling Commission. This licence allows you to operate an unlimited number of Category C and D gaming machines on a location that is open to all ages. However, Category C machines must be in a segregated part of the premises that is supervised, to prevent children and young people accessing those machines.

NEW

The cost of applying for this licence is £1,406, for premises with an annual gross gambling yield of up to £7.5m. If an application is successful, there is an annual fee related to the Annual Gross Gambling Yield which ranges from £1,150 for premises yielding up to £200,000 to £41,840 for premises yielding over £30m.

Unlicensed Family Entertainment Centres

If you want to run a Family Entertainment Centre that just operates Category D gaming machines, you do not need an FEC licence from the Gaming Commission. However, you will need an Unlicensed Family Entertainment Centre permit from your licensing authority.

Premises licence

If you have an alcohol licence for the premises, you are automatically entitled to install two Category C or D gaming machines upon notification to the local licensing authority of your intention to make gaming machines available for use. If you would like further machines, you need to apply to the licensing authority. Once you have installed machines you will also have to inform the licensing authority if you change the number or category of machines sited.

If the provision of gambling facilities is not the primary function of your business, and you would like to install just category D machines, then you will only need a gambling permit rather than a premises licence.

You should check the licensing requirements on your licencing authority's website as to the range of licences and permits available, and review their gambling statement or policy before you apply.

Further guidance

Alcohol licensing

Further information on all aspects of the Licensing Act 2003 is available on **Gov.uk**.

Pavement licences

Guidance on the updated process for pavement licences is available on **Gov.uk**.

Gambling Commission guidance

The Gambling Commission publishes guidance on all aspects of the Gambling Act 2005 and the requirements associated with installing gaming machines on their website: **gamblingcommission.gov.uk**

Your local authority

Information on licensing authority requirements is available from your local council.

The Purple Guide

The Events Industry Forum publishes *The Purple Guide*, with advice for staging events on your premises, from safety to waste disposal: **thepurpleguide.co.uk**

TV and copyright licences

KEY FACTS

- If you play recordings of any copyrighted music on your premises (this includes background music, or music made available on devices such as TVs and radios) or if the music is performed live, you may need TheMusicLicence from PPL PRS Ltd.
- If you play a TV in public areas with the sound on, you need TheMusicLicence from PPL PRS Ltd.
- If you offer short-stay accommodation (of any kind) to overnight visitors and have installed TVs in the accommodation, you need a 'Hotel and Mobile Units Television Licence' (hotel licence).
- If you offer a DVD film library, you need a DVD Concierge licence.
- If you operate an in-room entertainment system you need a Hotel Vision licence.
- If you show films or TV programmes, including channels such as ITV or BBC1, you need both an MPLC licence and a licence from AVLA.
- If you use images in your marketing, you must have permission to use them from the copyright owner.

Television licences

Do I need a special licence?

UPDATED

- **Maybe:** for non-accommodation businesses, you will need a licence if you provide a TV or a programme-streaming service such as NOW, ITVX or BBC iPlayer for either staff or customers on any part of your premises. If your premises is a single unit then you will only need a single TV licence at the standard rate of £169.50. However, if your business has multiple units (for example corporate boxes at a football stadium) then you will need a special Hospitality Licence which costs £169.50 for the first 15 units and £169.50 for each further five units.

LICENCES & CONSENTS
MARKETING
CUSTOMERS
FOOD & DRINK
ENVIRONMENTAL PROTECTION
HEALTH & SAFETY
STAFF
BUSINESS, MANAGEMENT & TAX
FURTHER INFORMATION

- **Yes:** if you offer short-stay accommodation to overnight visitors, whether in serviced or self-catering accommodation, and you provide a device on which your guests can view TV programmes, you need to apply for a 'Hotel and Mobile Units Television Licence' (hotel licence). It should be noted that a licence is required regardless of whether the TV programmes are viewed through a TV, computer, mobile phone, games console, digital box, DVD player or any other device.

Note: despite its name, the hotel licence encompasses accommodation ranging from hotels, guesthouses, bed and breakfasts and inns to holiday cottages, flats and chalets through to camping and caravan sites and narrowboats.

The TV Licensing Authority says that you should always take out a hotel licence if you are providing televisions for the use of paying guests. While staying on your property, guests are not covered by their home licence. There is one exception: long-term hotel residents (those staying more than 28 days) are not covered by a hotel licence, but they must have an ordinary television licence.

Note: while accommodation provided in sited caravans falls under the hotel licence scheme, there are different rules for touring caravans or mobile homes. The hirer of a touring caravan or mobile home may be covered by the licence for their home address, as long as the television receivers are not being used at their home and caravan or mobile home at the same time.

Hotel licence fees

UPDATED

Your licence fee will be based on the number of units of overnight accommodation that you have available to let:

- If you have up to 15 units with televisions installed, you will pay one full fee of £169.50.
- If you have more than 15 units, you will pay one full fee for the first 15, and an additional £169.50 for every extra five units (or fewer).
- The hotel licence is available only from TV Licensing. (See *Further guidance*, below).

What does the licence cover?

It will cover any equipment that can be used to watch or record TV programmes in:

- Hotels, inns, guest houses, holiday villages, caravans and campsites.
- The owner's private rooms on the site.
- On-site staff accommodation (if provided by the hotel/ accommodation owner).
- Lounges or other common rooms that are open to people staying on the site.

It does not cover:

- TV equipment which is not provided by the proprietor of the accommodation.
- TV equipment in long-term letting accommodation and for permanent residents.

Note: an important feature of the regulations is that a TV licence only covers one or more units if they are 'on the same site' or 'within the same premises'. That means a site or premises that is not divided or separated by any public thoroughfare such as a road or footpath or by another private property. For example, if you have a chain of businesses or your attraction spans two sides of a road, or your hotel has an annexe in a separate property next door or if you let holiday cottages in different locations, you will need a Company Group TV Licence.

If you have a TV in public areas, such as a bar or breakfast room, which has the sound turned on, you will also need TheMusicLicence from PPL PRS Ltd.

Copyright licences for music

The **Copyright, Designs and Patents Act 1988** states that any use of copyrighted music in public is possible only with the permission of the person who holds the copyright to the music being played.

'In public' means anything outside a family/domestic situation, and includes all areas of a tourism accommodation property, including guests' rooms. So, even if you just have a radio in the breakfast room or TVs in guests' rooms, you may require a licence.

There are two separate copyright licences that relate to the playing of copyrighted music on your premises. They apply regardless of the device provided by which the music is played, and even apply if the music is performed live.

The first music copyright licence fee is to pay the performers and record companies for the use of their recorded music. The fee for this licence is collected by PPL and is known as a PPL Licence.

The second music copyright licence fee is to pay the songwriters, composers and music publishers for the use of their musical compositions and lyrics. The fee for this licence is collected by PRS and the licence is known as a PRS Licence.

While PPL and PRS licences can be paid separately, the two collection companies also work together to provide a single licence that covers both copyright fees where this is required. This combined licence is called TheMusicLicence.

Do I need a music copyright licence?

No: You are exempt from requiring either a PPL or PRS music licence if:

- You have a bed and breakfast or guesthouse that has three guest bedrooms or less, and;
- The premises is the only holiday accommodation business that you own or operate;
- The premises is also your domestic residence;
- Facilities are only available to resident guests;
- You have a self-catering property which comprises fewer than four self-catering units (regardless of how many bedrooms there are in each unit), and:
  - The premises is the only holiday accommodation business that you operate;
  - Facilities are only available to resident guests.

Yes: you need a combined TheMusicLicence that covers both PPL and PRS copyright fees if you operate a business that is outside the exemptions detailed above.

Is a licence required for copyrighted music in customers' rooms?

Yes: a licence is required where music can be played in guests' rooms via TVs, radios and other devices that you provide for guests. A licence is not required where the guest provides their own device and, for example, plays music that they access through the internet.

The PPL PRS Code of Conduct clarifies the rights and responsibilities of PPL PRS and businesses that provide music. An ombudsman has also been established to oversee PPL PRS's performance and to adjudicate on complaints.

Tariffs

The tariffs relating to TheMusicLicence continue to be set by both PPL (representing the copyright for recordings) and PRS for Music (representing the copyright for songs being played) separately. Licence tariffs vary in accordance with the type of performance (live or recorded), the type of premises, the occasion and the frequency of performances.

There is a wide range of tariff rates depending on the type and scale of business you operate. They include separate tariffs for:

- Amusement parks, saloons, arcades, travelling showmen, funfairs;
- Parks, open-air places, pools;
- Cinemas;
- Theatres;
- Holiday centres;

- Holiday caravan parks;
- Hotels, restaurants and cafés;
- Pubs;
- Passenger ships and boats.

You can obtain more information by contacting the PPL PRS Customer Service Centre, on **0800 0720 808.**

Obtaining a licence

If a licence is required, you can find more information on the costs by viewing the separate tariff cards for each of the categories on the PPL PRS website.

PPL PRS has a dedicated section of its website for hotels, bed and breakfasts and guesthouses. You can view all the tariffs which relate to your establishment and a checklist of information needed to obtain a quote, which includes:

- Music in bedrooms;
- Number of bedrooms supplied or provided with recorded music;
- Background music – all premises;
- Areas where music is audible, such as receptions, bars, etc;
- Premises with 16 bedrooms or more;
- The square meterage of each area where music is audible;
- Number of seats in bar and restaurant areas where music is playing;
- Types of devices used to play music, such as radio, CDs, TV etc;
- Live events;
- Number and capacity of live events held per year.

Note: there are discounts available for businesses that are only open for part of the year, or only stage events or performances for part of the year.

Note: you are required by law to obtain a licence if you need one. If you apply for a licence before you start playing copyrighted music in a public place, you will be charged a standard rate. If you apply later, or are caught playing music without a licence, you will be charged a higher rate for the first year of the licence.

Discretionary charging policies

PPL and PRS for Music each separately operate a number of discretionary charging policies, setting out circumstances in which – while legally entitled to do so – they choose not to apply a charge. Due to the specific nature of these policies, it is advisable to contact them for more information and to check if any of them apply to you.

Copyright for showing films and TV programmes

A copyright licence is needed if customers can watch films on your premises, either on TV or via a service you provide, such as a supply of DVDs or streaming services such as Netflix.

There are three main film licensing companies. The first two, Motion Picture Licensing Company (MPLC) and Filmbankmedia, collect copyright royalties on behalf of different film studios in different circumstances. For example, though both MPLC and Filmbankmedia license the showing of films to audiences, MPLC collects the copyright for films shown on TV in commercial settings while Filmbankmedia provides films for businesses (such as hotels) to show on in-house entertainment systems.

Previously there has been an exemption for showing films and TV programmes via free-to-air services, for example if you have TVs that play films on channels such as BBC or ITV. However, you now need to gain a licence through the MPLC to provide this service to your customers. As with PPL PRS for audio copyright licensing, MPLC is a collection society which licenses rights on behalf of various film companies and TV producers.

There are three main licence types:

Showing films

If you have a business where you have a limited number of public screenings of films each year, or want to stage a one-off event, both MPLC and Filmbankmedia offer a Single Title Movie Licence with different rates – depending on the number of times the movie is shown, the size of the audience, and whether the audience pays an admission charge. For paying audiences, the MPLC cost is the greater of either £75 or 35% of the total ticket sales.

UPDATED

Communal areas

The MPLC operate an Umbrella Licence for businesses that show films on TV in public communal areas (e.g. bar, guest lounge, gym or reception) on an ongoing basis. The fee is set by the type of business and size of the area. For example, the fee for restaurants and cafés up to 500 sq m is £102.62 +VAT. A full table of the charges is available on the MPLC website: hotel.themplc.co.uk.

Alternatively, Filmbankmedia offers an annual Public Video Screening Licence (PVSL), which allows organisations to legally screen films to create background ambience within their premises.

Guest bedrooms

If you have TVs in guest bedrooms you will be required to pay the Hotel/Guest Bedroom tariff rate of £6.15 + VAT per bedroom per year, plus a charge of £126.10 for other areas of the premises where TVs are located which have a combined area of up to 500sqm. You can find more information on the MPLC website hotel.themplc.co.uk.

Note: an MPLC licence is not required if you only have a TV in a public area of your establishment that is locked onto a channel that does not play films or TV programmes (for example the BBC News channel or Sky Sports). However, you cannot just say 'we only show the news channel': the test is that the TV is not able to be switched to film-playing channels.

If you offer films to guests, either through an in-room entertainment system or by providing a DVD film library, you need a licence to do so.

Licences are taken out on a different basis, depending on the type of guest accommodation:

- Bed and breakfast accommodation, guesthouses, small hotels and boutique hotels are required to buy a licence on a per-room basis.
- Serviced apartments require one licence per apartment.
- Chalets and holiday homes require one licence per chalet/home.

The main form of licence applicable to small accommodation businesses is the DVD Concierge Licence which allows businesses to provide DVDs for their customers' use. There are two forms of this licence:

- Annual properties (those open year-round): £30 + VAT per room/unit.
- Seasonal properties (open for eight months or less): £20 + VAT per room/unit.
- The fees payable are for the licence only, and accommodation providers would continue to purchase DVDs as usual. The licence fees quoted for guest accommodation apply when no extra charge for the DVD is made to the guest. If a charge is levied, as in most hotels, then a higher licence fee applies.

The third copyright licensing company is AVLA (the Audio Visual Licensing Alliance), which represents the creators of audiovisual works, including producers, script writers, performers, directors and visual artists.

The standard AVLA tariff for accommodation businesses is £10 (+VAT) per annum for each bedroom that contains a TV. However, there is a 20% discount for businesses that have fewer than 15

NEW

bedrooms and a pro-rata discount for months when the business is not open. For example, if your business is closed for three months over winter, then you would only pay 75% of the applicable rate.

In addition to the per room rate, there is a communal area rate that applies when customers are able to watch films or programmes in communal areas which includes receptions, TV and games rooms, restaurants, bars and other areas of accommodation or attraction businesses where customers congregate. The tariff for these areas is dependent on their size, ranging from £120 (+VAT) for areas up to $500m^2$ to £280 (+VAT) for areas over $1{,}000m^2$. Again, the discounts for small establishments and businesses that are only open part of the year apply to this tariff.

Avoiding DVD licences

Smaller businesses may choose to avoid the purchase of a licence by removing DVDs. A licence is not required if guests bring their own DVDs to watch.

Please note: copyright licensing organisations such as MPLC, Filmbankmedia Ltd and AVLA are subject to the **Collective Management of Copyright (EU Directive) Regulations 2016**, which state that the organisations and users (i.e. businesses) must "conduct negotiations for the licensing of rights in good faith" and "provide each other with all necessary information". If you believe that these conditions have not been met, a complaint can be submitted to the IPO via their complaints procedure process: gov.uk/government/organisations/intellectual-property-office/about/complaints-procedure.

Imagery and copyright

The **Copyright, Designs and Patents Act 1988** treats all imagery – including photographs on websites – as 'artistic works' that are subject to copyright. This copyright applies to any image, whether it has been produced by a professional photographer or a member of the general public, and regardless of the image source (for example, the act applies to images found in an online image search).

Under the act, you need the permission of the copyright owner to use the image, for whatever purpose. If you use an image without permission you could be taken to court, and be required to compensate the copyright holder for the illegal use of the image.

To ensure that you are using images legally, you can:

- Take images yourself (meaning that you are the copyright owner);
- Hire a professional photographer, ensuring that image usage is included in your contract with them;

- Download licence-free images from online image libraries. However, check the conditions attached to any images you wish to use, as some may not have permission to be used for commercial use (for example selling something, which includes hotel rooms).

Further guidance

TV licensing

Check what type of licence you need, and pay online on the TV Licensing website **tvlicensing.co.uk**

Intellectual Property Office Guidance

The Intellectual Property Office is a Government agency which regulates copyright. They have produced guidance for businesses that explains how copyright applies to the showing of films and other programmes on TVs located in public spaces including business premises, *Changes to section 72: public showing or playing of broadcasts*, which you can find on **Gov.uk**.

PPL PRS

Find more about TheMusicLicence and how much it will cost on the PPL PRS website: **pplprs.co.uk**

Filmbankmedia

Research which licences you need to show films on the Filmbankmedia website: **filmbankmedia.com/licences**

Motion Picture Licensing Company

Find out if you need an MPLC licence via the Motion Picture Licensing Company website: **themplc.co.uk**

AVLA

More information about AVLA and the tariffs they charge is available on their website: **avla.uk**

Planning and building

KEY FACTS

- Planning permission and building regulations apply if you are considering starting a business, or if you plan to convert, extend or make structural alterations to an existing property or construct a new building.
- Contact the planning department of your local authority for advice on planning permission.
- Asbestos can be found in buildings and can pose a serious health risk. You must identify whether the building contains asbestos, keep an up-to-date record of the location and condition of asbestos-containing materials, assess any risk, and prepare a plan to manage that risk.

Essential first steps

Planning permission and building regulations are the essential first steps if you are considering starting an attraction or serviced accommodation business. Serviced accommodation includes:

- Hotels;
- Guesthouses;
- Bed and breakfasts;
- Farmhouses;
- Inns.

Planning permission

You should contact the planning department of your local authority for advice on planning permission at a very early stage if you are considering:

- Starting a new business;
- Converting or extending your premises.

Planning policies for tourism businesses – especially visitor attractions and accommodation – will be set out in your local authority's Local Development Framework.

'Change of use'

The Town and Country Planning (Use Classes) Order 1987 (as amended) puts uses of land and buildings into various categories known as 'Use Classes'.

Accommodation is Use Class C, with the provision of serviced tourism accommodation such as hotels and guesthouses being Use Class C1.

Attractions such as museums and galleries are Use Class F1, while attractions such as theatres, amusement arcades/centres or funfairs are outside this classification system and have their own specific Use Class. Always check with your council whether the property that you are planning to use for your business is the appropriate Use Class for your purpose.

If the existing Use Class is not appropriate for your intended use, you will have to apply to the Council for 'change of use' consent. This is required both within a Use Class (for example, changing a property from residential use (C3) to a guesthouse (C1)), or from one Use Class to another (such as changing a property from a retail store (E(a)) to a museum (F1)).

Depending on the specifics of any proposed change of use, including any building work associated with the proposal, it may require an application for planning permission or prior approval.

Even if you only wish to start offering a simple bed and breakfast in your home, or open a small museum or visitor centre in an outbuilding on your property where no structural alterations to the building will be carried out, you may need change of use planning permission to do so.

Change of use consent and bed and breakfasts

There is sometimes confusion about whether converting a property from a residential dwelling to a bed and breakfast establishment requires the owner to gain change of use approval. This confusion stems from two sources: the first being that there are no hard-and-fast rules as to what constitutes change of use, and the second from the fact that there are two change of use requirements:

- The first is related to planning permission.
- The second is related to building regulations.

Planning permission and change of use consent

In planning terms, consent from the council must be gained if there is any 'material' change of function to a property or building. In most cases, it is relatively straightforward as to what constitutes this (for example, converting a house into a commercial building or a block of flats).

However, there is a grey area as to how much alteration is allowed before that change materially affects the purpose for which the building is used. That is, at what point does a residential house become a premises whose main purpose is to offer accommodation for visitors? This issue is particularly relevant for bed and breakfast establishments where the property is simultaneously a residential property and a commercial property.

To clarify this area, local authorities have developed a range of measures to determine whether a material change of use has occurred and therefore planning consent is required. These rules generally relate to the proportion of the property that has been given over to the business. This can be determined in a number of ways, the most usual relating to:

- The number of bedrooms as a proportion of the total number of bedrooms in the property, or;
- The area of the building used for the business as a proportion of the total building.

However, some local authorities use the 'six-bed rule'; that is, change of use consent must be sought if the business provides six or more bed spaces (not to be confused with bedrooms) for customers.

If you are considering operating a bed and breakfast, you should consult with the local authority planning officers to determine whether change of use consent is required. Even if you have previously operated a similar bed and breakfast in another destination where no consent was required, you should contact the council as their interpretation of a material change to the use of a property could be different.

Building regulations change of use consent

The second change of use requirement is under the **Building Regulations 2000.**

Under the Building Regulations, there is a material change of use where there is a change in the purposes for which, or the circumstances in which, a building is used, so that after the change 'the building is used as an hotel or a boarding house, where previously it was not'. As with determining whether planning consent is required, different local authorities have different guidelines as to whether a property is deemed to be a hotel or boarding house under these regulations. Potential bed and breakfast operators should check with their local authority to determine whether change of use consent is required.

You should also note that the Building Regulations definition of 'material change of use' differs substantially from the meaning of

'material change of use' in the **Town and Country Planning Act 1990**, which has given rise to a great deal of litigation. Planning permission may be required for a change of use where Building Regulation approval is not needed, and vice versa.
If consent is required, you must make an application using the 'Full Plans' application process, as domestic buildings that are not exclusively used as private dwellings (for example holiday accommodation and bed and breakfasts) are subject to the **Regulatory Reform (Fire Safety) Order 2005.**

Note: even if planning consent is not required, you may still require building regulations consent. You may also require building regulations consent even if you are not contemplating any structural changes in turning your house into a bed and breakfast establishment.

Granting planning permission

Local authorities' policies on granting planning permission vary, and any proposal will be checked against these policies. When deciding whether or not to grant planning permission, where it is needed, the council will take into account the effects on neighbours and the environment, the loss of residential accommodation, traffic generation, access from the highway, car parking facilities and the number of bedrooms offered for letting.

Restrictions on what you can do are usually stricter in specially designated areas, such as:

- National parks;
- Green belts;
- Conservation areas;
- National Landscapes (previously known as Areas of Outstanding Natural Beauty).

Note: you may also need consent for any signage for your property (see the *Signs for Your premises* section).

Building regulations

Building regulations apply whenever a building is erected, extended, materially altered or made subject to a material change of use. They also cover other works and fittings such as:

- New drainage and sanitary installations;
- New heating installations;
- Structural alterations to a building;
- Alterations which have an effect on the existing means of

escape in fire;
- Replacement windows and external doors;
- Electrical installations;
- Change to a building's energy status, and renovation or replacement of thermal elements of a building (such as roofing, cladding, plastering, dry lining, external render and existing floors).

Permitted Development Rights

Permitted Development Rights are the ability to undertake certain types of building work without needing to apply for planning permission. In August 2020, the Government extended Permitted Development Rights to include the ability for homeowners to increase the size of their homes by adding:
- Up to two additional storeys, where the existing house consists of two or more storeys, or;
- One additional storey, where the existing house consists of only one storey.

However, there are a large number of restrictions on the operation of this right, including the following:
- The house was constructed before 1 July 1948 or after 28 October 2018.
- Additional storeys have already been added to the original house, whether by operation of this right or otherwise.
- Following the development, the height of the highest part of the roof does not exceed 18 metres.

Bear in mind that the Permitted Development Rights which apply to many common projects for houses do not apply to flats, maisonettes or other buildings. Similarly, commercial properties have different permitted development rights from dwellings.

It is important to note that Permitted Development Rights are more restricted in specially designated areas, such as national parks

Contact the planning department of your local council to check the Permitted Development Rights that apply to your area and your particular building.

Note: even if you are not thinking of altering a building and planning permission is not required, you may still be required to do work to your property in order to meet building regulations requirements. Again, you need to contact the building control department of your local authority as early as possible.

Energy Performance Certificates

All properties that are newly built, sold or rented are required to have an Energy Performance Certificate (EPC). These certificates provide information on a building's energy use and carbon dioxide emissions, and are accompanied by a report with suggestions on how to reduce them. A certificate is valid for 10 years, after which it must be renewed.

A building's EPC must be provided to any person who wishes to purchase or rent the building. However, an EPC is not required if a property is:

- Rented out for less than a cumulative period of four months within a 12-month period, or;
- Rented out through a licensing arrangement whereby the holidaymaker does not have exclusive use of the property during the period of their booking;
- A listed building;
- A stand-alone building with total useful floor space of less than 50 sq metres.

This means that accommodation operators are not required to gain and provide EPCs for customers, provided that the agreement under which the property is let is a 'licence to occupy'. A licence to occupy is the type of agreement that hotels have with customers, whereby staff can enter the property to undertake essential work, rather than a tenancy agreement whereby the landlord must gain the permission of the tenant to enter the property.

NEW

Note: the Government is currently consulting on changes to the legislation relating to EPC requirements. One of the proposals in the consultation document is that all short-term accommodation businesses will need a valid EPC when letting the property to customers, regardless of whether the customer or the operator pays for the energy required to heat the property.

Managing asbestos

Many buildings throughout the country contain asbestos, which can pose a serious health risk if not managed properly.

For non-domestic properties, the **Control of Asbestos Regulations 2012** provide a framework for the management of asbestos and asbestos-containing materials (ACMs), and any work activity involving asbestos. Duty holders must ensure that anyone who carries out any work in non-domestic premises and any occupants of the premises are not exposed to asbestos from ACMs that may be present.

The legal duty relates to its management – not necessarily its removal. The regulations require you to:

- Identify whether the building contains ACMs;
- Keep an up-to-date record of the location and condition of ACMs;
- Assess the risk and prepare a plan to manage that risk.

All parts of your property that are non-domestic will be subject to the regulations. Any private areas used only by the owner will be considered to be domestic and therefore not subject to the regulations.

If you think that your property contains asbestos, seek advice from an expert. Asbestos is only dangerous when disturbed: if it is safely managed and contained, it does not present a health risk.

Further guidance

Your local authority

Information and advice on whether you need planning permission is available from the Planning Department of your local authority.

Planning Portal

The Government's online service offers free guidance on all aspects of planning: **planningportal.co.uk**

Guidance on asbestos

Find official guidance from the Health and Safety Executive on asbestos, which can be found in any building built before 2000: **hse.gov.uk/asbestos**

Manage asbestos

Identify whether asbestos is present in your property and how to manage it on the Health and Safety Executive website: **hse.gov.uk/asbestos/managing/index.htm**

Signs for your premises

KEY FACTS

- If you display any outdoor signs and/or advertisements you may need to apply to the planning authority for consent to display the proposed sign.
- The need for consent from the planning authority depends on whether signs are fully, partially or non-illuminated and where they are situated.
- You will also need to ensure that any signs displayed are not misleading, as this could constitute a breach of unfair trading and misleading marketing legislation.
- The highways department of your local authority can advise on brown tourism signs.

Background

Do the regulations apply to me?

Yes, if you display any outdoor signs and/or advertisements, you need to comply with:

- The **Town and Country Planning (Control of Advertisements) Regulations 2007**
- The **Consumer Protection Regulations 2008** (CPRs) relating to unfair trading and misleading marketing (see the *Unfair Trading Practices* section).

Planning regulations and permission

The display of all outdoor signs and advertisements is controlled by local planning authorities under the provisions of **Town and Country Planning (Control of Advertisements) Regulations 2007**.

Local planning authorities are required to exercise their powers under the regulations with regard to amenity and public safety, taking into account relevant development plan policies in so far as they relate to amenity (including both visual and aural amenity) and public safety, as well as any other relevant factors.

These regulations can be complex and you are strongly advised to seek the advice of the planning department of your local authority (see *Further guidance* below) before commissioning and setting up any signs for your premises.

A very brief summary of the regulations is given here:

- 'express consent' means that you have to apply to the planning authority for consent to display the proposed sign
- 'deemed consent' means that consent is deemed to have been given by the planning authority and you do not have to apply for it.

Signs on your premises

Illuminated and non-illuminated signs

- **Fully illuminated signs** always require express consent from the planning authority (although this is not normally the case if the sign is displayed inside a window, rather than on the wall or doorway outside).
- **Partially illuminated signs** (e.g. where only letters, and not the background, are illuminated) may not require express consent.
- **Non-illuminated signs** can normally be displayed with deemed consent if they are fixed to the building, although there are limitations placed on the height of the sign and on the size of any characters or symbols on it.

Listed Buildings

If your property is a Listed Building, you will always have to obtain Listed Building consent before you put up a sign.

Signs at the entrance to your premises

You may normally put a non-illuminated sign by your gate, driveway or within the grounds of your establishment with deemed consent (subject to limitations on overall size, height and size of characters or symbols).

Signs in advance of your premises

If you wish to put up directional signs by the side of the roads approaching your establishment, e.g. in a field overlooking the road (with the landowner's permission, of course), you must always seek the express consent of the planning authority.

Flags

Provided that your premises are not within areas of special control or other areas with protective designations, flag advertisements that do not require express consent are restricted to:

- a single flag from a single flagpole projecting from the premises with either the company name or logo of the

company or the advertising of a specific event of limited duration, such as a sale;
- two flags on flagstaffs not attached to a building.

Special controls

In sensitive places, e.g. Conservation Areas, the deemed consent may be removed by an Article 4 Declaration. You will have to apply for consent for signs on or at the entrance to your premises. In some rural localities, an Area of Special Control Advertisements may restrict all outdoor advertising.

Ensuring signs are not misleading

You should also ensure that any signs displayed are not misleading. For example, it is illegal for a non-assessed property to display a Quality Grading Scheme sign or to display a sign showing an incorrect rating.

For more information on misleading signs, see the *Unfair Trading Practices* section.

Brown tourism signs

Both attractions and accommodation businesses can apply for brown tourism signs. However, in practice, accommodation establishments have been less successful with their applications than visitor attractions.

The first step is to contact the highways department of your local authority who will advise you about procedures, local policy and the cost of such signs. Each local highways authority will have its own guidelines that balance local environmental and road safety interests with those of the tourism industry.

Your local highway authority controls signs on the local roads in its area and sets local policy on brown signs. Highways England controls signs on trunk roads and motorways.

The standard for tourism signing on the trunk road network and guidance on signage on local roads in England is available on the Highways England website (nationalhighways.co.uk), along with an application form for signs on roads managed by Highways England. However, it should be noted that the application process can take up to nine months and a sign can be expensive - from £8,000 to £20,000 if it is on a single carriageway and from £17,000 to £40,000 if it is on a motorway.

Note: guidance on tourist signs has been modified to ensure that priority is given to genuine tourist attractions rather than wider retail, sport or leisure facilities. There has also been a move towards greater transparency in the application process and improving processing times. Whilst this guidance only applies to motorways and trunk roads, local highway authorities will be encouraged to apply similar standards.

Further guidance

Your local authority

For informal advice or to apply for consent for signage on your property, contact the planning department of your local authority.

Outdoor Advertisements and Signs

Outdoor Advertisements and Signs - A Guide for Advertisers can be downloaded from the Gov.uk website.

Applying for a brown tourism sign

The Highways England website contains a range of guidance publications related to tourism signage on both trunk and non-trunk roads: **gov.uk/guidance/apply-for-brown-tourist-signs-on-roads-the-highways-agency-manage.**

Find local support

Your local Destination Organisation/LVEP or your local authority may also be able to advise you on the local situation with brown signs: **visitbritain.org/business-advice/find-local-support.**

Direct marketing

KEY FACTS

- If you make direct marketing calls to individuals, or send direct marketing faxes to individuals or businesses, you are required to comply with direct marketing legislation.
- As a business, you are not allowed to make direct marketing calls to individuals who have declined to receive such calls or who have registered with the Telephone Preference Service (TPS).
- If you send email and text/picture/video marketing messages to advertise your business, the Privacy and Electronic Communications (EC Directive) Regulations 2003 apply.
- The Consumer Contracts (Information, Cancellation and Additional Charges) Regulations 2013 apply to goods and services sold over the internet, by phone or by mail order. However, they do not apply to contracts to provide accommodation, transport, catering or leisure services.

Direct marketing by telephone or electronic media

The **Privacy and Electronic Communications (EC Directive) Regulations 2003** were introduced to protect individuals, and in some cases businesses, against receiving direct marketing material by phone or electronic media (for example email or text messaging) without their prior approval.

Under the 2003 regulations you are not allowed, by law, to send unsolicited marketing material by email to an individual subscriber without previous consent, or send any marketing material by email (whether solicited or unsolicited) to any subscriber without revealing your full identity or a valid address to which the recipient can send an opt-out request.

The regulations are overseen and enforced by the Information Commissioner's Office. This is an independent authority established by the Government.

Do the regulations apply to me?

Yes: if you make direct marketing calls, emails, texts or other electronic communications to individuals or businesses.

What do the regulations cover?

Direct marketing phone calls

As a business, you are not allowed to make a direct marketing call to any individual (including sole traders and, except in Scotland, partnerships), if they have told you that they do not want to receive such calls or they have registered with the Telephone Preference Service (TPS). If you do undertake marketing calls, you are required to ensure that your phone number is displayed on the customers' phone (that is, you are not allowed to make calls using a private line).

The TPS is a service managed by the Data and Marketing Association (DMA). They maintain registers of all those who have stated that they do not want to receive direct marketing calls or faxes.

Emails and text messaging

The regulations define electronic mail as 'any text, voice, sound, or image message sent over a public electronic communications network' and this includes messages sent via social media.

The regulations require you to obtain individuals' prior consent before sending unsolicited direct marketing via email or text messages. When undertaking any marketing you must also identify your business and provide a valid address to which the recipient can send an opt-out request.

Customers must opt-in

There used to be an exemption called the 'soft opt-in', whereby you were allowed to send electronic communications such as emails or texts for marketing purposes to previous customers who had not opted-out of receiving these communications (that is, the customer had not actively indicated that they did not want to receive them).

This is no longer the case. Customers now have to actively indicate that they want to receive marketing communications. This means that you must provide an empty tick-box on a paper or online booking form for them to fill in, rather than a 'pre-ticked' box where they have to remove the tick.

If customers agree to you sending them marketing communications, the material you send them must relate to the similar products and services only (for example, you cannot send them advertising material for someone else's business). In addition, the material you send must also provide the opportunity for the person to opt-out of any subsequent communications.

How do I comply, and what are the costs?

If you intend to make any 'cold' direct marketing calls (calls where permission has not been given to do so beforehand) to individuals, you need to check the numbers first against the TPS register. If you make regular cold calls, you must check the numbers every 28 days.

The cost of access to the TPS register varies, depending on the type and level of access you require. In order to ensure that you have the most appropriate package, call the TPS information pack line (see *Further guidance* below). There is also useful information on the TPS website. If you use a telemarketing company to run a telephone campaign for you, you do not need to subscribe.

Penalties for non-compliance

The **Privacy and Electronic Communications (Amendment) Regulations** were introduced in 2018 following reports from the Information Commissioner's Office (ICO) that its penalty-imposing powers were not having the intended effect on unsolicited direct marketing. As a result, if a company cannot show that an individual did not 'opt-in' to receive direct marketing, and no other type of consent is obtained, it can be fined up to £500,000 by the ICO.

For information on other data protection regulations, see the *Registration, Data Protection and Surveillance* section.

UPDATED

Using premium rate numbers

Premium rate numbers generally begin with 09, 118 and 087 and also include five or six digit mobile voice and text shortcode numbers. They are usually used to enter competitions, vote on TV shows, give to charities or for the provision of online services such as IT support.

By contrast, 0800 and 0808 numbers are usually free-call numbers while 084 and 087 numbers and business rate numbers are charged at, respectively, up to 7p and up to 13p per minute.

Premium rate numbers are currently regulated by the Phone-paid Services Authority under an Ofcom-approved code of practice.

Pricing

Pricing information is to be clearly written wherever you display the number. It applies to electronic, website and print information.

Undue delay

There should not be an unfair delay before a caller can access the service required. Callers must be informed of the expected time it will take to have their call answered and, if applicable, of their position in any queuing system.

Prior permission licences

Some services require prior permission from the Phone-paid Services Authority before they can operate on a premium-rate line, such as international dial-through services. A list of services exempt from prior permission can be found on the Phone-paid Services Authority website: psauthority.org.uk

Customer care contact number

A number must be provided for customers with complaints or concerns to call. This number can be the same or an alternative 087 number.

For more information or to register a premium rate service, see the Phone-paid Services Authority website: psauthority.org.uk

The use of 'cookies' on websites

A 'cookie' is a piece of data stored by a website within a browser, and then subsequently sent back to the same website by the browser. Typically, a cookie remembers a user's preferences or settings when they revisit the website. More recently, businesses have introduced 'tracking cookies' as a way to compile long-term records of an individual's browsing history, so that products and offers can be targeted to specific customers, or so a picture can be developed of a customer's buying patterns.

You are not allowed to use cookies or similar devices unless:

- Customers are provided with clear and comprehensive information about the purposes of the storage of, or access to, that information, and;
- Customers have given their consent.

The Regulations are not prescriptive about the sort of information that you should provide, but the text should be sufficiently comprehensive and intelligible to allow customers to clearly understand the potential consequences of allowing storage and access to the information collected by the cookie should they wish to do so.

Guidance on the use of cookies and other similar devices is provided on the Information Commissioner's Office website:
The ICO also produces a guidance publication, *Guidance on the rules on use of cookies and similar technologies*, which can be downloaded from their website: ico.org.uk

Distance selling

In June 2014 the **Consumer Contracts (Information, Cancellation and Additional Charges) Regulations 2013** came into force.

These regulations apply to goods and services that are not sold in 'face-to-face' transactions. That is, items sold online, by phone or by mail order where the customer is not able to inspect the goods and services that they are purchasing.

The purpose of these regulations is to provide additional rights to consumers buying at a distance to encourage confidence in this method of transaction. The information that must be provided in these transactions includes details about:

- The business;
- The goods or services you are selling;
- Payment arrangements;
- Delivery arrangements;
- Consumers' right to cancel their orders.

The regulations also require the business to provide those goods or services within 30 days.

However, it is important to note that the regulations do not apply to contracts to provide accommodation, transport, catering and leisure services where the contract provides for a specific date or period of performance (for example, a concert or sports event that is only being staged on specific dates).

It should also be noted that the regulations do not apply to goods and services sold to other businesses (these are business-to-business contracts), and only apply to transactions that are normally undertaken at distance and where there are systems in place for trading in this way.

So even if you occasionally sell products and services other than the services listed as exempt above, the regulations only apply if this is your normal way of selling these products and services.

Further guidance

The Data and Marketing Association

The Data and Marketing Association runs the TPS, FPS and other preference services and provides further information on its website: **dma.org.uk**

Guidance on privacy and e-communications

Guidance on the *Privacy and Electronic Communications (EC Directive) Regulations 2003* can be downloaded from the website: **ico.org.uk**

Guidance on consumer contracts

Guidance on the Consumer Contracts (Information, Cancellation and Additional Charges) Regulations 2013 can be downloaded from **Gov.uk**.

LICENCES & CONSENTS
MARKETING
CUSTOMERS
FOOD & DRINK
ENVIRONMENTAL PROTECTION
HEALTH & SAFETY
STAFF
BUSINESS, MANAGEMENT & TAX
FURTHER INFORMATION

Phone-paid Services Authority

The UK regulator for content, goods and services charged to a phone bill: **psauthority.org.uk**

Telephone Preference Service

The official central register where consumers record their preference not to receive unsolicited sales or marketing calls: **tpsonline.org.uk**

Holiday packages

KEY FACTS

As the legislation currently stands, the Package Travel and Linked Travel Arrangements Regulations 2018 apply, with some exceptions, if:

- You offer, or allow customers to buy, at least two of the following elements: transport, accommodation, vehicle hire and other significant visitor service to the same customer within a 24 hour period.
- These regulations cover circumstances where you sell different elements yourself, work with another business to sell different elements, or provide the customer with a targeted offer to purchase an element from another business and include specific requirements relating to how you market, book and deliver these products.

NEW

Note: in 2023, the Department for Business and Trade undertook a Call for Evidence on proposals to reform the Package Travel and Linked Travel Arrangements Regulations 2018. However, this work ended with the 2024 election and it is unknown (as of January 2025) whether the Government will continue with this work.

Package Travel Regulations

The **Package Travel and Linked Travel Arrangements Regulations 2018** (commonly known as the 'Package Travel Regulations') were introduced on 1 July 2018 and greatly expanded the scope of the former Regulations. The Regulations now cover situations where the customer creates their own packages (dynamic packaging), and introduces the concept of a 'Linked Travel Arrangement', whereby a customer is provided with a targeted offer for a service provided by a separate business once they have completed a booking. These changes affect the activities of many accommodation providers.

These regulations concern the marketing, sale and performance of products that are sold together or through a linkage. They apply not only to large companies offering overseas package holidays, but also to accommodation businesses selling offers that combine or link products (for example, accommodation with tickets to an attraction, a spa treatment, a murder mystery weekend or a round of golf).

Enforcement and penalties

There are criminal penalties for non-compliance. Trading Standards are responsible for enforcing the legislation.

Do the regulations apply to me?

Yes: if you are offering a package of services for sale at an inclusive price which includes at least two of the services listed below, and the package lasts for at least 24 hours or includes overnight accommodation, you will probably be offering a 'package' that is subject to the regulations:

- Transport;
- Accommodation;
- Vehicle hire;
- Other visitor services that are a significant part of the package and not ancillary to transport or accommodation (for example excursions, access to a golf course and theatre tickets, but not educational, business or conference services).

Selling packages

There are two main circumstances in which an accommodation business may be deemed to be selling a package:

1. **You work with another business in order to provide a package that combines two or more elements.** This is the traditional package, where two businesses work together to develop a package that is then sold to the customer for an inclusive price. For example, if you sell accommodation and a ticket to a nearby attraction for an inclusive price.
2. **Your business sells two or more different elements to customers.** This applies in situations where you sell different products to customers on your premises – for example, if you operate a hotel which provides accommodation and other services such as restaurant meals, spa treatments, gym use or a round of golf. This covers two different situations:
   - Specific offers that your business puts together, such as a 'romantic weekend package' at a hotel which includes accommodation and a meal, or a 'New Year's Eve special' which includes entrance to a party with the accommodation.
   - Self-packaging by the guest where, either by phone or through

your website, they book a room and another service such as a spa treatment or meal in the restaurant at the same time.

Note: a package is only formed if the different elements can be purchased separately. Therefore, bed and breakfast businesses are exempt because the price of the breakfast is always included in the room rate.

Exemptions

There are two main exemptions to the Package Travel Regulations for accommodation businesses:

1. **If the 'Other Tourism Service' element does not form a 'significant part' of the package.** When the 'Other Tourism Service' element is combined with accommodation, a package is only deemed to have been formed if the 'Other Tourism Service' makes up 'a significant part' of the package.What constitutes a 'significant part' of the package is a bit of a grey area, but there are two main tests:
   - **If the 'Other Tourism Service' constitutes over 25% of the cost of the package.** This requirement provides accommodation businesses with the opportunity to review their pricing structure so that, where they provide a service alongside accommodation, the service is priced in such a way that it comprises under 25% of the overall cost to the customer, thus excluding the package from the regulations
   - **If the 'Other Tourism Service' is deemed to be an 'essential element' of the package.** It is important to note that even if the service is under 25% of the total cost, it could still be a 'significant part' of the package if it is deemed to be an essential element. This means that there is good reason to believe that the customer bought the package on the basis of this element. While this can be subjective, it is generally accepted that if the promotion of the package is based on the service, then it is an essential element, compared to where it is promoted as a 'bonus'. For example, if you sold a combination of accommodation and a round of golf as a 'weekend golf break', then the round of golf would be an essential element regardless of whether it represented over 25% of the total cost. However, if you simply said that use of a golf course was a benefit of staying at the hotel, this would probably not be deemed as an essential element.
2. **If the elements are purchased at least 24 hours apart.** The other main exemption is that a package or Linked Travel Arrangement is not formed if the two different elements are

purchased at least 24 hours apart. For example, if a customer books both their accommodation and a table at your restaurant at the same time, this would constitute a package. However, if they booked the accommodation and then called back two days later to book a spa treatment, this would not be a package. Similarly, if your guests purchase a meal at your restaurant after they arrive, or you sell them tickets to a local attraction or a round of golf at the local golf club, provided that they booked the accommodation more than 24 hours before arrival, then this would also be outside the scope of the legislation.

What do the regulations require?

The regulations contain significant provisions relating to the marketing, booking and delivery of packages and Linked Travel Arrangements, including the terms and conditions of contracts for providing these products.

If you are deemed to be selling a package or Linked Travel Arrangement, there are also significant requirements on the information you must provide to the customer, the terms and conditions that must apply to the sale, and the financial protection that you must have in place. The specific requirements vary between packages and Linked Travel Arrangements, but the main features are:

1. **Pre-contractual information**
   Before customers book the package, they must be provided with information on the main characteristics of the package (that is, what is included in the package and any exceptions, such as whether service charges are included or whether the offer of a meal includes drinks), the total price of the package, the name and details of the organiser and information on the cancellation policy.
2. **Standard information about the Package Travel Regulations**
   The pre-contractual information must be accompanied by standard information forms that make customers aware of the key protections associated with buying a package holiday, including telling them if they are not covered by the regulations.
3. **Contractual information**
   When the customer makes the booking, they must be provided with further information. This includes contact details if a problem is experienced during the course of the contract, the complaints resolution process, and the ability of the customer to transfer the booking.
4. **Insolvency protection**
   You must have insolvency protection that covers all reasonable costs, including the return of all payments for services not

performed and repatriation. This can be achieved through buying insurance, keeping customer payments in a trust account or becoming bonded.

Selling Linked Travel Arrangements

Separate from the rules related to the sale of packages, the regulations also address the sale of Linked Travel Arrangements. A Linked Travel Arrangement is deemed to have been formed if, on the basis of booking accommodation with you, the customer is provided with a targeted offer such as a discounted rate for purchasing something from another business, or access to facilities not generally available. This applies regardless of whether you gain financially from the arrangement. There are two forms of Linked Travel Arrangement:

Type A: This is where the customer, on completing a purchase on your website, is immediately invited to purchase another product on someone else's site. For example, someone purchasing accommodation is immediately offered the opportunity to purchase a hire car on a partner's website.

Type B: This is where you facilitate the customer purchasing additional services from another business, but that purchase does not take place within 24 hours of their booking with you. For example, if you provide the customer with a voucher to get 20% off a meal in a local restaurant when they arrive.

There has been confusion as to whether providing recommendations to customers on local businesses such as restaurants, pubs and attractions constitutes the creation of a Linked Travel Arrangement, but Government guidance states that you are entitled to provide recommendations without this being deemed to be included in the scope of the legislation

Further guidance

Your local Trading Standards office

Your local Trading Standards office can provide more information on the requirements of the Package Travel Regulations.

Government guidance

The Department for Business and Trade provides guidance for tourism businesses on the application of the Package Travel Regulations, *Package holidays: complying with regulations – guidance for businesses* on Gov.uk. Although the guidance offers a good assessment of what constitutes a package, you should seek specific advice if you believe that you are selling packages or Linked Travel Arrangements as this remains a complex area.

Unfair trading practices

KEY FACTS

- Businesses have a general duty not to undertake unfair trading practices under the Consumer Protection from Unfair Trading Regulations 2008 (CPRs).
- The CPRs aid in determining whether certain advertising and marketing practices are misleading, aggressive or lack due diligence.
- In addition to this general duty, there are 31 business practices that are banned outright, such as displaying a quality mark without authorisation.
- The Business Protection from Misleading Marketing Regulations 2008 impose further restrictions on how companies can compare their products to rival products from other companies.

Background

The **Consumer Protection from Unfair Trading Regulations 2008** (CPRs) encompass legislation preventing business practices that are unfair to consumers.

The aim of the legislation is to make it easier for customers to compare the products and services provided by businesses, and to make informed purchasing decisions. This is particularly relevant to the tourism sector, where the customer is unable to see the product before making a booking or deciding to visit.

The **Business Protection from Misleading Marketing Regulations 2008** tighten restrictions relating to how companies compare their products to rival products from other companies.

Do the regulations apply to me?

Yes: if you are either:

- Advertising your business using any form of media (including online and social media);
- Making statements about your facilities to the public.

LICENCES & CONSENTS
MARKETING
CUSTOMERS
FOOD & DRINK
ENVIRONMENTAL PROTECTION
HEALTH & SAFETY
STAFF
BUSINESS, MANAGEMENT & TAX
FURTHER INFORMATION

Unfair trading

What constitutes an unfair trading practice?

The aim of the CPRs is to provide a framework for determining whether certain practices are misleading, aggressive or lack due diligence on the basis that they would alter the behaviour of the average customer. In other words, if it can be determined that the customer made a purchase that they otherwise would not have done if they knew the full facts of the matter, then the business has engaged in unfair practices.

This covers engaging in misleading practices such as making false or deceptive statements in marketing material, or omitting important information that would have a bearing on the customer's purchasing decision.

Examples

False and deceptive statements could include statements made about:

- the quality of accommodation (see also *Practices banned outright* below);
- the amenities or services available;
- the location of the premises.

For example, it would be a false statement if you advertised that your accommodation was 'five minutes from the beach', when it is actually a half-hour drive, while a misleading claim would be that 'the art museum has the best collection of Turner paintings in the UK' when only one is on public display.

Similarly, if you omitted to notify customers that you were undertaking refurbishment work that either closed facilities or generated considerable noise or dust, or that you had to pay for rides within a theme park in addition to the admission charge, this could be deemed to be misleading.

Another aspect to be aware of in this area is the provision of food and descriptions of dishes on menus. For example, it would be a false statement if you say you provide a 'champagne breakfast' but you actually serve prosecco, or that all meals are organic if the produce used is not certified to be organic. Similarly, it would be misleading to state that seafood is sourced locally if that means that it came from a local supermarket.

Practices banned outright

While much of what constitutes an unfair practice will have to be determined through case law, the legislation lists 31 practices that are banned outright. These practices include:

- Displaying a quality mark (such as an accommodation grading scheme mark) without having the necessary authorisation. This includes displaying a quality mark that is out-of-date;
- Falsely claiming that a premises or product has been approved or endorsed by a public body such as VisitEngland;
- Falsely stating that an offer will only be available for a limited time;
- Luring the consumer by advertising special prices for a product you cannot offer, or with the intention of selling the customer a different product.

So, if you display on your premises an incorrect VisitEngland star rating, or an outdated tourist board rating such as a Crown or Diamond classification and grading, this is regarded as a breach of the regulations.

Unfair comparison

In addition to the CPRs, the **Business Protection from Misleading Marketing Regulations 2008** tighten the legislation relating to comparison marketing. These regulations specify that companies must not use advertising to:

- Compare products or materials that are not designed for the same period;
- Confuse people as to the advertiser and the competitor;
- Present imitations or replicas of products bearing a protected trademark or trade name;
- Take unfair advantage of the reputation of competitors' trademarks, trade names, other distinguishing marks, or country of origin information.

Examples

Unfair comparisons could include:

- Taking out an advertisement that unfavourably compares the cost of staying at a neighbouring hotel with staying at your hotel, if you fail to mention that the neighbouring hotel is a five-star property while yours is a three-star;
- Comparing your admission charge with that of another attraction, if their admission includes the use of all facilities but visitors to your attraction have to pay extra to use them;
- Comparing your low-season rate with a competitor's high season rate;
- Describing your guesthouse as 'the Torquay Hilton', even if you consider this to be a tongue-in-cheek description.

LICENCES & CONSENTS
MARKETING
CUSTOMERS
FOOD & DRINK
ENVIRONMENTAL PROTECTION
HEALTH & SAFETY
STAFF
BUSINESS, MANAGEMENT & TAX
FURTHER INFORMATION

Online reviews and endorsements

If your website allows customers to post reviews, the CPRs prevent you from managing or presenting the reviews you receive in a way that misleads your customers. This means that you cannot write or commission fake reviews. 'Commission' includes asking friends to write reviews and offering inducements to customers in return for writing positive reviews.

It also means that, in order not to mislead your customers, the review section of your website must accurately reflect your customers' views, regardless of whether they are positive or negative. Your process for collecting, moderating and publishing reviews must not hinder their impartiality, and you must publish all genuine and lawful reviews. For example, you cannot pick and choose which customers you ask to provide a review when they depart – you must either invite all of them or none – and you cannot choose which reviews to publish on your site.

For more detail, see the Competition and Markets Authority (CMA) online guide *Giving a balanced picture: dos and don'ts for online review sites.*

Note: The Government has announced that it will be strengthening the law on fake reviews by introducing new legislation that will make it illegal to:

- Commission someone to write or submit a fake review;
- Host consumer reviews without taking reasonable steps to check they are genuine;
- Offer or advertise to submit, commission or facilitate fake reviews.

Paid promotions

It is not illegal to pay a person or publication to promote your business online; however, potential customers need to know that the endorsement has been paid for. For example, while it is legal to pay a blogger to write a piece about your business, it must be clear that you have paid for this endorsement. This can be done by adding a statement such as 'Advertisement Feature' or 'Advertisement Promotion'.

The CMA has issued further guidance on this topic in their guidance *Online endorsements: being open and honest with your audience.*

Enforcement and penalties

Your local Trading Standards office is responsible for enforcing the regulations.

Anyone who breaches the regulations can be prosecuted for a criminal offence by a local Trading Standards office, be subject to a fine, and/or – in extreme cases – a prison sentence of up to two years. In addition, it could lead to a civil claim: see *Misrepresentation*, below.

Defence against a charge of unfair trading

Possible defences against a charge of unfair trading include:

- You made an honest mistake and were not given the opportunity to remedy the situation (for example, you thought that you had the oldest pub in the region).
- Your statement was based on information supplied by a third party.
- The statement was made by some 'other person', such as a guidebook or newspaper article ('other person' does not mean any of your employees).

However, in any defence, you would still have to show that you took all reasonable care and exercised all due diligence to check that the facts were true in any publication or statement. You should keep written records of those efforts so that you can prove what you did (for example, a copy of your brochure or information sheet marked to show the checks that you made).

Misrepresentation

Engaging in unfair trading practices can not only result in a criminal prosecution (see *Enforcement and penalties*, above) but it may also result in a civil claim being brought against you by any person who has suffered loss as a result of a false statement. This stems from what is referred to in law as 'misrepresentation'.

When misrepresentation occurs

Misrepresentation occurs where a party is induced to enter into a contract by certain statements that later turn out to be untrue. With respect to tourism businesses, these could again include statements regarding:

- Quality;
- Amenities;
- Location.

For example, if Mr Anderson and his family had booked into a bed and breakfast with an assurance that it was only 'five minutes from the beach' but it turned out to be a half-hour drive, he would be able to either:

- Refuse to continue with the booking and claim damages from you for any losses incurred as a result;
- Continue staying with you but claim damages for his and his family's distress and disappointment.

Other considerations

For any promotional material, you should also bear in mind the following:

- **Advertising codes** (for broadcast and non-broadcast media): these are issued by the Committee of Advertising Practice (CAP) and require advertisements and sales promotions to be legal, decent, honest and truthful. Advertising codes also deal with specific issues, including the availability of products at the advertised price and VAT inclusion in prices.
- The requirements of the **Package Travel and Linked Travel Arrangements Regulation 2018**: see the *Holiday Packages* section for more information.

Social media

Many operators advertise and market their business through social media – for example, having an Instagram account.

It is important to realise that while you may use a far more relaxed or 'chatty' style of communication when using social media than you would in print or on your main website, everything that you post via social media must still comply with all aspects of the CPRs. It is therefore essential to re-read anything that you are about to post on social media to ensure that it is accurate, is not open to misinterpretation and does not make unfair comparisons.

Further guidance

Your local Trading Standards office

Your local Trading Standards office, which is responsible for enforcing the regulations, should be able to give you further guidance.

Consumer Protection: a basic guide

Read the Gov.uk guidance publication *The Consumer Protection from Unfair Trading Regulations: a basic guide for business*.

Advertising codes and advice for small businesses

Further information on the advertising codes and guidance for small businesses can be found on the Committee of Advertising Practice (CAP) website: **asa.org.uk.**

CUSTOMERS

Pricing and charging

KEY FACTS

- It is a criminal offence for businesses to provide customers with misleading information on the prices charged for services or goods.
- It is an offence not to do everything reasonably possible to correct a price indication that has subsequently become misleading, if it is reasonable to assume that customers will still be relying on the original price information.
- Prices must include VAT if you are VAT registered.
- You cannot charge customers extra for paying by credit/ debit card.

Price statements

Does this apply to me?

Almost certainly yes: the **Consumer Protection from Unfair Trading Regulations 2008** covers all statements you make regarding the provision of products or services.

The regulations will normally apply to all businesses, regardless of whether the price is.

- Stated in an advertisement, a brochure, a leaflet or online;
- Given in an email or text message;
- Given by letter or over the telephone.

What does the legislation require?

It is a criminal offence for you to give customers misleading information on the prices charged for services or goods.

It is also an offence not to do everything reasonably possible to correct pricing information that has subsequently become misleading, if it is reasonable to assume that customers will still be relying on the original price information.

Good practice

The Chartered Trading Standards Institute's Business Companion website (businesscompanion.info) contains a series of quick guides and in-depth publications on all aspects of trading standards. Included on the site is a good practice guide on how to comply with the Consumer Protection from Unfair Trading Regulations. It also produces information specifically related to the pricing of goods and services, called *Guidance for Traders on Pricing Practices*. This gives practical guidance on how to avoid giving misleading prices. Compliance with the guide, while not an absolute defence, will assist you in showing that you have not committed an offence under the act.

One important point to note is that you are not allowed to separate out non-optional extras (such as a cover charge) from your headline price. If there is a non-variable charge that a customer cannot avoid paying, then this must be included in the headline price.

Where non-optional charges vary, you should give clear information about the charging structure at the outset to enable customers to easily calculate the total cost before agreeing to a purchase.

All prices given to customers should include VAT. The message is that customers should not get any surprises when it comes to paying the bill.

Displaying prices on your premises

The **Consumer Protection from Unfair Trading Regulations 2008** require you to be open and honest in your pricing, and not to mislead or leave out information that could affect the purchasing decision of your customers (see the *Unfair trading practices* section for further information).

While there is no specific regulatory requirement regarding the display of prices in reception, it is recommended guidance that you do so in order to fulfil your obligations under the regulations. This price list should be in a prominent position and be easy to read. It is suggested that the price list should include:

For accommodation businesses

- The cost of a bedroom for one person (for example £75 per night) if all the rooms are the same price, or the lowest and highest rates (for example £70-95 per night) if there is a range of prices;
- The price of a bedroom for two people;
- The price of any other type of bedroom;
- Whether or not accommodation prices are inclusive of breakfast or other meals and services.

For attractions

- The price of admission (for both adults and children);
- The price of admission for groups;
- Whether the price includes admission to all exhibitions/rides/activities;
- The price of components that are sold separately.

All prices must include VAT (if you are VAT registered) and any compulsory service charge. You must make it clear if meals are included in the price.

Further information on displaying prices is available from the Chartered Trading Standards Institute (businesscompanion.info).

The **Consumer Protection (Amendment) Regulations 2014** give consumers private remedies where a trader has committed a misleading or aggressive practice under the 2008 regulations. Under these regulations, consumers have simple, standardised recourse against traders who have misled or intimidated them into entering a contract or making a payment.

Importantly, they do not need to demonstrate any loss, or show that you have acted dishonestly, recklessly or even negligently. If the trader's actions were misleading or aggressive, then the remedies apply.

Under the regulations there are three remedies:

1. **Unwind a contract and get their money back**
   The right to unwind allows the consumer to undo the transaction that they entered into, restoring the consumer to the position he or she was in before entering the contract or making the payment. This must be done within 90 days of the start of the service being provided (that is, when they arrive at the property rather than when the booking was made), and it must be possible to reject the service (so this must be done before the booking ends).
2. **Receive a discount on the price paid**
   The right to a discount applies where the right to unwind has been lost, whether due to delay (with a claim made more than 90 days after the relevant day), or because the goods or services have been fully consumed.

   For goods or services that cost £5,000 or less, consumers have a right to a fixed percentage discount on the price. There are four pre-set bands of discount which can apply, depending on the severity of the misleading or aggressive practice:

   (1) 25% if it is more than minor;
   (2) 50% if it is significant;

(3) 75% if it is serious;
(4) 100% (full price) if it is very serious.

3. Claim damages for detriment caused

Consumers can claim damages if they have suffered losses that exceed the price paid for the relevant goods or service. Damages can cover distress and inconvenience, as well as losses suffered by the consumer because of the contractor payment they made as a result of the misleading or aggressive practice.

These damages can only be claimed upon proof of actual loss, or distress and inconvenience. In accordance with general principles, only reasonably foreseeable losses are covered.

Under the regulations, a defence can show that the misleading or aggressive practice happened as a result of a mistake or other cause beyond your control, and that you took all reasonable precautions to avoid the misleading or aggressive practice from occurring.

For more information, see the Gov.uk publication *Misleading and Aggressive Commercial Practices: New Private Rights for Consumers*.

Bonds/card payments in case of damage

The practice of accommodation businesses taking bonds (or damage deposits) is separate from taking a deposit on the payment for the booking.

This bond is protection against damages incurred while the guest is staying in the property, but is becoming increasingly uncommon as businesses tend to retain customers' credit or debit card details in case of damage. If you wish to either charge a bond or to retain customers' card details so that you can recoup any damages, you must notify customers of this prior to the booking being agreed (while this can be done verbally, it is far better to do it in writing in case there is any dispute).

It is important to note that you are only able to retain money from the bond, or charge a customers' card, if the damage has resulted from a deliberate act (such as kicking walls) or negligence (actions whereby it was reasonably foreseeable that damage would occur). You are not able to charge for damage that results from general 'wear and tear', for example marks on floors, an electrical item failing or a cup breaking during washing-up.

To protect against disputes, it is good practice to show a customer around a property so that any pre-existing damage can be recognised and agreed (as car hire companies do), and to get photographic evidence of any damage, in order to support your actions if the customer or their credit card company queries the charge. Also, three quotes should be gained on any repairs to show that the amount being charged is justified.

The requirement for guests to provide a bond or pay for damages must be applied in a fair and consistent manner that does not breach anti-discrimination law. That is, the requirement should be imposed on all guests and cannot just be imposed on the basis of race, disability, sexual orientation, age or gender. For example, you cannot require a bond from a group of young male customers if you do not require it from other groups of customers.

Credit and debit card charges

It is illegal to make any additional charge where payments are made using debit, credit or charge cards, such as American Express and electronic forms of payment such as PayPal.

In essence, this means that the price you advertise a product for must be the price that the customer pays at the end of the booking process. However, you are allowed to increase the headline cost of your product to compensate for not being able to charge the card fees if you wish.

The law also only applies to purchases made by personal consumers and not to purchases made by businesses. So, if your customer is a business (for example a company booking rooms for an away day or to use an attraction for an event) then you are allowed to charge a card-processing fee, provided that it is no more than the cost to you of processing the transaction.

However, in this situation it is important to note that a customer must be using a business card for you to charge a fee. You cannot charge a card-processing fee if the customer is using their personal card, regardless of whether they will reclaim the cost as a business expense later.

Further guidance

Guidance on pricing practices

Business Companion provides free, impartial legal guidance for businesses on Trading Standards law: **businesscompanion.info.**

Your local Trading Standards office

Check you are trading legally by contacting your local Trading Standards office.

Bookings and tickets

KEY FACTS

- Once you have accepted a booking from a customer, you normally have to honour the booking.
- All businesses should abide by good practice with regard to booking procedures.

Booking contract

Once you have accepted a booking from a customer, you normally have to honour the booking (see the *Accepting customers* section for circumstances where a booking does not have to be honoured). This is because once you have agreed the terms of the booking with a customer (for example the dates, accommodation type or services to be provided and price) and then accepted the booking, a legally enforceable contract exists between you and the customer.

This applies equally whether the arrangement has been made verbally over the telephone, by email or in writing. You may only change the terms of the booking at a later date if both you and the customer agree to the change of terms.

To avoid any problems with cancellations, no shows or curtailment (when a customer cuts their stay short), you are strongly recommended to have a cancellation procedure. For the cancellation procedure to be enforceable, you must make it clear to customers before accepting a booking. See the *Cancellations and no-shows* section for further details.

Booking terms and conditions

Larger businesses may have arranged for their lawyers to prepare full booking conditions, and any operator that needs to comply with the **Package Travel Regulations** will require them. However, it is recommended that all operators have a policy relating to deposits and cancellations.

If you have any special arrangements like these, you must give customers the full details before they book, to ensure that the arrangements are part of the booking contract and binding on the guest.

CUSTOMERS

In developing any terms and conditions for the provision of goods and services to customers, there are three important points to keep in mind:

- Regardless of your terms and conditions, the law requires you to use reasonable skill and care in providing the underlying services.
- You cannot contract yourself out of your legal responsibilities. For example, you cannot have a condition which states you are not responsible for any injury a customer may sustain when the Health and Safety Act says you have a responsibility for your customers' wellbeing. Similarly, you cannot say that you will only deal with complaints that are brought to your attention while the customer is on the premises.
- The law does not allow you to limit your liability to a customer for death or personal injury arising out of your negligence, or that of an employee or agent. In respect of any other loss or damage, you can only restrict your liability towards a guest as far as is reasonable.

The Competition and Markets Authority (CMA) provides guidance as to what constitutes unfair terms in contracts. In general terms, their guidance is:

- A deposit is just to reserve the goods/services, and should be no more than a small percentage of the total price.
- Advance payments should reflect the expenses of the business, and leave customers with a reasonable amount still to pay on completion.
- Customers should not lose large advance payments if they cancel.
- Businesses should set sliding scales of cancellation charges, so they cover their likely losses directly from the cancellation.

However, this guidance should be viewed 'in the round'. A special deal which requires a large deposit or payment in full could be justified if there were no cancellation charges, or if cancellation charges only applied within a few days of the customer arriving.

For more details, see the *Unfair contract terms* guidance on **Gov.uk**.

You can also see the *Cancellations and no-shows* section for more information.

Good practice

As a matter of good practice, you should keep a clear, accurate record of the arrangements for each of your bookings. You might also want to have a simple checklist by the telephone or computer, to remind you of the details you need to run through with each guest, for example:

- Pricing;
- Deposit;
- Cancellations;
- Data protection.

Ideally, you should confirm all bookings in writing to the guest, although this may not always be practical. However, you should confirm in writing/email the booking details for any longer stays, larger groups or bookings that are more complex than usual.

Selling tickets

Selling tickets for entry or for events is covered by the **Consumer Protection from Unfair Trading Regulations 2008**. This means that you must provide full and clear information, including:

- Any terms and conditions associated with the ticket;
- What the ticket entitles the customer to;
- Opening hours;
- The validity of the ticket (for example, whether it is for a particular day or can be used on any day);
- If the ticket is for an event, the timing of the event, the location and, if it is seated, where the seats are.

Under these regulations, it is illegal to give consumers misleading information or claims, and to mislead the customer by omitting information that the customer requires to make an informed choice. This could include:

- Additional charges not included in the ticket price (for example, where the price for entry to an amusement park does not include the cost of rides on its attractions);
- Advertising an event as 'A night with Michael Bublé' when the singer is only a guest that performs one song;
- The cancellation policy if an event cannot be held;
- Information on any part of an attraction that is closed for maintenance;
- Whether seating is allocated, and if so, where it is in relation to the stage and whether the view is restricted.

Pricing

For events where there is a range of pricing for tickets, you can advertise that 'prices start from £x'. However, when doing this, you must ensure that there are a reasonable number of tickets available at that price. Having a very limited number of tickets at the advertised price is called bait marketing, and is illegal.

It is also important to note that when you advertise and sell a ticket, the price must include all non-optional extra charges, such as booking fees.

Cancellations

It is important to have a cancellation policy if you are selling tickets ahead of an event, with terms and conditions that are fair to the customer. **The Consumer Contracts (Information, Cancellation**

and Additional Charges) Regulations 2013 applies to sales over the internet or by phone, and generally requires businesses to provide a 14-day period in which the customer can cancel a service or return goods.

However, there is an exemption for tickets for events held on a specific date or within a specific time period.

Further guidance

Guidance on ticketing for events

The Society of Ticket Agents and Retailers (STAR) has developed a code of practice for businesses selling tickets for events to the public: **star.org.uk**

Professional legal advice

Booking contracts and conditions are a complex area of law. For any detailed information or assistance, you should seek professional legal advice.

Registration, data protection and surveillance

KEY FACTS

- If you hold any personal information on customers or any other individuals, including employees, the Data Protection Act 2018 (DPA) applies.
- Unless you have an exemption, you are required to pay an Annual Data Protection Fee to the Information Commissioner's Office (ICO).
- The General Data Protection Regulation 2018 (GDPR) enhances consumer rights, including the ability to access the information that businesses hold.
- All serviced and self-catering accommodation premises must keep a record of all guests over the age of 16. The record should include their full name and nationality. You must keep each guest's details for at least 12 months.
- Surveillance equipment can only be used if there is a legitimate reason to do so. Customers should be made aware that they are being monitored, who is undertaking the activity, and the purpose for which that information is to be used.

Data protection

The holding and use of personal information of individuals is regulated by the **Data Protection Act 2018** (DPA), which sits alongside the **General Data Protection Regulation 2018** (GDPR). As the provisions are extensive, you should read the paragraphs below to see if they apply to you.

Note: the paragraphs in this section focus on personal data held on customers, as this is perhaps the most relevant situation for smaller tourism businesses. However, the Acts apply equally to personal data held on other individuals, including employees, although the specific provisions vary. For further information, contact the Information Commissioner's Office.

What is the purpose of the DPA?

The DPA is intended to protect the privacy of individuals (data subjects) by preventing the misuse or unauthorised use of personal information (personal data) that is held by others (data controllers). It achieves this by:

- Regulating the use of personal data held by data controllers, and;
- Giving rights to data subjects.

Does this Act apply to me?

The DPA applies to the 'processing of personal data' for any business purpose, regardless of the size of the business. This includes personal data on either employees or customers.

What is 'personal data'?

Personal data is any information that relates to an identifiable individual. It can range from their name, phone number or email address, through to more personal information such as their sexual orientation or whether they are disabled. It is important to note that personal information also includes images, including CCTV recordings. As a general rule, if it is possible to identify an individual directly from the information you process, then that information is personal data.

What is 'processing'?

Processing of personal data is pretty much anything you do with it: from collecting, storing, organising and using that data, through to deleting it.

What is a 'controller'?

A controller is the person that decides how and why to collect and use the data. Employees are deemed to be acting on behalf of the employer – meaning that, as the business operator, you are the controller even if you do not actually process the data yourself.

Data protection principles

Controllers are required to follow strict rules called data protection principles. You must ensure that all data is:

- Used fairly, lawfully and transparently;
- Used only for specified, explicit purposes;
- Used in a way that is adequate, relevant and limited to only what is necessary;
- Accurate and, where necessary, kept up to date;
- Kept for no longer than is necessary;
- Handled in a way that ensures appropriate security – including protection against unlawful or unauthorised processing, access, loss, destruction or damage.

I think the DPA applies to me. What must I do?

The three basic requirements are set out below. Please note that even if you are exempt from (a), you still need to comply with (b) and (c).

(a) Pay an Annual Data Protection Fee

No: if you only hold personal data on a manual filing system, you do not need to pay this fee.

Yes: if you hold personal data on a computer (or any other automated system), you must pay this fee. However, you are exempt if you only hold personal data for the following purposes:

- Staff administration (including payroll);
- Accounts and records (such as details of past or present customers or suppliers);
- Your own advertising, marketing and public relations (the information must be restricted to just what is necessary for your advertising, marketing and public relations), and your advertising, marketing and public relations are not undertaken by a third party;
- You are using the personal data for not-for-profit purposes.
- You are maintaining a public register.

It is important to note that if you use CCTV on your premises for crime prevention purposes (that is, security reasons), then you are required to notify the Information Commissioner's Office (ICO) and pay the Annual Data Protection Fee.

Under the **Data Protection (Charges and Information) Regulations 2018**, individuals and organisations that process personal data need to pay a data protection fee to the ICO. There is an annual fee of £40 if you have a turnover of less than £632,000 or fewer than 10 staff, and £60 for businesses with a turnover of up to £36 million or up to 250 staff.

Charities, regardless of their size, are only required to pay an annual fee of £40.

The ICO has an online assessment tool for determining whether you have to pay the Annual Data Protection Fee.

(b) Follow the data protection principles

All data controllers, whether their records are computerised, automated or manual, and whether they have to notify or not, must comply with the eight data protection principles set out in the DPA. In brief, personal data should be:

- Obtained and processed fairly and lawfully, and should not be held or used unless the data subject has given their consent, or it is necessary in performance of a contract to which the data subject is a party, or it is necessary for any other reason

specified in the DPA (see the ***Direct marketing*** section);
- Obtained only for specified and lawful purposes;
- Adequate, relevant and not excessive in relation to the purposes for which they are being held or used;
- Accurate and, where necessary, kept up to date;
- Kept no longer than necessary for the purposes concerned;
- Processed in accordance with the rights of data subjects (see (c) below);
- Subject to appropriate technical and organisational measures against unauthorised or unlawful processing and against accidental loss or destruction;
- Not transferred to a country or territory outside the European Economic Area, unless that country or territory ensures adequate level of protection for the rights and freedoms of data subjects in relation to processing personal data.

Consent

If you intend to hold information on a customer for any purpose other than handling their current booking or purchase (for example, you would like to send them marketing material in future), you must obtain their consent.

The DPA does not specify what form this consent must take. It may be an informal, spoken 'yes', but you should give customers enough information for them to make an informed decision (for example, by telling them what personal information you intend to hold and why).

Customers can give their consent at any time: on booking, on entry or check-in, or when they leave. You should keep a record of all consents in case a customer disputes that they granted their permission.

You may want to produce a simple form that can be used either over the telephone, on emails or in writing, which:
- Explains to customers the personal information on them that you want to hold, and why;
- Asks customers for their consent;
- Has a space, such as a tick box, to record whether or not consent is given.

If you intend to keep 'sensitive personal information', you must have the customer's explicit consent to hold and use their personal data for the purposes specified. Sensitive personal information includes the following:
- Race, ethnic origins;
- Religion;
- Political opinions;
- Physical or mental health (for example a disability);

- Sexual orientation;
- Criminal convictions or allegations.

(c) Complying with the rights of data subjects
All data controllers must comply with the rights given to individuals by the DPA in relation to the personal information held on them. The DPA gives eight distinct rights, of which the most applicable are as follows:

Right to access: individuals have a right to know what information you are holding on them, and why you are holding it (called a Subject Access Request). If you receive a written request from an individual for this information, you must respond within 30 days, stating:

- Whether you hold any personal data on them;
- What the data is, the reason you are holding it, and those to whom it has/may be disclosed, along with an intelligible copy of the information and details of the manner in which it was collected.

Right to prevent processing for the purposes of direct marketing: if you receive a request from an individual to cease using the personal data you hold on them for direct marketing, you must do so.

Right to prevent processing that is likely to cause damage or distress: if you receive a request from an individual to cease using the personal data you hold on them because it is causing, or likely to cause, substantial damage or distress to them or another, you must do so.

Right to compensation: any individual who suffers damage or distress as a result of a contravention of the DPA by you is entitled to seek compensation from you if you did not take reasonable care to comply.

Note: you have the right to require reasonable proof of identity from a person who is asking to exercise these rights. You should be satisfied that the person asking is the person concerned, but you must not use excessive identity checking as a way to deliberately complicate access to the data.

Caution! If you are buying-in any mailing lists, you should ensure that the provider has the consent of the individuals listed to pass on their details to third parties.

For more information, consult the ICO's guide to determining whether you are complying with the Data Protection Act on their website: ico.org.uk

The General Data Protection Regulation (GDPR)

The **General Data Protection Regulation (GDPR)** came into force on 25 May 2018. The main additional requirements of the GDPR are:

1. **The Right to be Forgotten**
   A customer can, at any time, request that you remove all of their personal data from your system. If the customer has previously agreed that you could provide their data to a third party, you must also stop doing this if you receive a Right to be Forgotten request. However, it is important to note that any Right to be Forgotten request does not override requirements to hold information under other legislation. For example, you are required by law to keep financial records for seven years, therefore a customer cannot request that you delete records of any financial transactions that they undertook within the last seven years.

2. **Improving Consent and Withdrawal of Consent**
   The conditions for consent were strengthened by the GDPR. You must be clear and upfront with customers about what exactly they are consenting to when they sign up. This is to stop companies from hiding the details in their terms and conditions. So, if you are planning to pass their information on to a third party and to email them a newsletter, you must tell them in simple and clear language next to the box that they are ticking.

   Importantly, it must be as easy for customers to withdraw consent as it is to give consent. So, if you have a simple tick-box online where customers give consent, then there should also be a simple tick-box online to withdraw consent.

3. **Right to Access**
   The GDPR also expands the rights of customers to access the information that you hold on them. This has two parts: first, on request from the customer, you are required to inform them if personal data concerning them is being processed, where it is being processed, and for what purpose. Second, if requested, you must provide a copy of all the personal data that you hold on the person – electronically and free of charge. This includes any information that you have made on the person's file, so if you have added notes such as, 'likes the Sunday Times', 'owns a Spaniel called Arthur' or 'gave a donation', you also need to provide this information. You need to supply it within 30 days.

4. **Notification of data breaches**
   The GDPR requires you to notify the ICO within 72 hours of first becoming aware of a data breach, where that breach is likely to 'result in a risk for the rights and freedoms of

individuals'. For any breach, you are required to notify the customers 'without undue delay' after first becoming aware of a data breach.

The ICO has produced several online resources to help businesses to comply with the GDPR:

- The *Guide to the General Data Protection Regulation (GDPR)*
- A small business toolkit to help you to check your compliance.
- A support helpline aimed at people who run small businesses or charities, designed to provide additional, personal advice. As well as GDPR advice, callers can ask questions about other legislation regulated by the ICO, including electronic marketing and Freedom of Information. People from small organisations should dial the ICO helpline on **0303 123 1113 (Monday to Friday between 9am and 5pm)** and select option 4 to be transferred to staff who can offer support.

Transferring personal data to and from the EU/EEA

UPDATED

The European Commission has found the UK data protection laws to be adequate to allow data to continue to flow as it did before the UK left the EU. This decision is expected to last until 27 June 2025.

More information on transferring personal data to and from the EU is available on the ICO website: ico.org.uk

Data security and credit cards

The DPA states that 'appropriate technical and organisational measures shall be taken against unauthorised or unlawful processing of personal data and against accidental loss or destruction of, or damage to, personal data'.

If you never receive a customer's card number (that is, you use a third party to deal with transactions) you probably have little to worry about, other than to ensure that the third party is a reputable organisation with a good knowledge of data security issues (for example Paypal or Worldpay).

If you do receive a customer's data, you should follow the standards of the Payment Card Industry Security Standards Council. This council is a global consortium of all major card payment companies, including Mastercard and Visa. Its function is to promote standards of data security that make it harder for criminals to steal data. These standards are quite demanding, but compliance is mandatory for retailers who accept card payments. The requirements of the Payment Card Industry Data Security Standard are contractual rather than the law of the land but, if you follow them, you will also be meeting the legal requirement.

CUSTOMERS

If you do handle card data, you must ensure that you know and follow the rules that are applicable to your circumstances. There are 12 requirements, some of which are of limited relevance to small businesses:

1. Install and maintain a firewall. Your computer operating system probably has this built in, for example Windows Firewall.
2. Do not use default passwords. If your password is 'password', change it. Passwords should not be obvious.
3. Protect stored cardholder data. Do not leave personal data on your laptop and then travel with it, due to the risk of losing it. Keep it secure at all times.
4. Encrypt internet transmission of cardholder data. Never use ordinary email to send credit card information.
5. Use and regularly update anti-virus software. This is essential: set it to update automatically if you can.
6. Develop and maintain secure systems and applications. This is likely to apply only to larger businesses who have developed their own systems.
7. Restrict access to cardholder data on a need-to-know basis. Ensure that card data is not available to your visitors, all staff, etc.
8. Assign a unique ID to each person with computer access. Do not share identities or passwords or run a database of past clients shared between several people with the same login.
9. Restrict physical access to cardholder data. Do not leave a print-out of data in an unlocked location (or in a file of manual card data records).
10. Track and monitor all access to network resources and cardholder data. This is relevant to businesses with larger systems, but all businesses should record who has access to card data.
11. Test security systems and processes regularly. At the very least, check that your security measures are being adhered to.
12. Maintain a policy that addresses information security. For small businesses, the key point is that you give this topic some serious thought, rather than writing a formal policy.

For small businesses, the above list can be summarised as making sure that access to card data – both on paper and electronically – is very well controlled, restricted to people who really need it, and that any computer on which you store it has proper defences such as a firewall and anti-virus software.

Although not a legal requirement, your acquirer may also require you to complete a PCI DSS Self-Assessment Questionnaire (SAQ) in order to validate your compliance to the standards.

Accommodation: keeping a register of your guests

Does this apply to me?

Yes: under the **Immigration (Hotel Records) Order 1972**, all serviced and self-catering accommodation premises must keep a record of all guests over the age of 16.

What do I need to record?

To comply with the **Immigration (Hotel Records) Order 1972** you need to collect the following information from guests on their arrival:

- Full name;
- Nationality.

> **Note:** you are not legally required to take a guest's home address or contact number.

For all guests who are not British, Irish, or nationals of Commonwealth nations:

- Passport number and place of issue (or other document which shows their identity and nationality);
- Details of their next destination (including the address, if known) on or before departure.

> **Note:** diplomats, their family and staff do not have to register.

What about the format of the register?

There is no set format for the register, but you must keep each guest's details for at least 12 months and have the register available for inspection by a police officer or duly authorised person at all times.

It may be, of course, that you are given the necessary details at the time of booking – but you should check them when the guests arrive, and ensure that you have all the information that you are required to collect. Even if your local police force has traditionally shown no interest in these records, circumstances could change.

Using surveillance equipment on your premises

Over recent years, the cost of buying and installing surveillance systems has dropped considerably. Their use is now becoming more prevalent in small businesses who want to safeguard their property and their customers.

However, it is very important to get the right balance between justifiable reasons for surveillance and a customer's right to privacy.

There are two main acts that cover the use of CCTV and other surveillance equipment: the **Protection of Freedoms Act 2012** and the **Data Protection Act (DPA)**. The first covers when and where it is justifiable to use CCTV equipment, and the second covers the treatment of the data that is gained from its use.

Protection of Freedoms Act

The starting point of the Protection of Freedoms Act 2012 is that people have a fundamental right to privacy, and this can only be encroached upon if there is a legitimate reason to do so. It is not acceptable to install surveillance equipment simply because you 'want to keep an eye on what is going on'.

You **must also only use surveillance equipment if there is no other practical way to solve a problem that does not impact on customers' right to privacy**. For example, if there had been thefts from a particular area, ways of restricting access to that area should be considered before you install surveillance equipment.

Surveillance equipment can only be used if the encroachment on people's right to privacy is proportionate to the purpose for which the equipment is being used. However, there are no hard-and-fast rules as to what is proportionate because each circumstance will involve differing levels of both justification and privacy.

For example, installing CCTV cameras to protect possessions in a museum or to monitor customers' safety in an animal park would be justifiable, but it would not be justifiable to put CCTV in guest bedrooms or in changing rooms where customers would expect a very high level of privacy.

Conversely, installing CCTV in a communal lounge would not normally be justifiable, but could become justifiable if there had been a spate of thefts in this area. However, it is important to note that in this situation the justification would end once the person committing the thefts was identified or the thefts ended.

Importantly, **when you do use surveillance equipment, customers should be made aware that they are being monitored, who is undertaking the activity, and the purpose for which that information is to be used**. Again, the greater the extent that a customer's privacy is being encroached, the more important it is that they are fully aware of the surveillance that is being undertaken.

Data Protection Act

Provided that the use of surveillance equipment is justified, there is then the issue of how to use, handle and store the data you collect.

This comes under both the Protection of Freedoms Act 2012 and the Data Protection Act.

Again, the handling and storage of this data need to be proportionate to the justification for collecting it in the first place. **You must have very clear guidelines as to who has access to the monitoring equipment and the stored data**. The greater the extent that you are encroaching on customers' privacy, the greater the restrictions should be on access to the monitoring equipment and the data.

The length of time that you keep the data should also be proportionate to the justification for using the surveillance equipment. For example, if the equipment is being used to monitor a pool to ensure that there are no accidents, then there would be little justification for storing the data beyond the period that the pool was being used (that is, it should be deleted at the end of each day as its storage is no longer warranted). However, if the equipment was being used to monitor the car park, then it could be justifiable to keep the data for longer in case a customer returned home and later found a dent that they thought happened while at your premises.

To help businesses in their use of surveillance equipment, the Home Office has produced the following 12-point code of practice:

1. Use of a surveillance camera system must always be for a specified purpose which is in pursuit of a legitimate aim, and necessary to meet an identified pressing need.
2. The use of a surveillance camera system must consider its effect on individuals and their privacy, with regular reviews to ensure its use remains justified.
3. There must be as much transparency in the use of a surveillance camera system as possible, including a published contact point for access to information and complaints.
4. There must be clear responsibility and accountability for all surveillance camera system activities, including images and information collected, held and used.
5. Clear rules, policies and procedures must be in place before a surveillance camera system is used, and these must be communicated to all who need to comply with them.
6. No more images and information should be stored, other than that which is strictly required for the stated purpose of a surveillance camera system, and such images and information should be deleted once their purposes have been discharged.
7. Access to retained images and information should be restricted, and there must be clearly defined rules on who can gain access, and for what purpose such access is

granted. The disclosure of images and information should only take place when it is necessary for such a purpose or for law enforcement purposes.

8. Surveillance camera system operators should consider any approved operational, technical and competency standards relevant to a system and its purpose, and work to meet and maintain those standards.
9. Surveillance camera system images and information should be subject to appropriate security measures to safeguard against unauthorised access and use.
10. There should be effective review and audit mechanisms to ensure that legal requirements, policies and standards are complied with in practice, and regular reports should be published.
11. When the use of a surveillance camera system is in pursuit of a legitimate aim, and there is a pressing need for its use, it should then be used in the most effective way to support public safety and law enforcement with the aim of processing images and information of evidential value.
12. Any information used to support a surveillance camera system which compares against a reference database for matching purposes should be accurate and kept up to date.

Further guidance

Information Commissioner's Office (ICO)

The ICO provides extensive information on data protection, including a free toolkit for businesses to check their GDPR compliance: **ico.org.uk**

Credit card data

Information on complying with data protection for credit card data can be found on the Payment Card Security Standards Council website: **pcisecuritystandards.org**

Surveillance camera code of practice

The Home Office's *Surveillance camera code of practice* provides information and guidance on the use of surveillance cameras.

Cancellations and no-shows

KEY FACTS

- All businesses are strongly recommended to have a cancellation procedure in order to avoid any problems with cancellation, curtailment and no-shows.
- If a customer cancels a booking or checks out early from accommodation, they are in breach of the booking contract that they have with you.
- If you cancel a booking that you have already accepted, you are in breach of the booking contract.

Cancellation by customers

Cancellation provisions in the booking conditions

To avoid any problems with cancellation or curtailment (when a guest cuts their stay short), you are strongly recommended to have a cancellation policy. To rely on the procedure, you must make this policy clear to customers before you agree on the booking, whether on the telephone, by email or in writing. It is also prudent to obtain confirmation from the customer that they understand and accept the policy. Finally, your booking conditions and cancellation policy should also be clearly stated on your website.

It is recommended to include a cancellation clause in your standard booking terms and conditions (see the *Bookings* section). Common cancellation procedures are to either charge customers a cancellation fee that varies according to the amount of notice given of cancellation, or to forfeit any deposit provided at the time of booking. It is important to note that any cancellation terms and conditions need to be fair to the customer. For example, demanding full payment in advance and having a cancellation policy that would see the customer forfeit the entire payment, regardless of when the cancellation was made, would be deemed to be unfair.

On cancellation or curtailment, you will need to send an invoice to the guest for the amount due. In spring 2019, HMRC changed its guidance on the VAT treatment of deposits when customers cancel a booking or do not arrive (no-shows). The revised guidance states that

LICENCES & CONSENTS
MARKETING
CUSTOMERS
FOOD & DRINK
ENVIRONMENTAL PROTECTION
HEALTH & SAFETY
STAFF
BUSINESS, MANAGEMENT & TAX
FURTHER INFORMATION

VAT is still chargeable because the deposit was a payment for the opportunity to use your goods or services. Therefore, you will need to send an invoice to the guest for the amount due, inclusive of VAT and include the revenue in your VAT filing.

Please note that VAT only applies to deposits that are made by the customer. If the customer cancels and you have a separately payable cancellation charge as part of your terms and conditions, this is exclusive of VAT as this is a penalty payment rather than a payment for the opportunity to use your goods and services.

Cancellation insurance

One option that is often given to customers on booking is to take out cancellation insurance. A premium covers any payments they are obliged to make for their accommodation in the event of them having to cancel. A typical policy will cover claims as a consequence of illness or injury to the guest or a member of their family, redundancy, a burglary, fire or jury service.

If you need to comply with the **Package Travel and Linked Travel Arrangements Regulations 2018** (see the *Holiday packages* section), you are required to tell the customer about the possibility of taking out cancellation insurance in good time before the start of their holiday.

You can contact a local insurance company or broker for details of how to offer this facility.

Deposits

Increasingly, businesses are taking deposits or asking for credit card details to reduce their exposure to cancellations.

Typically, this charge is a 25% deposit at the time of booking, with the balance paid between six to eight weeks in advance of arrival – but this will vary depending on the type of business and the ease of replacing lost custom. For example, accommodation providers will charge a higher deposit and require a greater lead-time for full payment than attractions, due to it being more difficult to replace cancelled bookings.

If you are VAT registered, you need to remember that any deposit is inclusive of VAT. This means that if you withhold a deposit as compensation for a guest cancelling, you must return the VAT component of the deposit as no service has been provided.

If a customer cancels and refuses to pay

If the guest refuses to pay:

- You may be able to charge the amount to their credit or debit card, but if not, you will need to consider taking the matter to the Small Claims Court.

Charging a credit card following cancellation or no-show

If you accept a telephone booking made by a credit or debit card and the customer later cancels the booking or fails to turn up, you can charge the customer's card **provided that** you can prove you clearly communicated to them when they made the booking that their account would be charged in the case of a cancellation, and that they accepted this condition.

One way to do this is to include the condition in your cancellation policy within the booking terms and conditions. Ideally, you should confirm this arrangement in writing or, at least, keep a record of the conversation as proof for the credit card company should the customer later challenge the charge.

If the guest refuses to acknowledge having made a booking or claims that they were not made aware of your cancellation conditions, and there is no proof to the contrary, banks will tend to refund their money and debit your account. If you take bookings online, it is a good idea to have a 'tick-box' where the guest has to confirm that they have read and accepted the cancellation conditions.

Claiming damages if a customer cancels

If a customer cancels a booking or leaves early when staying in accommodation, they are in breach of the booking contract that they have with you. You may be entitled to claim damages for any losses you have suffered from the cancellation/curtailment. This applies regardless of whether you have cancellation/curtailment procedures as a booking condition.

Procedure

If you do not have a cancellation policy and want to make a claim for damages, the procedure is as follows:

- **Minimising your loss:** You must first make every reasonable effort to minimise your loss. This may be by trying to re-let the accommodation or reselling a ticket on which only a deposit was paid. If you re-let the room or resell the ticket at the same price, you should have not suffered a loss and so cannot make a claim.
- **What amount can I claim?** If, despite your efforts, you cannot re-let the accommodation or resell the ticket, you will be entitled to claim damages that reflect the losses you have incurred as a result of the cancellation. This is the value of the booking less the cost of any items that you did not supply. For example, you cannot charge for food, heating, electricity or cleaning as you did not supply these products or services. You are also not able to include any service charge.

Note: there is a general rule of thumb for accommodation businesses that your loss will be about two-thirds of the value of the booking, but individual cases differ.

- **What about the deposit?** You may keep the deposit, off-setting it against the amount claimed.
- **How soon can I make a claim?** You must wait until the period of the booking has elapsed before you can send the customer an invoice for the amount claimed (this should be exclusive of VAT, as no services have been provided).
- **What happens if the customer does not pay the claim?** If you have difficulties with a customer refusing to meet your claim, you could consider pursuing the claim through the small claims procedure in the County Court. A small claim can be for any amount up to £10,000. You will have to pay a fee to start your claim, which is related to the size of your claim, but this will be added to the money that you are already owed. The appropriate forms and a booklet advising you on how to pursue your claim can be obtained from any County Court.
- **What happens if I lose?** Be aware that if you lose the case, the customer can seek to recover expenses from you (although not the cost of any legal fees they have paid). These expenses include £95/day for loss of earnings or leave to attend a hearing, plus reasonable travelling expenses for each of the other side and any necessary witnesses they take along to court. You can also be required to pay £750 if the judge gave them permission to get evidence from an expert.

What if a customer does not accept your product or service?
Should a customer refuse to accept a product or service that they have booked or any other suitable alternative that you may offer, then, depending on the reasons given by the customer, you may be able to treat this as a cancellation.

Generally, you will not be able to do this if the customer rejects the product or service because they booked it on the basis of untrue statements made about it by you or your staff, or if the alternative does not meet the criteria of the customers booking (for example, if the guest specifically asked for a room with a sea view when booking and the only room available when they arrive overlooks the car park, or the customer booked a dinner/dance on the basis that there was a vegetarian option but it was not available)

What if I cancel a customer's booking?

If you have to cancel a booking that you have already accepted, you are in breach of contract and must refund the customer. For accommodation businesses, if you cannot accommodate a guest who has made a booking, you must find them alternative accommodation of the same or higher standard.

The guest is entitled to claim damages as compensation for any losses incurred in finding alternative comparable accommodation (for example, extra taxi fares or any extra accommodation costs). However, the guest has a legal duty to keep losses to a minimum, so if your establishment is a bed and breakfast they cannot book into a luxury hotel and expect you to pay the difference.

Note: an issue that came to prominence during the COVID-19 pandemic was the situation where, due to rules introduced by the Government, businesses were required to close or customers were prevented from travelling to certain destinations. The Competition and Markets Authority ruled that if Government legislation prevented a contract from being fulfilled, the customer should be refunded any payment made, minus any amount used for services that had already been provided (for example, the purchase of flowers for a wedding reception). Similarly, if the business was allowed to remain open but was unable to provide the services booked by the customer because of legislation, then the entire booking should be cancelled and any deposit refunded (for example, if a customer booked a room for a party for 100 people but Government rules stated that only 10 people could socialise together).

However, it is important to remember that this does not apply if Government restrictions are only guidance and not legal requirements.

Further guidance

Professional legal advice

If you have any detailed questions on cancellations or any problems with a guest, you are advised to seek professional legal advice.

Your local Trading Standards office

Your local Trading Standards office may be able to offer some guidance, particularly on cancellation terms.

Accepting customers

KEY FACTS

- You cannot discriminate against any customer on the basis of a range of characteristics including race, religion, sexuality and disability.
- A hotel can refuse guests who appear unable or unwilling to pay, or who are not in a fit state to be received.
- You are bound to honour a booking unless the booking was made on the basis of false statements that impact on the provision of services or facilities.

Can I turn customers away?

As a service provider, the **Equality Act 2010** applies to your business. This means that it is unlawful to discriminate against customers on the following 'protected characteristics':

- Disability;
- Gender reassignment;
- Pregnancy and maternity;
- Race – this includes ethnic or national origins, colour and nationality;
- Religion or belief;
- Sex;
- Sexual orientation;
- Marriage and civil partnership;
- Age – this applies to guests aged 18 and above (for example, you cannot have a policy excluding under 25s).

Discrimination does not just mean refusing to provide services to people on the basis of their 'protected characteristics'. It also means providing them with different standards of service, different products, charging different prices or having different terms and conditions. For example, it would be discriminatory to only allow gay couples to have a twin bedroom rather than a double bedroom, or to prevent groups of more than 10 men from entering an attraction.

However, you are allowed to provide different products and services for disabled customers, as long as there is an objective justification

LICENCES & CONSENTS
MARKETING
CUSTOMERS
FOOD & DRINK
ENVIRONMENTAL PROTECTION
HEALTH & SAFETY
STAFF
BUSINESS, MANAGEMENT & TAX
FURTHER INFORMATION

for doing so. Objective justification is said to occur when the difference in the goods or service provided is 'a proportionate means of achieving a legitimate aim'. For example, it could probably be considered justified to only sell ground floor rooms in a listed building to a wheelchair user if the upper floors were only accessible by a staircase. Similarly, it would probably be considered justified to advise pregnant women not to undertake a particularly violent ride at an adventure park on the basis of medical risk.

It should be noted that it is the inability to make alterations rather than the cost of making alterations that provides objective justification – that is, you cannot provide a discriminatory service on the basis of cost alone.

In addition to not being able to discriminate against customers on the above grounds, you cannot discriminate against anyone on the grounds of association. This means not discriminating against the parent, partner, friend or carer accompanying someone with one of the 'protected characteristics' listed above.

Indirect discrimination

You must be careful not to have booking conditions or rules that would constitute indirect discrimination. Indirect discrimination occurs when any requirement, which in itself is not discriminatory, would have a disproportionate impact on people with a protected characteristic. For example, if you have a requirement that all-male groups had to pay a higher booking fee because you had problems with stag parties in the past, this could be deemed to be indirect discrimination as it would always apply to gay couples but would not apply to heterosexual couples.

To help ensure that you do not discriminate, you are required to undertake reasonable adjustments to your premises or to the way you deliver your services. This, for example, could mean providing improved access, undertaking staff training on equality or providing meals that comply with the religious requirements of guests.

For more information on accepting disabled customers, see the *Disabled Customers* section.

Requirements for accommodation providers

For accommodation businesses, there are further requirements related to accepting guests.

Guests with prior bookings

A booking is a legal contract for the provision of a service. Therefore, when a guest makes a booking, you must honour that booking unless there are legal grounds for not doing so. Such legal grounds include accepting the booking on the basis of false statements made by the guest or that the guest does not comply with the conditions associated with the booking. For example, if you state that pets are not allowed at your establishment and the guest arrives with a pet, or if they book a room for two adults and they arrive with children who they want to sleep on the sofa. In these situations, you can turn the guests away and you may also be able to claim damages from them if you are unable to re-let the room.

'Walk-in' guests

Under the **Hotel Proprietors Act 1956**, aa hotel can only refuse to let a room to a walk-in guest with no booking if that guest appears unable or unwilling to pay, or is not in a fit state to be received. This would be the case, for example, if the guest was drunk or if you had reasonable grounds for believing that the guest would be a nuisance to other guests.

However, you have complete discretion to decide which room to allocate to a guest, provided that the guest has not booked a specific room.

Note: the Hotel Proprietors Act 1956 defines a hotel as 'an establishment held out by the proprietor as offering food, drink and, if so required, sleeping accommodation, without special contract, to any traveller presenting himself who appears able and willing to pay a reasonable sum for the services and facilities provided and who is in a fit state to be received'. As such, it is possible for an operator whose premises do not fit this definition to refuse walk-in guests.

Accepting bookings from under 18s

Anyone under the age of 18 does not have the same legal capacity as an adult to enter into a contract, such as booking a room. You can accept bookings for someone under 18 to stay, but you should be careful. For example, the booking itself should be made by someone 18 or over – such as a parent, guardian or another adult who can take responsibility for payment or damages.

Further guidance

How to comply with equality legislation

The Equality and Human Rights Commission (EHRC) provides comprehensive advice for accommodation providers on how to comply with equality legislation: **equalityhumanrights.com**

Under 18s and the law

The Children's Legal Centre website has a service that answers questions in relation to under 18s and the law: **childrenslegalcentre.com**

The Equality Act: a quick start guide

This guide includes specific advice, FAQs and examples of where the Equality Act 2010 could apply in real-life situations and is available on **gov.uk**

Guide to the ban on age discrimination

This summary guide for accommodation providers covers what you can and can't do in relation to age discrimination is available on **gov.uk**

Guidance on single sex spaces

The EHRC provides online guidance on how the Equality Act 2010 relates to single sex spaces, including separate or single-sex toilets: **equalityhumanrights.com**

Disabled customers

KEY FACTS

- The **Equality Act 2010** applies to all businesses.
- The act protects anyone who is disabled, is thought to be disabled, or is associated with someone who is disabled.
- The act gives these people rights of access to goods, facilities and services (including tourist attractions and accommodation) and ensures that they are treated no less favourably than other customers.
- You are also required to make reasonable adjustments to the way you deliver your services and to the physical features of your premises to make it easier for disabled customers to use them.
- It would be unlawful to refuse access to a disabled person accompanied by an assistance dog, except in the most exceptional circumstances.

The Equality Act 2010

The **Equality Act 2010** was introduced to consolidate and strengthen all anti-discrimination legislation (including disability discrimination legislation). The act builds on the Disability Discrimination Act 1995 (DDA) which gives disabled people rights of access to goods, facilities and services, which includes tourism businesses, by specifically banning discrimination against people associated with disabled people (for example carers, friends and family) and people presumed to be disabled. These rights are enforceable by any individual through the Courts, if necessary.

Does the Act apply to me?

Yes: if you provide any sort of goods or services to the public, the act applies to you.

How is 'disabled' defined?

For the purpose of the law, disabled people are all those whose physical and mental impairments have a substantial and long-term adverse effect on their ability to carry out normal, day-to-day activities.

LICENCES & CONSENTS
MARKETING
CUSTOMERS
FOOD & DRINK
ENVIRONMENTAL PROTECTION
HEALTH & SAFETY
STAFF
BUSINESS, MANAGEMENT & TAX
FURTHER INFORMATION

This includes those who have cancer, HIV and multiple sclerosis, and those who have other progressive conditions likely to result in an impairment which has a substantial adverse effect. These people become covered by the act from the time they are diagnosed.

Note: a disability may not always be apparent, so it is important not to make assumptions.

Types of discrimination

There are four types of disability discrimination covered by the Equality Act 2010. They are:

- Direct discrimination;
- Indirect discrimination;
- Discrimination arising from a disability;
- Discrimination by association.

Direct discrimination

This is discrimination directly associated with a person's disability. As a 'service provider', you need to make sure you treat disabled customers the same as you treat other customers. You would be treating customers with disabilities less favourably if you:

- Refuse to serve them;
- Offer less favourable terms;
- Offer a lower standard of service compared with what you normally offer.

It is important to note that the Equality Act does not allow any justification for direct discrimination. If you treat someone less favourably, the act allows them to seek damages from you.

An example of unequal treatment would be if a guesthouse or attraction refused access to someone who has a neurological impairment, on the basis that they felt the person would upset other customers.

Indirect discrimination

This is where a business policy, while applying to all customers, would have a greater impact on disabled customers. Examples could include:

- Serving breakfast only in a room that is down a set of stairs;
- Providing information on an attraction that was only in writing.

The **Equality Act** does allow indirect discrimination if there is 'objective justification'. For example, it may be justified to only allocate loft rooms to people who are able to move unescorted, on the grounds of fire safety. If there is no objective justification (cost is generally not acceptable), then reasonable adjustments (see below) need to be undertaken to adapt to the circumstances of the disabled customer. For example, information in large font sizes or audio tours could be provided.

Discrimination arising from a disability

This is where the discrimination is based on a consequence of the disability rather than the disability itself. Examples would include:

- Banning a person with Tourette's syndrome from an event or area because their outbursts may offend other customers;
- Providing plastic cups and plates to a person with muscular dystrophy because you think that they might break items.

Discrimination by association

This is discrimination against someone associated with a disabled person, such as a carer, friend or member of the family. Examples may include:

- Refusing the booking of a non-disabled couple because it was known they have a disabled child which they might bring with them;
- Making the carer of a disabled person sleep in the same room to ensure that they don't disturb other guests.

How does the Act impact on me?

To ensure that you do not discriminate against disabled people or their associates, the law requires you to make reasonable adjustments to both your property and business practices.

Reasonable adjustments

You should make **reasonable** adjustments to the way you deliver your services to make it easier for disabled guests to use them.

The duty is anticipatory, meaning you should consider in advance how to make your services accessible to disabled customers. Waiting for customers to ask you to do something may not be enough.

You should make reasonable adjustments where, if the adjustment were not made, a disabled person would be at a substantial disadvantage compared to people who are non disabled. The question is whether the adjustment is a reasonable one to make in all the circumstances.

The Equality Act 2010 sets out the three requirements for making reasonable adjustments:

1. Adjustments to a policy or procedure

- Monitor your policies and procedures to ensure that they are not putting disabled people at a substantial disadvantage in comparison to non-disabled people when accessing goods, facilities and services.
- Take reasonable steps to ensure that any policies or procedures that put disabled people at a substantial disadvantage are changed or ended.

Note: even if you do not allow animals, you must allow assistance dogs.

2. Adjustments involving the provision of auxiliary aids and services

- Anticipate what auxiliary aids or services you need to make available to disabled individuals who would otherwise be at a substantial disadvantage compared to non-disabled people. For example, provide large-print menus for visually-impaired guests, or a hearing loop at a service counter for customers who use hearing aids.

3. Adjustments to physical features

- You have a duty to take reasonable steps to remove, alter or provide a way of avoiding any physical barriers that make it impossible or unreasonably difficult for disabled people to make full use of facilities. This can include, for example, providing ramp access at steps, or a lift if reasonable. If this is not possible, you must look at how the service can be provided by an alternative method.

The need for reasonable adjustments also applies to your website, which may be the first point of contact for a disabled person.

What is reasonable?

Often simple measures can make your facilities more accessible, for example taking more time to help disabled guests, letting them know how to ask for help, and arranging appropriate training for you and your staff.

You are only required to do what is 'reasonable'. What might be considered reasonable for a national hotel chain may not be so for a small attraction. What is a reasonable step for a particular service provider depends on all the circumstances of the case. It will vary according to:

- The type of service being provided;
- The nature of the service provider and its size and resources;
- The effect of the disability on the individual disabled person.

However, without intending to be exhaustive, the following are some of the factors which might be taken into account when considering what is reasonable:

- Whether taking any particular steps would be effective in overcoming the substantial disadvantage that disabled people face in accessing the services in question;
- The extent to which it is practical for the service provider to take the steps;

- The extent of any disruption which taking the steps would cause;
- The extent of the service provider's financial and other resources;
- The amount of any resources already spent on making adjustments.

The Act permits service providers to justify less favourable treatment (and in some instances failure to make a reasonable adjustment) when there is no possibility to do so, despite the fact that this would mean that a disabled person is treated less favourably. An example is where an historic listed building would have to change the structure of the building to allow step-free access to all floors. Service providers do therefore have flexibility when considering how to make their services accessible to disabled people. In this example, a video tour of the inaccessible floors could be made available as a reasonable adjustment.

It is important to note that you are unable to pass on the cost of making reasonable adjustments to your disabled customers.

NEW

Assistance dogs

Assistance dogs are not pets. Thousands of people rely on an assistance dog to help them with day-to-day activities that many others take for granted. It is not only blind people who are helped by assistance dogs; they are also trained to help those with hearing loss, epilepsy, diabetes, physical mobility problems and more. Assistance dogs carry out a variety of practical tasks for people, as well as supporting their independence and confidence.

Assistance dog owners are protected by the act in a number of ways:

1. **Reasonable adjustments**
   It will almost always be reasonable not to apply a 'no dogs' policy for assistance dog owners, and a failure to do so would amount to unlawful discrimination.
2. **Discrimination arising from disability**
   You must not treat a disabled person unfavourably because of something connected to their disability. For example, if a hotel or attraction has a 'no dogs' policy and they bar someone who uses an assistance dog, not because of their disability but because they have a dog with them, this would be discrimination arising from disability unless the business can objectively justify what it has done.

Guidance from the Equality and Human Rights Commission (EHRC) states: 'It would be unlawful to refuse access to a disabled person accompanied by an assistance dog except in the most exceptional circumstances'.

CUSTOMERS

Tourism providers will understandably wish to ensure that only genuine assistance dog users are able to access these rights. However, in determining the legitimacy of assistance dogs, providers should note:

- There is no definition of an assistance dog in the act (other than in relation to carriage of an assistance dog in taxis).
- The act does not specify acceptable standards of training, behaviour or health; assistance dogs can be owner-trained.
- The act does not state that assistance dogs have to be registered (there is no regulatory system for the registration of assistance dogs).
- The act does not state that assistance dogs require any identification documents or an identifying harness or jacket.
- There are no blanket exceptions in the act to cover assistance dogs in food service (or preparation) areas, refusal due to allergies, or refusal due to owners' pets.

There is no reference in the Equality Act (or supporting Statutory Code of Practice) to 'support animals' – including therapy animals or comfort animals that people may have to help them cope with illness, anxiety, or mental health issues. However, it is important to note that the Act protects any person that has a physical or mental impairment which has a long term and substantial adverse effect on their ability to carry out normal day-to-day activities (the Act's definition of disability). Therefore, you should attempt to accommodate the needs of someone who has a support animal for such conditions, and have a valid, justifiable reason if you refuse to allow the animal on the premises.

Ultimately, only a court can determine whether a refusal of service is unlawful, and such a determination would be highly dependent on the specific facts and circumstances of the particular case.

Good practice

IIn terms of what you should do in relation to disabled customers, good practice includes:

- Thinking and planning ahead;
- Not making assumptions based on stereotypes;
- Asking a disabled person or organisation what is required if you are in doubt;
- Respecting the dignity of your disabled guest;
- Establishing a positive policy and practices;
- Training staff accordingly.

Note: a willingness to help and an attentive ear can help when considering how to make your services accessible to disabled customers. Disabled people will tell you what you need to do to help them best. Also bear in mind that accessibility is often about making compromises, as a feature that will make things easier for one person might make them more difficult for another.

Providing accessibility information

Disabled people, their family and friends need accurate accessibility information to make informed decisions as to where to stay and visit, in view of their requirements.

VisitEngland research carried out in 2022 showed that to save time and energy when researching a trip, people with accessibility requirements want to easily find out what key accessibility features are available at tourism venues. Many people then require more detailed information in an Accessibility Guide to empower them to make personal choices.

Key accessibility features

Free questionnaires are available to help tourism businesses identify the key accessibility features at their venue and promote them in the accessibility section of their website. Download the questionnaire specific to your business type from VisitEngland's Accessible and Inclusive Tourism Toolkit for Businesses at **visitengland.org/access**.

Accessibility Guides

AccessAble's Detailed Access Guides allow tourism operators to provide a quality assured description of their venue's facilities and services, specifically in relation to individuals with accessibility requirements. Go to the Your Accessibility Guide Portal at **visitengland.youraccessibilityguide.co.uk** to get a quote for a professional surveyor to undertake either a Guided or On Site Assessment of your venue and produce a Detailed Access Guide.

NEW

Further guidance

Equality Act: good practice

More information on the Equality Act and help with good business practice is available on the EHRC website: **equalityhumanrights.com.**

What the Equality Act means for you

The Government has produced a series of guides to help operators understand what the act may mean for their business, available on **gov.uk**

Make your business accessible

Find a range of guidance, tools and resources to help increase engagement with the accessible tourism market in VisitEngland's Business Advice Hub, including a comprehensive Accessible & Inclusive Tourism Toolkit: **visitengland.org/access**

Luggage and belongings

KEY FACTS

- If you run a hotel*, you are required by law to take responsibility for the safekeeping of all reasonable items of luggage brought in by guests.
- Hotel* owners have the legal right to detain guests' property until their bill is settled.

Rights and responsibilities

If you operate a hotel* and you accept a guest into your accommodation for at least one night, you are required by law to take responsibility for the safekeeping of all reasonable items of luggage brought in by the guest.

* The **Hotel Proprietors Act 1956** defines a hotel as 'an establishment held out by the proprietor as offering food, drink and, if so required, sleeping accommodation, without special contract, to any traveller presenting himself who appears able and willing to pay a reasonable sum for the services and facilities provided and who is in a fit state to be received'. It is worth noting that this definition of a hotel is somewhat antiquated, and the Courts are likely to apply the same rights and responsibilities to the operator of any serviced accommodation, even if it does not technically meet the definition.

If a guest's property is lost or damaged, the extent of your liability will vary as follows:

You may not be liable, where the loss or damage to the guest's property is caused by an act of negligence on the part of the guest or by an 'Act of God' (such as a flood).

You may be fully liable, where:

- The loss or damage to the guest's property is caused solely by your negligence or wilful act (or that of your staff), or;
- The goods have been entrusted to you for your safekeeping, or;
- The goods have been offered to you for safekeeping but refused by you.

You may limit your liability to £50/£100, where the loss or damage to the guest's property does not fit into either of the above categories and you have displayed the statutory notice set out below in a prominent area of your establishment (near the main entrance or reception area). You may then be liable for a minimum amount of £50 per article and £100 maximum per person.

Since the maximum liability has not increased since 1956, many operators now choose to reimburse their clients to a higher value and claim the cost from their hotel insurance.

> **Note:** under the **London Local Authorities Act 2004**, the limits in Greater London are £750 and £1,500 respectively.

The statutory notice is as follows (the second version of the notice is for Greater London only).

NOTICE:
Loss of or damage to guests' property

Under the Hotel Proprietors' Act 1956, a hotel proprietor may in certain circumstances be liable to make good any loss of or damage to a guest's property even though it was not due to any fault of the proprietor or staff of the hotel. This liability however:

- Extends only to the property of guests who have engaged sleeping accommodation at the hotel.
- Is limited to £50 for any one article and a total of £100 in the case of any one guest, except in the case of property which has been deposited, or offered for deposit, for safe custody.
- Does not cover motor cars or other vehicles of any kind or property lost in them, or horses or other live animals

This notice does not constitute an admission either that the act applies to this hotel or that liability thereunder attaches to the proprietor of this hotel in any particular case.

NOTICE:
Loss of or damage to guest's property
(Greater London only)

Under the Hotel Proprietors' Act 1956 and the London Local Authorities Act 2004, a hotel proprietor may in certain circumstances be liable to make good any loss of or damage to a guest's property even though it was not due to any fault of the proprietor or staff of the hotel. This liability however:

- Extends only to the property of guests who have engaged sleeping accommodation at the hotel.
- Is limited to £750 for any one article and a total of £1,500 in the case of any one guest, except in the case of property which has been deposited, or offered for deposit, for safe custody.
- Does not cover motor cars or other vehicles of any kind or property lost in them, or horses or other live animals.

This notice does not constitute an admission either that the act applies to this hotel or that liability thereunder attaches to the proprietor of this hotel in any particular case.

What if the guest did not stay overnight?

If you provide serviced accommodation of any kind and the guest did not stay overnight (for example, they just visited the restaurant or bar), then you will usually be liable for the loss or damage to your guests' property only if you or your staff have been negligent or if the guest handed the property over to you for safekeeping.

It is difficult to be more specific regarding your liability for the loss of guests' property, as each case depends on the circumstances of the loss or damage.

Returning guests' property

If a guest accidentally leaves an item behind, you have both a duty to look after the item (you can be liable for any loss or damage that occurs while it is in your possession) and a duty to reunite the owner with their property. Therefore, you should make every effort to contact the guest to inform them that you have an item belonging to them, rather than just putting it in a lost property box.

If you are able to contact the owner, you can mutually agree on what to do with the item (for example, whether to post it to them, hold it for collection or to simply dispose of the item). You are within your rights to charge the guest for posting the item back, should you wish to do so, as this is an additional service outside the contract you have with them to provide accommodation. However, the charge should be limited to actual justifiable costs.

LICENCES & CONSENTS
MARKETING
CUSTOMERS
FOOD & DRINK
ENVIRONMENTAL PROTECTION
HEALTH & SAFETY
STAFF
BUSINESS, MANAGEMENT & TAX
FURTHER INFORMATION

If it is not possible to contact the guest, your actions should depend on the nature of the item. For most relatively low-value items (for example clothes) it is sufficient to retain the item for a reasonable period before disposing of them (usually around three months). However, items such as bank cards or driving licences should be handed to the appropriate issuing authority, and high-value items should be handed to the police.

Your right to retain a guest's luggage

Hotel owners

Hotel owners (see note above) have the legal right to detain a guest's property until they settle their bill. This right does not extend to the guest's car or any property left in it, or to the clothes that the guest is wearing.

When the bill is paid, the property must be returned to the guest. No storage charge may be made, and you must reimburse the guest accordingly if the property has been damaged while in your possession.

Selling guests' property

If the bill has not been paid in full after six weeks, you may then sell the guest's property. The sale must be by public auction and it must be advertised at least four weeks in advance in both a London and a local newspaper. The adverts must set out your intention to sell the property, give a full description of the goods, name the guest to whom they belonged, and give full details of the forthcoming sale.

The proceeds of sale, less the amount owed to you and the costs of the advertisements and organising the auction, must then be returned to the guest on demand.

This right is in addition to any other right that you have, such as that of pursuing a claim for non-payment through the Small Claims Court.

> **Note:** you cannot detain a guest except to await the arrival of the police.

Owners of self-catering accommodation

Operators of self-catering properties have no legal right to detain and sell a guest's property.

If a guest does not pay a bill, and further contact or correspondence does not result in payment, then you have the option of pursuing a claim for non-payment through the Small Claims Court (see the *Cancellations and no-shows* section).

Further guidance

Professional legal advice

For more detailed advice, or if a serious claim is made against you, you are advised to obtain professional legal advice.

CUSTOMERS

Childcare

KEY FACTS

- If you regularly provide day care for children under the age of eight for more than two hours in any day, then registration with Ofsted may be necessary.
- The registration process involves filling in an application form and providing details about other people associated with the care.
- Ofsted will need to be satisfied that you are a suitable person and will expect certain qualifications or recommend some training.

Childcare facilities and the Children Act 1989

UPDATED

Under Part X (Child Minding and Day Care for Young Children) of the **Children Act 1989**, you are required to register with Ofsted if you are offering certain types of care facilities for children under the age of eight for more than two hours. This applies regardless of whether the child belongs to a member of staff (for example, a crèche for employees) or a customer (such as a childcare service or kids' activity group). If you are looking after children older than their 8th birthday, you can voluntarily sign-up to be on Ofsted Child Care Register.

Does this apply to me?

No:

- If the child is aged eight and above, or;
- If the child is in your care for less than two hours.

Yes:

UPDATED

- If you are caring for a child at any time between the first September following their 5th birthday (from the first day of the month) and their 8th birthday and the child is in your care for more than two hours – you have to be on the **Ofsted Child Care Register**.
- If you are caring for a child at any time between their date of birth and the end of the August following their 5th birthday and the child is in your care for more than two hours – you have to be on the **Ofsted Early Years Register**.

CUSTOMERS

If you are looking after children that are aged eight and above, you can voluntarily sign-up to be on Ofsted Childcare Register.

You can apply to join one register or both registers at the same time.

You cannot voluntarily register if you look after each child for under two hours a day – even if your business is open for longer than two hours.

The only exception to this is if you provide before- or after-school care for less than two hours a day in total. In this case you can, if you wish, register on the voluntary part of the Childcare Register.

Exemptions

There are various exemptions from the need to register. These include:

1. If you provide tutoring or coaching in either one or two of the following activities to children aged three and over:
   - Sports;
   - Performing arts;
   - Arts and crafts;
   - School study support or homework support;
   - Religious, cultural or language studies.

However, you cannot look after children under five for more than four hours in any one day.

2. If you look after children under eight from one place for 14 days or less in any year.

3. If you operate a crèche and all of the following apply:
   - You look after children under eight for four hours or less each day;
   - The children's parents plan to stay in the immediate area (close by, where they can be summoned immediately);
   - There is no long-term commitment to provide childcare;
   - The crèche is offered to parents or carers as a short-term convenience, for instance, while they are undertaking an activity.

This is particularly relevant to activity and holiday centres where care facilities are offered so that parents can undertake an onsite activity.

However, it is important to note that the **Children Act 1989** says that you have a duty to ensure that the children are well cared for, even if you are not required to be on a register.

Are baby-sitting and baby listening services covered?

Baby-sitting is not specifically covered by the Children Act 1989. This is because care that is provided on the parent's own premises is not normally treated as childminding, unless you care for the children of more than two sets of parents in the home of one of them.

Baby-listening services do not come within the scope of the **Children Act 1989**. However, if you provide baby-sitting services on a regular basis on particular premises, such as a hotel's baby-sitting service, then you may need to register.

If you need to apply for registration, or are in any doubt as to whether you need to register, you should contact Ofsted.

Registration with Ofsted

In the first instance, you should contact your local authority for information about pre-registration briefings and an application pack. Ofsted recommends a briefing session with your local authority before making your application.

The registration process starts as soon as Ofsted receives your form. They aim to complete the process within 12 weeks for childminders and 25 weeks for day care providers.

During this time, Ofsted will arrange a registration visit and a 'suitable person' interview with one of their inspectors. They will carry out a number of checks, including with the Criminal Records Bureau, on everyone associated with an application such as the applicant, day care manager or those who live on the premises where the applicant proposes to provide child-minding.

The registration process is explained in the Ofsted leaflets mentioned below in *Further guidance*.

After registration, Ofsted will conduct the first inspection within seven months of you starting to care for children. Regular inspections of the quality of care follow this first inspection at least once every three years and, in some cases, more often.

Training

The Department for Education's Early Years Foundation Stage (EYFS) is the statutory framework which sets the standards that all Early Years providers must meet, in order to ensure that children learn and develop well and are kept healthy and safe. This is a comprehensive framework that sets the standards for learning, development and care of children from birth to five years old, and was revised in 2014. All registered early years providers are required to use the EYFS.

Further guidance

Ofsted registration

The Ofsted website gives information on registration for day care providers and childminders: **gov.uk/government/organisations/ofsted**. You can also call their helpline on **0300 123 1231**.

Early Years Foundation Stage

The *Early Years Foundation Stage handbook* can be downloaded from the Foundation Years website: **foundationyears.org.uk**.

Alternative dispute resolution

KEY FACTS

- If you are unable to resolve a dispute with a customer, you must provide the customer with the name and web address of a certified Alternative Dispute Resolution (ADR) provider, and whether you are willing to use this provider to settle the dispute.
- All businesses must provide an email address for customers on their website.

Alternative dispute resolution

The traditional means of adjudicating on a dispute between a business and a customer who have been unable to reach an agreement has been via the court system (usually the Small Claims Court). However, this route can be both expensive and time-consuming.

The **Alternative Dispute Resolution (ADR) Regulations 2015** established a new low-cost means to resolve these disputes, by detailing independent alternative dispute resolution providers that businesses can use to provide adjudication. Although there is no requirement in the regulations for ADR providers to be certified, it is recommended that you use a certified ADR provider to help ensure the quality of the service.

ADR providers are organisations or individuals who can act as an independent adjudicator and make a decision on the dispute. Normally, before using an ADR provider, you will agree with the customer as to whether the decision will be legally binding. If you sign an agreement that the ADR provider's decision is legally binding, then the decision can be enforced in the same way as adjudicated/arbitrated decisions.

If either you or the customer do not agree to the decision being legally binding, then either side is still able to go to a court or tribunal to seek redress.

While it is not compulsory for businesses to use an ADR provider, all businesses that undertake the sale of goods and services to customers (the regulations do not cover business-to-business transactions) are required to provide customers with information on the ADR.

The dispute resolution process

If you enter into a dispute with a customer, the first course of action is to try to negotiate a resolution that is acceptable to both yourself and the customer. The ADR Regulations only come into effect if your negotiations with the customer have reached an impasse.
At this point, the ADR Regulations require you to inform the customer via a 'durable medium' such as a letter or email (that is, not verbally) of:

- The name and web address of a certified provider, and;
- Whether you are willing to use this ADR provider to settle the dispute.

Note: if you are a member of a trade association or another organisation that requires members to use an ADR scheme, you must consent to using the ADR provider whose details you provide.

Once you have sent the customer this information, and providing that you have stated that you are willing to use this ADR provider, both sides have 12 months in which to send evidence to the ADR provider.

Within three weeks of receiving the evidence from both sides, the ADR provider will inform both parties as to whether they will adjudicate over the dispute and, if so, will then provide a decision within 90 days.

If you trade online

Up until 1 January 2021, if you traded online, you were also required to provide a link on your website to the European Commission's Online Dispute Resolution (ODR) platform. With the UK now having left the EU, UK businesses no longer have access to the ODR platform and must use a UK-based ADR provider instead.

Providing an email address

A final requirement of the ADR Regulations 2015 is for all businesses to provide a contact email address on their website. This means that it is now insufficient to just have an online contact form on your website which does not show the email address.

Further guidance

Alternative Dispute Resolution providers

A list of certified ADR providers, and the sectors they cover, is available from the Trading Standards website: **tradingstandards.uk**

Guidance on the Regulations

A copy of the *Alternative Dispute Resolution Regulations 2015 guidance for business* is available on the Business Companion website: **businesscompanion.info**

FOOD & DRINK

Food safety and hygiene

KEY FACTS

- If you supply food to customers you must comply with the provisions of food safety and hygiene legislation. The word 'food' is defined as including drink.
- You should not provide food that is unsafe (for example, injurious to health) or unfit for human consumption.
- You must put in place and implement a food safety management system to ensure that the food you provide is safe to eat. These procedures must be based on the Food Standards Agency's Hazard Analysis and Critical Control Point (HACCP) principles.
- You must not keep foods at a temperature that might make them unsafe to eat. There are specified temperatures that different hot or chilled foods must be kept at.
- Registration with the local authority is required for accommodation businesses that serve or supply food or drink of any description, including bed and breakfasts.

Food safety legislation

The most important food safety and hygiene legislation applying in the UK comprises:

- The **Food Safety Act 1990**, which provides the framework for food legislation and creates offences in relation to safety, quality and labelling.
- The **General Food Law (Amendment etc.) (EU Exit) Regulations 2019**, which created general principles and requirements of food law.
- The **Food Safety and Hygiene (England) Regulations 2013**, which revoke and re-enact with some minor changes to the **Food Hygiene (England) Regulations 2006** and certain provisions of the **General Food Regulations 2004**.

Does food safety legislation apply to me?

Yes: if you supply food to customers, you must comply with the provisions of the legislation. The word 'food' is defined as including drink.

Main provisions of the legislation

General Food Law Regulation (EC) 178/2002

The General Food Law Regulation (EC) No 178/2002 covers the placing of unsafe or unfit food on the market. You should not place food on the market (that is to sell or supply food, or hold it with intent to supply) which is:

- Unsafe (that is, injurious to health).
- Unfit for human consumption (for example, food that is rotten, 'gone off' or has been subject to considerable contamination).

The regulation also covers traceability. You should keep records of businesses which have supplied food to you and any businesses you supply food to. The Food Standards Agency (FSA) guidance says this should include:

- Address of customer or supplier.
- Nature and quantity of products.
- Date of transaction and delivery.

This is to help when a food manufacturer needs to coordinate a withdrawal of unsafe food. There are offences for breaches of these provisions in the **General Food Regulations 2004** (as amended).

Offences under the Food Safety Act 1990

- **Rendering food injurious to health.** Not only is it an offence to place food on the market which is harmful to health, but it is also an offence to do anything which would make food harmful by adding something to it or removing something from it. This may apply even if you did not realise the effect of what you were doing at the time.
- **Selling 'to the purchaser's prejudice' food which is not of the nature, substance or quality demanded.** 'To the purchaser's prejudice' means to his or her disadvantage. This includes things like supplying lemonade when low-calorie lemonade has been requested, or supplying a beef casserole when the customer has ordered lamb casserole.
- **Falsely or misleading describing, advertising, or presenting food.** This offence can be committed when statements or pictures concerning food are untrue. It can also cover statements that are strictly speaking correct but presented in such a way that the customer is led to the wrong conclusion. Bearing this in mind, you should take care with the descriptions of dishes on your menus. There is a similar provision about this in the General Food Law Regulation.

General food hygiene

Do the regulations apply to me?

Yes: if you supply food to customers, you must register with your local authority at least 28 days prior to trading and comply with the regulations. It does not matter if you are a small bed and breakfast, a five-star hotel or you provide meals in other circumstances. As a food business operator, the onus is on you to make sure you supply safe food.

If you are not sure whether you should register as a food business, you should speak to your local environmental health department for advice.

How do I comply?

Food safety management procedures

You must put in place and implement a food safety management system to ensure that the food you provide is safe to eat. These procedures must be based on the HACCP principles, although they can be proportionate to the nature and size of the business and should not be burdensome on small businesses. HACCP stands for:

- **H**azard;
- **A**nalysis;
- **C**ritical;
- **C**ontrol;
- **P**oint.

This means that you must:

- Analyse all potential **food hazards:** a hazard is anything that might hurt the consumer.
- Identify the **points in operation** where hazards might occur.
- Decide which of the points identified are **critical** to ensuring food safety.
- Identify and implement effective **control and monitoring** procedures at those critical points.
- Determine what **corrective actions** must be taken if your procedures are not working.
- Keep appropriate **records** to show your procedures are working.
- **Review** all of the above periodically and whenever your food operations change.

Records

The amount of paperwork you will need to keep as part of your safety procedures will also depend on the size and nature of your business. Larger businesses will need to maintain some documented procedures in addition to their records.

The Food Standards Agency offers a number of models to help you comply with the record-keeping part of the procedures (for more details, see the *Safer food, better business for caterers* section of the FSA website. You can also contact your local authority for advice.

Food premises

As a basic requirement, food premises must comply with the following:

- They must be kept clean, be well maintained and designed to enable good hygiene practices to be adhered to.
- They must have adequate hand-washing facilities available, with supplies of hot and cold water, and drying facilities suitably located and designated for cleaning hands. Toilets must not open directly into rooms where food is handled.
- They must have adequate means of ventilation, lighting and drainage.

What is adequate in any situation will depend on the nature and size of the business. In addition, the following requirements apply to all rooms, except dining areas, in which food is prepared:

- Surface finishes to walls, doors, floors and equipment should be easy to clean and, if necessary, to disinfect.
- There must be adequate facilities for cleaning work tools and equipment and for washing food.

Slightly scaled-down, but broadly similar, requirements apply to premises that are only used occasionally for catering purposes.

The full list of requirements are detailed in the *Safer food, better business for caterers* section of the FSA website **food.gov.uk**

Domestic premises

Premises 'used primarily as a dwelling house but where foods are regularly prepared' (for example, this might include some bed and breakfasts) are subject to slightly different requirements with regard to the rooms where food is prepared (*Regulation (EC) 852/2004*, Annex II Chapter III). Speak to the environmental health department of your local authority for guidance.

Further requirements

Equipment: all equipment and other items which come into contact with food must be kept clean and well maintained and installed in such a way as to allow adequate cleaning of the surrounding area.

Food waste: waste must not be allowed to accumulate and, as a general rule, must be kept in closed containers which are easy to clean and disinfect. The waste must be eliminated in a hygienic and environmentally-friendly way and must not constitute a direct or indirect source of contamination.

Water supply: there must be an adequate supply of drinking water. Generally, this water supply should be used to make sure that food is not contaminated, and any ice should be made from it.

Cleaning agents: cleaning chemicals must not be stored in areas where food is handled.

Personal hygiene: everyone working with food must maintain a high level of personal cleanliness, including clean clothing. You must not allow anyone suffering from an illness which could contaminate food to work in a food handling area. Additionally, staff working in food handling areas are required to report such illnesses to you. You should also ensure that good hand washing routines are maintained.

Raw materials: you should not buy, or supply, any raw material that will not be fit for human consumption.

Protection against contamination: all food must be protected against any form of contamination, including pests, which would make it fail food safety requirements.

Training: all staff handling food must receive training commensurate or appropriate to the work they do. The *Industry Guide to Good Hygiene Practice: Catering Guide* includes a table that sets out the training requirements for four different categories of food handlers within a business. All food handlers must receive induction training in the essentials of food hygiene prior to starting work. The level of supervision and instruction and/or training required to comply with the legislation can only be determined by the work activities that they perform. Other staff who are not food handlers may also need some instruction or training as a matter of good practice.

The full list of requirements are detailed in the in the *Safer food, better business for caterers* section of the FSA website **food.gov.uk**

Food and temperature control

The temperature control rules are found in **Food Hygiene (England) Regulations 2006** (and equivalent legislation in Scotland, Wales and Northern Ireland).

Do the regulations apply to me?

Yes: if you are an accommodation provider that offers food to guests, you must comply with the regulations. Just as with the hygiene regulations, it does not matter what type of premises you are – all food operators as defined need to comply with the temperature requirements.

UPDATED

What are the requirements?

You must not keep foods at a temperature that might make them unsafe to eat. Foods which need temperature control for safety must be held either:

- Hot (at or above a minimum temperature of 63ºC).
- Chilled (at or below a maximum temperature of 8ºC).

In addition to this, foods that are likely to support the growth of harmful bacteria or the formation of toxins should not be kept at temperatures which would result in a risk to health.

Exemptions

Some foods are exempt from the 8ºC limit, such as:

- Bakery products which are to be used quickly;
- Most unopened canned foods;
- Dried foods;
- Food which is ripening or maturing at room temperature (for example soft cheeses).

Serving and display of food

The regulations also have a degree of flexibility in the serving and display of food. For example, food that should normally be kept at or below 8ºC may be kept above that temperature for a single period of four hours to allow it to be served or displayed (for example, food on a buffet table or a cheese trolley). After this period it should either be thrown away or chilled back to 8ºC or below until used.

Likewise, food which will be served hot may be kept on display out of temperature control (63ºC and above) for a single period of two hours. If any food is left after this time, food should either be discarded, reheated to 63°C or above (in Scotland, food must be reheated to 82° or above), or cooled as quickly as possible to 8°C or below until final consumption. Guidance on temperature control legislation in the UK is available on the FSA website **food.gov.uk**

Handling ready-to-eat foods safely

It is important to handle ready-to-eat foods carefully as they could, if mishandled, lead to cases of food poisoning. They include sandwiches, salads, desserts, cold cooked meats and foods you have cooked in advance to serve cold. The following controls should prevent this from happening:

- Check that the temperature of purchased frozen and chilled ready-to-eat foods is correct (under 8ºC for chilled foods, -18ºC for frozen foods).
- Check products are within the date code and that the packaging is not damaged.
- Do not use products after their 'use by' date.
- Store ready-to-eat foods separately from raw foods, such as

meat, poultry, eggs, etc. Store at the correct temperature and stock rotate.

- Follow the manufacturer's instructions on storage and preparation.
- Wash and dry hands before the preparation of ready-to-eat foods.
- Use clean knives, utensils and separate boards for the preparation of ready-to-eat foods.
- Sanitise boards, surfaces and utensils after use.
- Keep ready-to-eat foods covered after preparation.
- Once prepared, do not allow ready-to-eat foods to remain at room temperature for any longer than necessary.
- Buy a thermometer to monitor temperatures.

Enforcement and food hygiene inspections

Local authorities are responsible for enforcing food hygiene laws and authorised enforcement officers have the right to enter and inspect food premises (registered or not) at any reasonable time without having to make an appointment – they will usually come without notice.

They carry out routine inspections and the frequency varies, depending on the degree of risk posed by the business and its previous record. Inspectors may also visit as a result of a complaint.

Inspectors (that is, 'authorised officers') will look at the way you operate your business to identify any potential hazards and to make sure that you are complying with the law. They will discuss problems with you and advise on possible solutions. They also have the following powers:

- To take samples and photographs and to inspect your records.
- To write to you informally, asking you to rectify any problems that they have found. If a breach of the law has been identified, they may serve you with a 'hygiene improvement notice'.
- To detain or seize suspect foods.
- To recommend a prosecution (although this is normally done only in serious cases).
- To serve a 'hygiene emergency prohibition notice' which forbids the use of the premises or equipment if there is an imminent health risk to the public. Such a notice must be confirmed by the Courts (or a Sheriff in Scotland).

Read further guidance on food hygiene inspections on the FSA website food.gov.uk

Allergies

A small percentage of the population is allergic to, or intolerant of, certain foods. In the UK, it is estimated that around 2% of the population suffer from food allergies and each year some people become seriously ill and even die from extreme reactions to foods such as peanuts, shellfish and eggs.

Under the **Food Safety Act 1990** and the **General Food Law (Amendment etc.) (EU Exit) Regulations 2019** you are responsible for ensuring that the food customers eat is safe and the quality is what they expect. This means you should understand exactly which foods can cause problems.

The following is a list of the 14 most common allergens:

- Cereals containing gluten, namely: wheat (such as spelt and Khorasan wheat), rye, barley, oats;
- Crustaceans, for example: prawns, crabs, lobster, crayfish;
- Eggs;
- Fish;
- Peanuts;
- Soybeans;
- Milk (including lactose);
- Nuts, namely: almonds, hazelnuts, walnuts, cashews, pecan nuts, Brazil nuts, pistachio nuts, macadamia (or Queensland) nuts;
- Celery (including celeriac);
- Mustard;
- Sesame;
- Sulphur dioxide/sulphites, where added and at a level above 10mg/kg or 10mg/L in the finished product. This can be used as a preservative in dried fruit;
- Lupin, which includes lupin seeds and flour and can be found in types of bread, pastries and pasta;
- Molluscs, for example: mussels, whelks, oysters, snails and squid.

You must be aware of any use of these allergens in the food that you prepare, and communicate this use to your customers. From October 2021, the way food businesses must provide allergen labelling information for **Prepacked for Direct Sale (PPDS)** has changed. Foods must have a label with a full ingredients list with allergenic ingredients emphasised within it. See the *Food labelling* section for more information on your requirement to inform customers of any use of allergens in food you serve customers.

Food Hygiene Ratings – 'Scores on the Doors'

In 2010, the Food Standards Agency introduced a National Food Hygiene Rating Scheme. This scheme ranks the cleanliness of premises that sell food between '0' (meaning urgent improvement is needed) and '5' (meaning very good and complies with all legal requirements).

The National Food Hygiene Rating Scheme covers all businesses that supply food directly to consumers, which includes hotels, bed and breakfasts, restaurants, cafés, takeaways and attractions that provide a food offering.

It is not mandatory for you to display the score that you have received if your business is in England (it is a legal requirement to display the rating in Wales and Northern Ireland). However, even if you do not display your rating, it is available to the public on the FSA's searchable online database.

If you believe that the food hygiene rating that you have been given is unfair, you have:

- A right to appeal within 21 days of being notified about your food hygiene rating.
- A 'right to reply' which allows you to publish an explanation of any actions you have taken to improve hygiene standards at your premises since your inspection, or to say if there were unusual circumstances at the time of the inspection that might have affected your rating, alongside your rating on the FSA's public database.
- An opportunity to request a re-visit when improvements have been made in order to be re-assessed for a new rating.

Note: Food Standards Scotland operates a different Food Hygiene rating scheme in Scotland, which comprises three ratings: Pass, Improvement Required and Exempt Premises.

Further guidance

Your local authority

For information and advice about food safety and hygiene, or 'Scores on the Doors', contact your local environmental health department.

Food Standards Agency (FSA)

FSA produces a range of useful publications on its website, including advice on food allergens and food hygiene: **food.gov.uk**

Food hygiene ratings

For more information on the National Food Hygiene Rating Scheme visit the FSA food ratings website: **ratings.food.gov.uk.**

Guide to good hygiene practice

UKHospitality has produced guidance on your legal obligations and the practical requirements to comply with food hygiene law, available on their website: **ukhospitality.org.uk**

Food labelling

KEY FACTS

NEW

- If you provide food for customers that contains genetically modified (GM) ingredients, you need to comply with GM food legislation.
- You need to provide information to customers on 14 allergens that may be used as ingredients in any food you sell.
- If you are providing pre-packaged food, any allergens must be highlighted on the Ingredients List on the label.
- Calorie labelling is only required if your business has more than 250 staff, or you run a franchise where the total number of people employed in different companies under the franchise is more than 250.

Pricing food

For details on pricing food, see the *Pricing and charging* section.

Food labelling and genetically modified food

To allow food providers and consumers to make informed decisions about the food they use or eat, there are food labelling regulations in place.

The rules covering genetically modified (GM) foods are outlined in:

- The **European Regulations (EC) No. 1829/2004, (EC) No. 1830/2004.**
- The **GM Food (England) Regulations 2004.**
- The **Genetically Modified Organisms (Traceability and Labelling) Regulations 2004** (and equivalent Regulations in Scotland, Wales and Northern Ireland).

Do the regulations apply to me?

No: if there are no ingredients containing, consisting of, or produced from genetically modified organisms in the food you offer to customers, the regulations do not apply to you. Foods produced with the help of GM technology do not have to be labelled. For example, cheese produced with the help of GM enzymes does not need to be labelled as the enzymes are not ingredients in the cheese.

LICENCES & CONSENTS
MARKETING
CUSTOMERS
FOOD & DRINK
ENVIRONMENTAL PROTECTION
HEALTH & SAFETY
STAFF
BUSINESS, MANAGEMENT & TAX
FURTHER INFORMATION

Also, if animals are fed on GM animal feed, the products produced from them (for example meat, milk and eggs) do not need to be labelled.

Yes: if you are providing food for customers that contains ingredients containing, consisting of, or produced from genetically modified organisms, whether or not there is any GM material in the final product (for example oil produced from GM soya or maize), you need to comply. Any intentional use of GM must be labelled, but there is a tolerance level (of 0.9%) for the accidental inclusion of EU-authorised GM material. For further information, see the ***genetically modified food*** section of the Food Standards Agency website **food.gov.uk**

Any food bought by you to prepare food for customers should be similarly labelled for GM ingredients, so you should be able to tell whether or not you need to comply.

What do the regulations require?

The words 'genetically modified' or 'produced from genetically modified [name of organism]' must be displayed on a notice, menu, ticket or label which can be easily read by customers. For example: 'Products on the menu marked * contain ingredients produced from genetically modified soya.'

Allergies and labelling

It is estimated that around 2% of the population suffer from food allergies, and each year some people become seriously ill and even die from extreme reactions to foods such as peanuts, shellfish and eggs.

Under the **Food Safety Act 1990** and the **General Food Law (Amendment etc.) (EU Exit) Regulations 2019** you are responsible for ensuring that the food that customers eat is safe, and the quality is what they expect. This means you should understand exactly which foods can cause problems.

The 14 most common allergens are:

- Cereals containing gluten, namely: wheat (such as spelt and Khorasan wheat), rye, barley, oats;
- Crustaceans, for example: prawns, crabs, lobster, crayfish;
- Eggs;
- Fish;
- Peanuts;
- Soybeans;
- Milk (including lactose);
- Nuts, namely: almonds, hazelnuts, walnuts, cashews, pecan nuts, Brazil nuts, pistachio nuts, macadamia (or Queensland) nuts;
- Celery (including celeriac);
- Mustard;

- Sesame;
- Sulphur dioxide/sulphites, where added and at a level above 10mg/kg or 10mg/L in the finished product. This can be used as a preservative in dried fruit;
- Lupin, which includes lupin seeds and flour and can be found in types of bread, pastries and pasta;
- Molluscs, for example: mussels, whelks, oysters, snails and squid.

Pre-packaged food

Food labelling requirements for prepacked for direct sale food changed on 1 October 2021 in England, Wales and Northern Ireland, as a result of a number of high-profile cases where people with food allergies have died as a result of inadequate labelling on pre-packaged food.

The allergen labelling requirements apply to a category of food called 'prepacked for direct sale'. This is food which is packaged at the same place as it is offered to consumers. The food should also be in the packaging before it is ordered or selected.

It includes food that customers select themselves (for example packaged sandwiches from a display) and pre-wrapped products kept behind a counter (such as bottled drinks, or meat and cheese products produced on-site). It can also include some food sold at mobile or temporary outlets.

Prepacked for direct sale food is determined by three criteria:

1. **When it is packaged**
   It needs to be packaged before the consumer selects or orders it.
2. **Where it is packaged**
   It needs to be packaged at the same premises, or at the site it is offered or sold to consumers. This includes food packaged by the same business and sold at a temporary or mobile site, such as a food truck or market stall. It also includes making food at home to take to sell at a café on the business premises.
3. **How it is packaged**
   It needs to be fully or partly enclosed by packaging, so that it cannot be altered without opening or changing the packaging in some way. In addition, the food must be ready for final sale to the consumer (for example, not ingredients that you have packaged to take to a shop or café).

All prepacked for direct sale food that meets the requirements above will need to have a label showing:

- The name of the food.
- A full ingredients list, with the 14 allergens required to be declared by food law emphasised on the ingredients list (for example in capitals or a bold font) if they are present in the food.

More information on the requirements and how to comply is available on the *introduction to allergen labelling changes* page on the FSA website **food.gov.uk**

Unpackaged food

You need to provide information to customers on any of the 14 allergens used as ingredients in foods that are sold without packaging or wrapped after ordering. This information could be written down on a chalkboard or menu, or provided orally by a member of staff. Where the specific allergen information is not provided upfront, clear signposting to where this information could be obtained must be provided (for example, a note on your menu telling customers to ask a server regarding the use of allergens in any of the items on the menu).

It is therefore very important that your staff are trained and regularly updated on the use of any allergens in food that you serve.

These rules only cover information about major allergens intentionally used as ingredients. They do not cover allergens present following accidental contact.

Calorie labelling

In 2021, the Government introduced the **Calorie Labelling (Out of Home Sector) (England) Regulations**. The purpose of these regulations is to make consumers more aware of the calorific content of food that is prepared for them for immediate consumption either on site (for example in restaurants and pubs) or off the premises (such as takeaways), so that they can make more healthy choices.

At present, the regulations only apply to large businesses with more than 250 employees. These employees do not have to all be on the same site, so if a restaurant chain has 10 branches with 30 staff at each one, then their total number of employees is 300 and they must comply with the regulations. The same applies to franchised businesses where the total number of employees across all the franchise agreements is more than 250.

The main requirements of the regulations are:

- The calorific content of each food offering has to be displayed at the 'point of choice' – that is, on a printed or electronic menu, blackboard or a display if the food is provided for self-service.
- Reference the size of the portion to which the calorie information relates.
- Display the statement that 'adults need around 2000 kcal a day'.

While it is not a legal requirement for businesses with fewer than 250 employees to undertake calorie labelling, the Government is encouraging smaller businesses to adopt calorie labelling on a voluntary basis. The Government also plans to review the regulations in 2026 with the intention of determining whether the requirement for calorie labelling should be extended to smaller businesses.

Further guidance

Allergen guidance for businesses

Further information on GM foods, food allergies and intolerance is available from the FSA website: **food.gov.uk**

Allergen toolkit

The Nationwide Caterers Association has published free guidance about allergens on its website: **ncass.org.uk**

UKHospitality

UKHospitality has a free Q&A document on allergen labelling, as well as allergen guidance for its members, on its website: **ukhospitality.org.uk**

Your local authority

Contact your Trading Standards department at your local authority for more information on food labelling.

ENVIRONMENTAL PROTECTION

Single-use plastics

KEY FACTS

- It is illegal to provide plastic drink stirrers and cotton buds to customers.
- There are significant restrictions on providing customers with plastic straws.
- The ban on single-use plastics was extended in October 2023 and now includes plates, cutlery and other items.

To reduce the level of plastic waste, the Government introduced the **Environmental Protection (Plastic Straws, Cotton Buds and Stirrers) (England) Regulations 2020.**

These regulations make it an offence to provide customers with three different types of single-use plastic products: straws, cotton buds and drink stirrers. The regulations treat these different products in slightly varying ways.

Plastic drink stirrers

It is an offence to sell or supply drink stirrers to end-users and businesses in England. This means that it is an offence for you to be sold plastic drink stirrers by a supplier and for you to supply them to your customers.

Plastic cotton buds

It is an offence to sell or supply plastic cotton buds to end-users in England, but they can still be supplied to businesses. This means that you are to purchase plastic cotton buds if you need them for a purpose such as cleaning fixtures and fittings, but it is an offence for you to provide them to your customers.

Plastic straws

It is an offence to sell or supply plastic straws to end-users in England, but they can still be supplied to businesses.
However, there is an exemption to this regulation for catering establishments, which includes restaurants, pubs, bars, cafés and hotel dining rooms. If you are providing food and/or drink for immediate consumption, you are allowed to continue to provide

customers with single-use plastic straws, provided that:

- The straws are not kept in a place where they are visible to customers;
- The straws are not kept in a place where customers have access to them, and;
- The straws are not offered or provided to customers unless requested by the customer.

This means that you can provide a plastic straw to a customer if they specifically ask for one. You cannot serve a drink with a plastic straw in it or put a box of straws on a counter for customers to help themselves.

It is also illegal to sell products such as cartons of drink with plastic straws attached.

The ban on single-use plastics was expanded in October 2023 with the inclusion of the following products:

NEW

Single-use plastic plates, trays and bowls

This includes any item regardless of the type of plastic (including recycled, compostable and biodegradable plastics) or how much plastic the item contains. For example, if the item is a paper plate with a plastic film to stop liquid penetrating the paper, it will still be banned.

There are two exceptions to this ban:

1. Business to business sales.

If you are supplying another business and not the end consumer, the use of these items is still permitted.

2. Packaged food

This is food that is either pre-packaged or packaged at the point of sale, such as a plate filled at the counter of a takeaway.

Single-use plastic cutlery

Single-use plastic cutlery includes any item used to consume food, so it includes Sporks and chopsticks.

Balloon sticks

These are the plastic sticks that attach to the nozzle of a balloon to enable children to carry the balloon.

Ready-to-consume food and drink in polystyrene containers

This includes polystyrene boxes for takeaway food such as fish and chips and burgers, trays provided for food at food stalls, and polystyrene cups used to serve tea, coffee and soup.

There is, however, an exemption for providing food or drink in a polystyrene container if the item needs further preparation before it is consumed. So, for example, raw meat can be provided on a polystyrene tray because it needs to be cooked, and a cup containing coffee granules and sugar can be provided because it needs hot water to be added before it can be consumed.

The ban on single use plastics is enforced by Local Authority inspectors who have the power to inspect premises, obtain samples of the items in which the food and drink are being provided and impose fines for non-compliance. Customers are also able to complain about non-compliance to Trading Standards.

NEW

Further guidance

Single-use plastics

Guidance on the regulations for single-use plastics is available on Gov.uk.

Coal and firewood

KEY FACTS

- It is illegal to sell house coal and wet wood in quantities of under 2 cubic metres.
- Businesses that provide coal or wood products to guests must ensure that the products they supply conform to certification requirements.

The **Air Quality (Domestic Solid Fuels Standards) (England) Regulations 2020** were introduced to reduce pollution caused by domestic fireplaces as part of the Government's Clean Air Strategy. This strategy aims to reduce emissions of very small particulate matter under 2.5 micrometres in size (PM2.5), which can have many adverse health impacts. In the short term, these particles can irritate the eyes, nose and throat, and cause coughing, sneezing and shortness of breath. In the longer term, prolonged exposure to these small particles can cause permanent respiratory problems such as asthma, chronic bronchitis and heart disease.

The burning of fuels such as wet wood and house coal is known to produce large amounts of PM2.5, so to address this, the regulations place restrictions on the sale of domestic coal and wood products.

The restrictions are:

- It is unlawful to sell traditional bagged house coal
- It is unlawful to sell wet wood in units under 2 cubic metres.
- Wet wood in larger volumes must be sold with advice on how to dry it before burning.
- All manufactured solid fuels (e.g. coal-based briquettes) must have a low sulphur content and only emit a small amount of smoke.

To support these restrictions, a certification scheme called Ready to Burn requires wood and coal products to be certified and labelled by suppliers, to ensure that they can be easily identified. Retailers such as hardware depots or specialist fuel suppliers are only able to sell fuel that is accompanied by the correct label, so businesses that buy wood and coal products from these suppliers will automatically be purchasing products that comply with the regulations.

If you provide your own logs to guests or buy products directly from someone who splits their own logs, you will need to ensure that the product you are buying is certified or that you properly store and dry the wood before providing it to your guests. To meet the requirements of the regulations, this means storing the wood until its moisture content falls below 20%.

In this context, it is important to note that any product you provide to a guest – even if it is not separately charged for – is deemed to have been sold to them, because its cost has been factored into the price charged for the accommodation. As such, providing traditional coal to guests would be to 'resell' the coal and would therefore be illegal. Similarly, providing 'free' wood to guests is a sale, and the wood must therefore have a moisture content of less than 20%.

Further guidance

HETAS website

Further guidance on the regulations is available from the HETAS website: **hetas.co.uk**

HEALTH & SAFETY

Health and Safety at Work Act

KEY FACTS

- The Health and Safety at Work etc. Act 1974 (HSWA) places general duties and responsibilities on all people at work, including employers, employees and the self-employed.
- You are responsible for ensuring, so far as is reasonably practicable, the health, safety and welfare of all your employees at work, plus anyone else who could be affected by your work activities – for example customers, casual workers and contractors.
- You are required to consult with employees, or their representative, on issues that may affect their safety.
- Your employees also have a responsibility to take reasonable care of their own health and safety.
- If you employ more than five people you must have a written health and safety policy.
- You must carry out a risk assessment to identify and manage any risks

Does the Health and Safety at Work etc Act apply to me?
The Act applies to all businesses that have employees. In 2015, an exemption was introduced for self-employed people with no employees whose activities do not impact other people. However, if your work activity poses a risk to the health and safety of others, then the law applies to you. Because accommodation and attraction businesses have customers who enter the premises, it is therefore unlikely that this exemption will apply to your business.

Your responsibilities as an employer to employees and others

It is your duty to protect the health, safety and welfare of your employees and other people who might be affected by your business, including customers and contractors who enter the premises to undertake work for you – such as cleaners and people undertaking maintenance work. You are required to do whatever is reasonably practicable to achieve this.

The Health and Safety at Work Act etc.1974 (HSWA) sets the framework for health and safety regulations in the workplace. It places general duties and responsibilities on all people at work, including employers, employees and the self-employed. There are two important responsibilities for an employer:

- You are responsible for ensuring, so far as is reasonably practicable, the health, safety and welfare of all your employees at work (your employees also have a responsibility to take reasonable care of their own health and safety).
- You have a wider responsibility to ensure, again so far as is reasonably practicable, the safety of other people who are affected by your business – for example customers, casual workers and contractors.

All of the health and safety legislation covered in this section relates to employers, employees, the self-employed and the workplace.

Health and safety law seldom prescribes specific rules for you to follow. Rather, it requires you to undertake whatever measures are necessary to manage safety on your business premises. There are severe penalties for not doing so, which include the possibility of a jail sentence. It is mandatory that you devote time and careful attention to the management of safety in your business; this is at the heart of the law, and you cannot fulfil your legal duties by form-filling or cursory treatment of the topic.

It is important to note that under the **Safety Representatives and Safety Committees Regulations 1977** and the **Health and Safety (Consultation with Employees) Regulations 1996**, you have a duty to consult with your employees, or their representatives, on health and safety matters. You must consult on:

- The introduction of any measure which may substantially affect their health and safety at work, for example the introduction of new equipment or new systems of work;
- Arrangements for getting competent people to help them comply with health and safety laws (a competent person is someone who has the necessary knowledge, skills and

experience to help an employer meet the requirements of health and safety law);
- The information you must give your employees on the risks and dangers arising from their work, measures to reduce or remove these risks, and what employees should do if they are exposed to a risk;
- The planning and organisation of health and safety training;
- The health and safety consequences of introducing new technology.

Further information on your requirements regarding consulting employees can be found on the HSE website: hse.gov.uk

Additional health and safety legislation

Other health and safety legislation supplements the HSWA's general responsibilities with specific requirements. The key regulations are covered in the following sections:
- *Fire safety (general);*
- *Fire safety of furniture and furnishings;*
- *Safety management;*
- *Hazards in the workplace;*
- *Hazards from work activities;*
- *Swimming, gym and outdoor safety.*

Policy statement and risk assessment

At the heart of health and safety legislation is the requirement for you to undertake a health and safety assessment of your premises, identifying:
- Any significant health and safety risks;
- Any group of employees identified as being especially at risk.

On the basis of this assessment, you must develop and implement a safety policy to manage any risks that you identify.

NEW

If you employ five or more people, your health and safety policy must be written down, including details of any groups of employees particularly at risk such as older, younger, pregnant or disabled employees and the arrangements you are putting in place for the management of safety in your business.

Even if you do not employ five people, it is still good practice to make a written record of your assessment and policy statement. If you do not, it may later be difficult to demonstrate that you have fulfilled your duties under the HSWA.

For information about how to do a risk assessment, see the *Safety management* section.

Health and safety notices

If you employ anyone, you are required by the **Health and Safety Information for Employees Regulations 1989** to display the HSE-approved Health and Safety Law poster.

Alternatively, you can provide your employees with individual copies of the same information, in a leaflet entitled *Your health, your safety: A brief guide for workers*.

Mental health

Under the HSWA, you also have a legal duty to assess risks related to work-related stress, and to adopt practices aimed at safeguarding the mental health of your staff. There are six main areas where all employers need to assess the impact on the mental health of their employees, to ensure that they are fulfilling their duty of care:

1. Demands on employees

This means assessing each employee's workload, target setting, work requirements and the workplace environment to make sure that they are not causing undue stress.

2. Control

This means assessing how much control staff feel they have over the way they work and their work environment.

3. Relationships

This means promoting a positive working environment that avoids conflict or harassment, either between employees or between employees and customers or contractors. It must be remembered that one person's 'jokes' or 'banter' is another person's harassment.

4. Support

This means that if an employee does encounter a problem, the organisation will provide support either through procedures or at least by having an environment where they feel that they can voice their concerns – and that these concerns will be treated seriously.

5. Role

This means ensuring that employees have the confidence to know what their role is and the training to fulfil it successfully, as well as knowing the roles of other employees so that conflict is avoided.

6. Change

This means having management, communication and support plans in place when the business is going through change (for example redundancies, expansion or being sold) and that staff understand their individual situation and can plan accordingly.

To help managers undertake this assessment, the Health and Safety Executive (HSE) has produced a publication called *Tackling work-related stress using the Management Standards approach: A step-by-step workbook*.

Enforcement

Local Environmental Health Officers (EHOs) are responsible for enforcing health and safety.

Further guidance

Introduction to health and safety

There is a section on the HSE website that provides an overview of what health and safety management means, as well as advice on finding the right guidance for your business and practical steps to manage health and safety in small, low-risk businesses: **hse.gov.uk/managing/introduction/index.htm**

Health and safety basics for your business

There is a section of the HSE website that provides advice on how to undertake a risk assessment and control risks in the workplace: **hse.gov.uk/simple-health-safety**

Contact your local authority

Contact the environmental health department of your local authority for further assistance.

Safeguarding employee mental health

Learn how to tackle workplace-related stress with the *Safeguarding employee mental health* guide from HSE, available on its website: **hse.gov.uk**

Consulting employees on health and safety

The guide *Consulting employees on health and safety: A brief guide to the law* can be downloaded from the HSE website: **hse.gov.uk**

Guidance on safety for vulnerable and temporary workers

Guidance for employers on the safety of disabled, pregnant, temporary, lone, young and remote workers can be found on the HSE website: **hse.gov.uk**

Health and safety liabilities

KEY FACTS

- If you have control over your premises, the Occupiers' Liability Act 1957 and Occupiers Liability Act 1984 apply to you.
- The person who controls the premises (the 'occupier') is liable for the physical safety of everyone who comes onto the premises.
- Under the Employers' Liability (Compulsory Insurance) Act 1969, employers must have insurance to cover their liability for any harm suffered by an employee at work.
- Public liability insurance is not compulsory, but is strongly recommended.

Your liability to customers and the public

Under the **Occupiers' Liability Act 1957** and **Occupiers' Liability Act 1984**, the person who controls the premises (the 'occupier') is liable for the physical safety of everyone who comes onto the premises. In some cases, this liability also extends to trespassers and other 'uninvited' guests.

Occupiers have what is known as a 'duty of care' to customers and other visitors, and must ensure that the premises are reasonably safe for the purpose for which customers were invited to use them. If there is a specific danger on the premises, then this danger must be highlighted to all visitors (including trespassers). This could include ponds, wells or areas where machinery is operating.

Does the legislation apply to me?

Yes: if you have control over your business premises, either through ownership, rental or leasing arrangement.

These Acts create a liability; that is, you can be sued for compensation. You cannot be prosecuted and fined, sent to jail or receive a criminal record under this legislation, but you could be prosecuted under other legislation if you do not take proper precautions.

What does this mean in practice?

You must make sure that the premises are 'reasonably safe.' For example, you should ensure:

- Floors, walkways and paved areas are not slippery;
- Passageways are clear;
- Cables are tucked away;
- Furniture and wall fixtures are secure;
- Equipment (for example playground equipment) is well maintained and serviced:
- Any outdoor structures are sound;
- Trees on the property are well maintained;
- Customers are acquainted with emergency procedures and the layout of the premises.

Note: special attention needs to be taken to make sure your premises are safe for disabled people and children.

Duty of care

Your duty of care in relation to customers does not normally extend to parts of your premises that are clearly marked as being out of bounds (such as the kitchens, machine-operating plants or electrical control rooms).

Generally, you are also liable for accidents caused as a result of the actions of your staff or other visitors. For example, if a member of staff leaves a bucket on the stairs, or if a visitor leaves the gate to a swimming pool open, you may be held responsible.

No matter how many notices you put up to the contrary, and whatever your booking conditions or conditions of entry may say, the law does not allow you to exclude or restrict your liability for death and injuries to guests arising from your negligence (or that of your staff or agents). However, you can take out public liability insurance to cover your risk.

You will not normally be liable for customers who injure themselves while involved in an activity that is not something they might reasonably have been expected to do on the premises, such as trying to jump from the roof of a building into the swimming pool.

Each guest has a duty to take care of his or her own safety. If the guest's own negligence led to an accident, this would reduce, or could even override, any liability that you would otherwise have.

The transportation of customers

If you transport customers, even if this is only occasionally driving people to or from a train station, there are three issues that need consideration:

- Whether a licence is required;
- What insurance is required;
- Health and safety considerations.

Occasional transport

At the lowest level, you do not need a licence for occasional transport if:

- You very occasionally help out a customer by providing a lift;
- You do not charge for this, and;
- Your vehicle has no more than eight seats.

However, you will need to ensure that you have business insurance for your vehicle as, regardless of the lack of payment from the customer, you are still undertaking a business activity.

You should also undertake a quick health and safety assessment prior to transporting the guest – for example, is the car roadworthy at the time, has the guest put on a seatbelt, and is any luggage stowed safely.

Regular transport

If you are providing a lift for your customers to and from their point of arrival as a regular or standard service (for example, running a shuttle service from a local railway station), then regardless of whether there is a separate charge for this service, you will require a special operating licence and appropriate vehicle insurance.

In this case, you will need a Passenger Service Vehicle (PSV) licence. There are two forms of this licence: restricted and full.

Restricted PSV licence

A restricted licence allows you to operate up to two vehicles that have up to 16 seats, provided that you do not use them as part of a passenger transport business, or you are operating your vehicles as part of your accommodation business and that it is not your main occupation. To gain a licence you will have to provide evidence that you:

- Have sufficient money to undertake a passenger service business;
- Have no convictions;
- Have a maintenance and safety programme in place for your vehicle;
- Understand the legislation relating to the maximum hours that you can work driving the vehicle;
- Have the relevant category of driving licence for the vehicle.

For each vehicle with more than nine seats, you will also need a Certificate of Initial Fitness for the vehicle, to prove that it was properly constructed for the purpose of transporting passengers.

You will require this even if you buy the vehicle second-hand.

Separately from the requirements for the PSV licence, you will also need to undertake a written health and safety assessment of the operation and keep this updated.

Full PSV licence

If you wish to operate more than two vehicles, or a vehicle with more than 16 seats, you will require a Full or Standard PSV licence. In addition to the requirements for a restricted PSV licence, you will also need a certificate of professional competence.

On-demand transport

If you wish to provide customers with an 'on-demand' service that transports them to wherever they request to go, you will require either a Taxi or Private Hire Licence. This is an expensive and time-consuming process requiring, among other things, a Criminal Records Bureau check, a knowledge test of roads and destinations in the area, a medical examination and special insurance.

The costs and stringent requirements associated with this form of licence mean that it is not generally recommended for accommodation providers.

Your liability to employees

Under the **Employers' Liability (Compulsory Insurance) Act 1969**, every employer must have insurance to cover their liability for any bodily injury or disease sustained by an employee at work. Failure to do this is a criminal offence.

How does this apply to me?

If you employ at least one person, you are required to take out and maintain employers' liability insurance cover with a minimum of £5 million for any one claim (most policies available offer £10 million cover).

You must display a copy of the certificate of insurance at your place(s) of business so that it can be seen and read by all of your employees. The policy document, or a copy of it, must also be kept available for inspection by Health and Safety Executive inspectors or Environmental Health Officers and, for future reference, all policy documents should be retained permanently.

Operating a business at home

If you start operating a business at your home, whether it be serviced, self-catering or caravan accommodation, or you are thinking of opening a visitor centre or museum in your garage, you need to consider whether you have appropriate and adequate insurance to cover, for example, your potential liability under the Occupiers' and Employers' Liability Acts.

Most household policies will not cover:

- Your use of the premises for business purposes;
- Your legal ability to employees or paying guests;
- Any theft or damage to your property by guests.

In any event, you should contact your existing insurers as soon as possible.

Public liability insurance

One type of insurance cover you should consider, particularly as the public becomes increasingly claims-conscious, is public liability insurance. This covers your liability to customers and other people such as contractors and business visitors for injury, loss or damage sustained while on your premises (for example, under the Occupiers' Liability Acts).

There is no legal requirement to take out public liability insurance, but it is strongly recommended that you have this type of cover as injury claims can be extremely high. Having public liability insurance is also a requirement for participation in all VisitEngland Quality Assessment Schemes.

Public liability insurance must not be confused with employers' liability insurance. It also does not cover any loss or damage that occurs to your property and is therefore not a substitute for business, property and contents insurance.

Taking out insurance

Most insurance brokers have special business insurance packages available that will protect you against losses suffered in the course of normal business activities, particularly when the business faces a compensation claim. These business insurance packages generally include:

- Public liability insurance;
- Employers' liability insurance;
- Property and contents insurance.

A broker will be able to advise you on these types of comprehensive packages, or about adding extra cover to an existing policy.

Your local destination management organisation (DMO) or Local Visitor Economy Partnership (LVEP) may be able to recommend local insurance brokers who have specific experience in arranging cover for accommodation and attraction operators. Insurance brokers should be registered with and regulated by the Financial Conduct Authority, and you can check brokers via its website: **fca.org.uk**

Insurance for transporting guests

Ensure that you have adequate insurance cover for your vehicle if you transport guests for any reason. See The *transportation of customers* section above for more details.

Legionnaires' disease

Guidance on your obligations in minimising the risk of Legionnaires' disease can be found in the *Legionnaires' disease* section.

Further guidance

Seek professional legal advice

If anyone makes a claim against you, you should seek legal advice immediately.

Understand Employer Liability Insurance

Download *A brief guide to the Employers' Liability (Compulsory Insurance) Act* from the HSE website: **hse.gov.uk**

Contact your local authority

For Taxi and Hackney Carriage information, contact your local authority.

The Purple Guide

Guidance from the Events Industry Forum for businesses staging events on their premises, from safety to waste disposal, can be found in *The Purple Guide*: **thepurpleguide.co.uk**

Running an event safely

Guidance from the HSE on running an event safely can be found on its website: **hse.gov.uk**

Safety management

KEY FACTS

- The Management of Health and Safety at Work Regulations 1999 place general duties and responsibilities on all employers at work.
- Employers must carry out a 'suitable and sufficient' assessment of the health and safety risks to employees and others arising from work activities.
- If you have five or more employees, you must keep a record of any significant findings of the assessment and your health and safety arrangements.
- Employers, the self-employed and those in control of work premises must report certain work-related accidents, diseases and dangerous occurrences.
- Employers must provide first aid equipment and facilities appropriate to the circumstances in the workplace.

Main provisions of the regulations

The **Management of Health and Safety at Work Regulations 1999** follow on from the general responsibilities outlined in the **Health and Safety at Work etc Act 1974**, by covering in more detail how an employer should manage health and safety at work in order to avoid accidents and ill-health.

Risk assessment is the key to effective management of health and safety, and is a legal requirement. The main tasks relating to an employer are as follows:

Carry out a risk assessment

Employers must carry out a 'suitable and sufficient' assessment of the health and safety risks to employees at work, and any other people, arising from work activities. The assessment allows you to identify any extra measures that you need to take.

Doing a risk assessment

A risk assessment is nothing more than a careful examination of what, on your premises, could cause harm to people – so that you can weigh up whether you have taken enough precautions, or should do more to prevent harm. You also have to do a risk assessment for fire safety (see the *Fire safety (general)* section, below), and it is acceptable to combine the fire risk assessment into the general one. There are five basic steps:

- **Step 1: Look** for the hazards: that is, anything that can cause harm. For most accommodation premises the hazards are few and simple, but assessing them thoroughly is a necessity. You probably know already if, for example, you have steps that are awkward or kitchen furniture that is unstable. Always consider electricity, gas, carbon monoxide poisoning and falls especially carefully, as these are potential causes of serious injury or even death. Do not neglect the garden or grounds.
- **Step 2: Decide** who may be harmed and how, including those especially at risk (see the section below).
- **Step 3: Evaluate** the risks. Consider in particular:
  - How likely a mishap is to happen, and;
  - How serious the consequences might be.

  The more likely and the more serious the potential accident, the higher the risk and the more you need to do to prevent it. Decide whether the existing precautions are adequate or whether more should be done. The test of whether you should do more is whether it is 'reasonably practicable' (see section below) to carry out the possible additional measure.
- **Step 4: Record** your findings.
- **Step 5: Review** your assessment and revise it if necessary.

You don't need to overcomplicate the process. Check that you have taken the precautions you can to avoid injury. You can probably do the assessment yourself. If you need assistance, you can contact your local environmental health officer, although they cannot do the assessment for you.

Consider those especially at risk

You must consider visitors and members of the public who might be affected by your work. You also need to give special consideration to:

- Workers who are young;
- Workers who are inexperienced or new to a particular job;
- Trainees doing work experience;
- Disabled workers;
- Customers who are children, elderly, or disabled.

Members of staff at special risk

If you have members of staff who are at special risk, any risk assessment and health and safety arrangements must address them specifically.

- **Disabled staff:** if you have disabled staff, you must ensure that you undertake a risk assessment that takes into account their impairment and, as well as undertaking any adjustments, ensure that you have systems and emergency procedures in place that do not expose them to undue risk.
- **Staff with poor English:** if you have staff whose first language is not English, you must ensure they understand, for example, all the preventative health and safety measures, signs and emergency procedures.
- **Young people:** there are special requirements covering young people (under the age of 18), which require employers to do a specific risk assessment and give specific information to the young person and their parents or guardians (see the *Employing Under 18s* section).
- **New and expectant mothers:** there are special requirements and considerations, which are explained in the HSE guide for new and expectant mothers on their website: **hse.gov.uk**

Reasonably practicable

This is a balance between the cost and inconvenience of undertaking actions to reduce risk, and the benefits of improved safety.

For example, if the cost of repairing a loose carpet is small, and the risk of tripping or falling down stairs is high, then you must make the repair. At the other extreme if the removal of an awkward step would involve rebuilding part of the house, and the consequences of any foreseeable trip are minor, it would not be reasonably practicable to do it (although, of course, warnings might well be needed).

Health and safety arrangements

You must put into place any extra measures identified in the assessment, along with arrangements for:

- Organising health and safety in the workplace;
- Ensuring safety procedures are followed;
- Reviewing and updating the measures and procedures.

Health surveillance

Health surveillance is a system of ongoing health checks which are required if you have employees who are exposed to noise or vibration, ionising radiation, solvents, fumes, dusts, biological agents and other hazardous substances. If your employees are exposed to hazardous substances, you must provide health surveillance appropriate to the risks identified in the assessment.

Competent person

Employers must appoint a competent person, preferably a member of staff with the necessary training or experience, to assist in health and safety matters.

Recording

If you have five or more employees, you must keep a record of:

- Any 'significant findings' of your assessment;
- Your health and safety arrangements (best included in your overall 'health and safety policy statement'): a template form is available on the HSE website: **hse.gov.uk**

Even if you have fewer than five employees, it is still sensible to keep a record. This will give you increased legal protection if there is an accident by being able to show that you complied with health and safety legislation.

Emergency procedures

Employers must draw up procedures for dealing with emergencies and establishing contact with the emergency services (such as fire and medical care).

Information, instruction and training

You must give your employees information on the risks, the preventative measures, and the emergency procedures so they can understand them.

You need to consult with your employees on these and any other key health and safety issues.

You also need to ensure that when a new employee starts, you give them sufficient health and safety training so that they can go about their work safely. For example, if you have a new cleaner starting, you must explain how to use all of the different cleaning agents safely.

The staff training needs to be repeated or updated as appropriate; it should take place during working hours and must not be paid for by employees.

Agency workers

If you hire agency workers, you must tell the employment agency about:

- Risks to the worker's health and safety, and steps you have taken to control them;
- Any necessary legal or professional qualifications or skills;
- Any necessary health surveillance.

Temporary staff

Employers must inform temporary staff, before they start work, about any special qualifications or skills required to do the work safely, and any health surveillance that you are required to provide.

Employees' duties

Employees have a duty to follow health and safety instructions and to report dangers.

Accident reporting

If you are an employer, self-employed or in control of work premises, you are required by law to report certain work-related accidents, diseases and dangerous occurrences. Details of the types of accidents that you need to report can be found on the RIDDOR website: **hse.gov.uk/riddor**

All incidents can be reported online, but a telephone service remains for reporting fatal and major injuries only: call the Incident Contact Centre on **0845 300 9923**.

You will be sent a copy of the final report for your own records; this meets your statutory obligation to keep records of all reportable incidents for inspection, and also allows you to correct any error or omission.

First aid

Employers must provide first-aid equipment and facilities appropriate to the circumstances in the workplace. The minimum would be a suitably stocked first-aid box and a person appointed to take charge of first-aid arrangements.

First-aid provision should be part of your risk assessment process under the **Management of Health and Safety at Work Regulations 1999** (see the *Carry out a risk assessment* section above).

You have no responsibility to administer first aid to customers or the public at large, although you should be familiar with local medical facilities.

Other regulations

Other health and safety legislation supplements these general responsibilities with specific requirements. For further information, see the following sections:

- *Fire safety (general);*
- *Fire safety of furniture and furnishings;*
- *Hazards in the workplace;*
- *Hazards from work activities;*
- *Swimming, gym and outdoor safety.*

Further guidance

An introduction to managing health and safety
The HSE website provides an overview of what health and safety management means, advice on finding the right guidance for your business and practical steps to manage health and safety in small, low-risk businesses: **hse.gov.uk**

Basic health and safety for your business
The HSE toolkit can help you write a health and safety policy, control risks, and provide the right facilities: **hse.gov.uk/simple-health-safety**

How to write a health & safety policy
Find an example health and safety policy, and guided templates that you can download and complete, on the HSE website: **hse.gov.uk/simple-health-safety/policy/index.htm**

Guidance for catering and hospitality businesses
There is a range of guidance publications for the catering industry on a dedicated HSE web page: **hse.gov.uk/catering/guidance.htm**

Employing new or expectant mothers
Detailed advice if you employ new or expectant mothers, who are especially at risk, can be found on the HSE website: **hse.gov.uk/mothers**

Employing young workers
Detailed advice if you employ young people, who are especially at risk, can be found on the HSE website: **hse.gov.uk**

How to report an accident
For guidance on accident reporting, go to the RIDDOR website: **hse.gov.uk/riddor**

Guidance on first aid
You can download *Basic Advice on First Aid at Work* from the HSE website: **hse.gov.uk**

The Purple Guide
Guidance from the Events Industry Forum for businesses staging events on their premises, from safety to waste disposal, can be found in The Purple Guide: **thepurpleguide.co.uk**

Running an event safely
Guidance from the HSE on running an event safely can be found on its website: **hse.gov.uk/event-safety/running.htm**

Hazards from work activities

KEY FACTS

- All employers must consider the risks to staff arising from the hazards associated with work activities. A hazard is something with the potential to cause harm.
- Any work equipment must be safe and suitable for the job, as required by the Provision and Use of Work Equipment Regulations 1998.
- If staff habitually use computers or other kinds of display screen equipment, the Health and Safety (Display Screen Equipment) Regulations 1992 (as amended) apply.
- If staff lift and carry objects, the Manual Handling Operations Regulations 1992 (as amended) apply.
- Under the Work at Height Regulations 2005 (as amended), employers are required to avoid work at height where possible, or, where it cannot be avoided, to take measures to ensure that the person working at height does not fall.
- If you are an employer you must assess all hazardous substances.
- These are the main regulations to be aware of, but other health and safety legislation may apply, depending on the work activity being done.

Work equipment

The **Provision and Use of Work Equipment Regulations 1998** cover the safety of work equipment (including an employee's own equipment and equipment used by a self-employed person, for example a self-employed cleaner who works on your premises).

The general duties of an employer include:

- Making sure that equipment is suitable – for example, selecting the right equipment for the job;
- Making sure equipment is properly installed and safe to operate;
- Giving proper training and instructions on the use of the equipment and following manufacturers' or suppliers' instructions.

- Making sure that there are suitable health and safety measures, including protective devices and controls such as guards over moving parts, emergency stop devices, adequate means of isolation from sources of energy, clearly visible markings and warning devices;
- Making sure equipment is maintained and in good repair through regular maintenance, inspection and – if appropriate – thorough examination;
- Providing equipment that conforms to any relevant product safety standard.

Display screens

The **Health and Safety (Display Screen Equipment) Regulations 1992** apply where staff habitually use computers or other kinds of display screen equipment (also known as visual display units or VDUs) as part of their normal work.

Employers have to:

- Analyse workstations and assess and reduce risks;
- Ensure workstations meet minimum requirements set out in the regulations;
- Plan VDU work so that staff have breaks or changes of activity;
- Provide eye and eyesight tests for VDU users who request them and provide spectacles if special ones are needed;
- Provide health and safety training and information for VDU users.

Safe manual handling

More than a third of all 'over three day' injuries reported each year to HSE and local authorities are the result of manual handling. In the catering industry alone, it is the second most common cause of injury.

As seen in the *Safety management section*, the **Management of Health and Safety at Work Regulations 1999** require an employer to assess the risks in any work activity and take the appropriate precautions.

In addition, the **Manual Handling Operations Regulations 1992** require an employer to:

- Ensure, so far as it is reasonably practicable, that employees are not required to undertake any manual handling operations at work if there is a risk of them being injured.
- If any hazardous operations cannot be avoided, thoroughly assess the risks and take steps to minimise the risks of injury as far as reasonably practicable.

Work at height

Falls from a height account for around 30 fatalities each year, and account for around a quarter of all worker deaths. One of the main causes is falls from ladders.

The regulations and types of work at height

'Work at height' means working where a person could fall and be injured. It therefore includes working at ground level next to a well or cellar opening, etc. There is no fixed height that is considered dangerous. This depends partly on where the person might land (for example on grass or concrete).

The **Work at Height Regulations 2005** require employers to avoid work at height where possible or, where it cannot be avoided, to take measures to ensure that the person working at height does not fall. A risk assessment must be carried out before a person works at a height.

Light work of short duration may be carried out using ladders if conditions are suitable, there are adequate hand-holds and the ladder can be secured.

People involved in working at a height must be competent and adequately trained and supervised.

You must:

- Avoid work at height if you can;
- Use equipment or take other measures to prevent a fall if you cannot avoid work at height;
- As a last resort, if no more can be done to prevent a fall, take measures to minimise the consequences of a fall.

Window cleaning and painting are common reasons for working at height. Although very common, window cleaning using ladders has led to many deaths in the past. A ladder is not usually a safe way to clean first-floor windows and above. If you decide to have work done by a person standing on a ladder, you must ensure you have measures in place to prevent him or her from falling off, or the ladder from slipping. There are alternatives, such as:

- Water-fed hose cleaning;
- The installation of interior eye bolts by a specialist company, which enables windows to be cleaned using a harness.

Things to consider

To ascertain the risk of falling from height, consider these questions:

- How far would a person fall?
- Are there adequate hand-holds?
- Are there any fragile surfaces (for example roof lights) involved?

- Where might the person land? (For example, on grass, concrete, spiked railings.)
- What is the nature of the work to be done? (Consider especially any leaning, stretching or carrying that might increase the risk of falling.)
- Is the ladder or other equipment secured, top and bottom, to prevent it from slipping?

Falling off a ladder carries a significant risk of severe injury or death. Ladders are best regarded as a means of access and not as a place from which to do work.

Reducing risks from working at height

To help prevent falls from a height you should assess and reduce the risks to all your workers, and ensure they are:

- Trained and have suitable and safe equipment for the task(s);
- Properly managed and supervised;
- Provided with sufficient protection measures (for example suitable and sufficient personal protective equipment) while they are working at height.

Hazardous substances

Hazardous substances can generally be identified from the product label. Most small businesses will only use domestic cleaning materials, but some products used for drain cleaning, pest control, gardening, cleaning pools or hot-tubs or other purposes may also be hazardous. For larger businesses, more concentrated commercial cleaning products are likely to be used, and these will pose a greater hazard to staff and customers.

COSHH assessment

If you are an employer you must assess all hazardous substances under the **Control of Substances Hazardous to Health Regulations 2002 (COSHH)**. The employer has a duty to remove employees' exposure to hazardous substances, for example powerful commercial cleaning agents or, where this is not possible, to adequately control it.

To help with the assessment, you may need to obtain a Safety Data Sheet (SDS) from the supplier or manufacturer of the hazardous substance. (This will not be necessary for very common products such as household bleach, for which plenty of information is readily available.) The SDS describes the substance and the dangers it may pose. You will only then be in a position to plan the measures that you will need to take to control the substance and prevent harm. It will usually be best to keep it in a secure location, especially if there are children on the premises.

COSHH Essentials

You can carry out a free, quick and simple risk assessment via *COSHH Essentials* on the Health and Safety Executive website (**hse.gov.uk**). *COSHH Essentials* is also available in a paper version, which you can purchase from HSE Books.

You will need to enter some very basic information about the chemicals or products that you use, and the system will automatically work out the correct control procedures for you. Alternatively, for some tasks such as cleaning, you can simply refer directly to the control advice.

Other legislation

The regulations mentioned above are the main ones to be aware of, but other health and safety legislation may apply, depending on the work activity.

Further guidance

Providing and using work equipment safely

You can download *Providing and using work equipment safely: A brief guide* from the HSE website: **hse.gov.uk**

Working with display screen equipment

You can download *Working with display screen equipment (DSE): A brief guide* from the HSE website: **hse.gov.uk**

Preventing injury to catering staff

You can download an information sheet on preventing manual handling injuries to catering staff from the HSE website: **hse.gov.uk**

Safety relating to musculoskeletal disorders

Find up to date information on health and safety relating to musculoskeletal disorders, for example back pain and repetitive strain injury on the HSE website: **hse.gov.uk**

Working from height

You can download *Working at height: A brief guide* from the HSE website: **hse.gov.uk**

Using ladders

You can download *Safe use of ladders and stepladders: A brief guide* from the Ladder Association website: **ladderassociation.org.uk**

Lifting equipment at work

You can download *Lifting equipment at work: A brief guide* from the HSE website: **hse.gov.uk**

Working with hazardous substances

You can download *Working with substances hazardous to health: A brief guide to COSHH* from the HSE website: **hse.gov.uk**

Legionnaires' disease

KEY FACTS

- Legionella bacteria is classified as a 'hazardous substance', and you are required to undertake a risk assessment, and any subsequent remedial actions, in order to protect both your staff and customers.
- If you have five or more employees, you must record what assessment and actions you undertake.

Legionnaires' disease is a potentially fatal form of pneumonia caused by Legionella bacteria. While these bacteria are common in natural water systems, they usually occur in numbers too small to cause health problems. However, in particular conditions, these bacteria can multiply quickly and cause a significant health risk.

These conditions are where water is maintained between 20 and 45°C, is stored or recirculated, where there is a source of nutrients in the water (including rust or scale) and where there are aerial water droplets. This means that water tanks, spas or hot tubs, air conditioning units and showers are the most common places for the bacteria to breed.

Legionella is classified as a 'hazardous substance' and, therefore, you are required to undertake a risk assessment, and any subsequent remedial actions, in order to protect both your staff and customers.

If you have five or more employees, you must record what assessment and actions you undertake. While it is not a legal requirement to record the assessment and actions if you have fewer than five employees, it is always recommended that you do so in case you are challenged at a later date.

If you have a self-catering or bed and breakfast property with a normal residential water system, this risk assessment will be straightforward as the risk of Legionnaires' disease should not be high. A full specialist assessment is generally only needed if you have a large commercial property or if you are uncertain of the property's water system.

LICENCES & CONSENTS
MARKETING
CUSTOMERS
FOOD & DRINK
ENVIRONMENTAL PROTECTION
HEALTH & SAFETY
STAFF
BUSINESS, MANAGEMENT & TAX
FURTHER INFORMATION

The main things to check for are:

- Ensure that no debris is entering the system (for example, ensure that any water tanks have a tight-fitting lid);
- Ensure that the hot water cylinder is set to at least 60°C;
- Ensure that there is no redundant pipework in which water could become stagnant;
- Ensure that showerheads are regularly cleaned and disinfected.

If you have machinery that contains water, such as air conditioning units or a spa/hot tub, then special attention needs to be paid to ensure that this is regularly serviced and cleaned.

If you operate a property where the water system is not in regular use (for example, a self-catering property that has long void periods or closes over winter) then additional precautions need to be undertaken to ensure that the water in the system does not stagnate. If your property is going to be vacant for a significant period, you should either drain or flush the system before the guests arrive.

Further information on Legionella and how to control it in water systems is available on the Health and Safety Executive website: hse.gov.uk

Further guidance

Legionnaires' disease: a brief guide

You can download *Legionnaires' disease: a brief guide* from the HSE website, which is aimed at employers and people in control of premises: **hse.gov.uk**

How to control legionella

You can download the approved code of practice and guidance *Legionnaires' disease: The control of legionella bacteria in water systems* from the HSE website: **hse.gov.uk**

Legionella and spa-pool systems

You can download *The control of Legionella and other infectious agents in spa-pool systems* from the HSE website: **hse.gov.uk**

Safe water supplies

There is a guidance document *Safe water supplies: information for organisations* on the Gov.uk website: **Gov.uk**

Hazards in the workplace

KEY FACTS

- All employers must consider the risks to staff arising from the hazards associated with aspects of the workplace. A hazard is something with the potential to cause harm.
- The working environment must be suitable, at a reasonable temperature, have adequate lighting and ventilation, and include sufficient rest facilities.
- Employers should reduce the risk of slips, trips and falls by cleaning spillages, keeping walkways clear and organising work more efficiently.
- All electrical systems in places of work must be maintained 'so far as is reasonably practicable', to avoid danger to all who use the premises (including customers).
- Although Health and Safety can be a complex area of legislation, there are two main sets of regulations that you need to be aware of: the Workplace (Health, Safety and Welfare) Regulations 1992 and the Management of Health and Safety at Work Regulations 1999.

The Workplace (Health, Safety and Welfare) Regulations 1992

The **Workplace (Health, Safety and Welfare) Regulations 1992** cover your employees' working environment, setting out the requirements in respect of:

- The quality of the working environment (for example reasonable temperature, lighting and ventilation);
- Suitability of the environment (for example room dimensions, space, passageways and windows);
- The facilities for your employees (for example toilets, washing and eating facilities, drinking water, changing and rest areas and rest facilities for pregnant women);
- The maintenance and cleanliness of the workplace, equipment and facilities.

The Management of Health and Safety at Work Regulations 1999

The main requirement of the **Management of Health and Safety at Work Regulations 1999** is that employers must carry out risk assessments to eliminate or reduce risks. Employers with five or more employees need to record the significant findings of a risk assessment; it is not necessary to record risk assessments for trivial or insignificant risks. In addition, employers must also:

- Make arrangements for implementing the health and safety measures identified as necessary by risk assessments;
- Monitor and review those arrangements;
- Appoint people with sufficient knowledge, skills, experience and training to help them to implement these arrangements;
- Set up emergency procedures and provide information about them to employees;
- Provide clear information supervision and training for employees, and ensure that suitably competent people are appointed who are capable of carrying out the tasks entrusted to them;
- Work together with any other employer(s) operating from the same workplace, sharing information on the risks that other staff may be exposed to – for example cleaning, catering or maintenance contractors;
- Take particular account of risks to new and expectant mothers.

Use of safety glass

The **Workplace (Health, Safety and Welfare) Regulations 1992** include the use of safety glass or materials in the workplace.

These regulations will not normally apply to self-catering accommodation unless someone works there, for example a cleaner. However, the **General Product Safety Regulations 2005** could potentially be applied to self-catering businesses (see *Product Safety* section) and could be taken to cover glass in doors, windows and elsewhere. Always be sure that the glass in your property is adequate for the use to which it is being put.

If there is a large pane of glass, especially if it extends to below waist height, you need to consider the risk of it being broken or walked into. If the circumstances lead to the conclusion that there is no risk, no action needs to be taken, but if there is a risk of it being broken it should be glazed with safety glass and also marked so that it is obviously present (for example with an etched design).

What glass is covered by the regulations?

The regulations do not apply to all glazing. In the past, a number of glaziers have misrepresented these regulations in attempts to persuade businesses to replace or modify all windows, glazed doors, walls or partitions. The actual requirement is detailed below.

Windows and transparent or translucent doors, gates and walls
Where necessary for reasons of health or safety, every window or other transparent or translucent surface in a wall or partition – and every transparent or translucent surface in a door or gate – should:

- Be of safety material, or be protected against breakage of the transparent or translucent material;
- Be appropriately marked or incorporate features so as, in either case, to make it apparent.

General guidance to the regulations then adds that transparent or translucent surfaces in doors, gates, walls and partitions should be of a safety material or be adequately protected against breakage in the following cases:

- In doors and gates, and door and gate side panels, where any part of the transparent or translucent surface is at shoulder level or below;
- In windows, walls and partitions, where any part of the transparent or translucent surface is at waist level or below, except in glasshouses where people there will be likely to be aware of the presence of glazing and avoid contact.

Safety glass or materials are only necessary in certain cases, where a particular need or risk has been identified. Indeed, the chances are that it will already have been fitted as a matter of routine. Wholesale replacement of windows and glazed doors or partitions is not implied by the regulations.

Slips and trips

Accidents as a result of a slip or trip are the most common causes of injuries at work. Resulting falls can be serious. They can happen in all kinds of businesses, but sectors such as the food and catering industry report higher than average numbers of incidents, and it is a particularly important subject if members of the public use your premises.

What are the chances of slips and trips at your workplace?

To identify problems and prevent accidents from happening, consider the following questions:

- Do you have floors that are, or can become, slippery – for example when wet?
- Does spillage or contamination occur and is it dealt with quickly?
- Do people use unlit areas, such as paths or yards, in the dark?
- Might temporary work such as maintenance or alterations take

place? This could introduce slipping and tripping hazards, such as trailing cables.
- Do you use floor-cleaning materials anywhere?
- Are the right methods and materials being used?

Reducing risk

Effective solutions are often simple, cheap and lead to other benefits. You should ensure that you:
- Clean up spillages, organise work more efficiently and keep walkways clear;
- 'Design-in' safety equipment and materials;
- Obtain help and advice, for example from the Health and Safety Executive, publications and guidance, or your local environmental health officer.

Electricity at work

The **Electricity at Work Regulations 1989** are wide-ranging. Operators should be aware of one objective in particular: that all electrical systems in places of work must be maintained 'so far as is reasonably practicable' to avoid danger to all who use the premises (including customers).

These regulations only apply to self-catering accommodation if you have one or more employees working on the premises. Of course, your general duties under the **Health and Safety at Work etc. Act 1974** include ensuring that guests are protected from electrical hazards and these still apply to self-catering businesses.

The safety of electrical equipment in self-catering accommodation is also covered in the *Product safety* section.

Which electrical equipment is affected?

All electrical systems are covered by the regulations, whether they are used solely by:
- You and your staff;
- You, your staff and customers;
- Your customers.

'Electrical systems' means the mains wiring and all mains-powered electric equipment.

Electrical equipment brought in by customers is not affected by these regulations, which are restricted to matters within your control.

NEW

Testing and maintenance

There is no specific requirement for the regular routine testing of systems under these regulations. Nevertheless, you do have a duty of maintenance under the regulations, and regular testing is the only practical way for you to be sure that you are complying with this duty. The new Home Office guidance for small accommodation businesses on how to comply with the Fire Safety Order 2005 (see *Fire safety (general)* section) states that fixed electrical systems should be inspected by a qualified contractor every five years, while electrical appliances should be subject to periodic in-house service and testing.

- The **fixed wiring installation** should be tested every few years; exactly how often will depend on its age and the likelihood that it has been damaged. It is important to remember that while there are no specific rules requiring testing every so often, if you never have it tested you will most probably not be carrying out your general duties to ensure the safety of your customers.
- You will often be able to tell from a quick visual inspection whether a piece of **portable equipment** is faulty or damaged. Regular visual inspection is the most important measure you can take. This will detect a large proportion of common faults such as damaged plugs, frayed or damaged cables, or cracks in a casing.

If you wish to have your electrical systems tested professionally, you should ensure that those doing the work are competent. This can be done by using electrical contractors who belong to either the Electrical Contractors' Association or to the National Inspection Council for Electrical Installation Contracting (NICEIC). However, portable appliance testing can be carried out by a trained, competent person who need not be a qualified electrician.

Records of testing and maintenance

Keep a record of all the testing and maintenance that has been carried out. In the event of an accident involving the electrical systems on your premises, this record should enable you to demonstrate that you have complied with your duty of maintenance under the regulations.

Cold callers

Health and safety legislation is an area that has been targeted by disreputable firms trying to sell products and services. Do not be intimidated by sales people who may be misrepresenting the regulations in an attempt to win your custom. Remember, the regulations do not generally specify what materials you must use, what tests you should undertake, or how often you should undertake them.

Further guidance

Guidance for managers

You can download *Workplace Health, Safety and Welfare: A Short Guide for Managers* from the HSE website: **hse.gov.uk**

Guidance on welfare provisions

You can download *Welfare at Work: Guidance for Employers on Welfare Provisions* from the HSE website: **hse.gov.uk**

Preventing slips and trips

You can download *Preventing Slips and Trips at Work* from the HSE website: **hse.gov.uk**

Maintaining portable electrical equipment

You can download *Maintaining Portable Electrical Equipment in Low-risk Environments* from the HSE website: **hse.gov.uk**

Brief guide to electrical safety

You can download *Electrical Safety and You* from the HSE website: **hse.gov.uk**

Product safety

KEY FACTS

- Operators of all domestic, residential and sleeping accommodation have a responsibility to ensure that gas appliances and flues in the premises are safely maintained and checked. All safety checks must be carried out by a Gas Safe registered engineer.
- Electrical equipment safety regulations require that all electrical equipment supplied 'in the course of business' is safe. There is no specific requirement for annual maintenance, but to ensure electrical equipment remains safe, you should have it checked and serviced regularly by a registered electrician.
- The essential requirements are to ensure that you supply only safe products to your customers, and to ensure that a product remains safe throughout its period of use. The general product safety regulations also apply if you provide self-catering accommodation.

Gas safety

Installing and maintaining gas appliances

Each year there are fatalities from carbon monoxide poisoning caused by poorly installed or badly maintained gas boilers, appliances and flues – as well as complaints from guests about the safety of gas appliances provided in accommodation premises. **The Gas Safety (Installation and Use) Regulations 1998** are there to protect your staff and your customers.

They supplement any responsibilities you may have under the **Health and Safety at Work, etc Act 1974** and the **Management of Health and Safety at Work Regulations 1999.**

Registration schemes for gas engineers

The CORGI registration scheme for gas engineers ended on 1 April 2009 and was replaced by the Gas Safe registration scheme. It is illegal for any engineer to undertake work under the **Gas Safety (Installation and Use) Regulations 1998** unless they are Gas Safe registered.

What do the gas safety regulations cover?

- The regulations specifically deal with the installation, maintenance and use of gas appliances and fittings and flues in domestic, residential and commercial premises.
- The regulations place duties on a wide range of people, including gas suppliers and those installing and working on gas equipment.
- The regulations include extensive duties on business operators for ensuring appliances and flues in their premises are safely maintained and checked.

What types of premises are affected?

The premises affected include all attractions and tourist accommodation including:

- Commercial installations generally;
- Self-catering properties;
- Hotels, guesthouses, hostels and bed and breakfasts;
- Permanently sited caravans;
- Touring caravans and inland waterway boats hired out in the course of business;
- Restaurants at attractions.

What are my main duties?

Duties as a business operator

You are required to:

- Ensure all gas fittings and flues are maintained in a safe condition;
- Ensure an annual safety check is carried out on each gas appliance/flue by a Gas Safe registered engineer (see *Registration schemes for gas engineers*, above, for more details);
- Keep a written record of the inspection for two years, containing information such as the following:
  - The date of the check;
  - Location and details of the appliance/flue;
  - Any defects found and action taken;
  - A confirmation that the check was made in accordance with the regulations.
- Issue a copy of the record to any person staying for more than 28 days – or if the premises is let for 28 days or less, display a copy of the record prominently in the premises.

Duties as an employer

You have a duty to ensure that gas appliances under your control are 'maintained in a safe condition so as to prevent injury to any person'. This includes staff or people that you contract to work on your premises (such as security guards and cleaners).

Other important provisions

Other important provisions include the following:

- Anyone carrying out work on gas appliances or fittings not as part of their business (for example as a favour to you) must still be competent. Do-it-yourself work can be dangerous and illegal.

Note: employers can only use Gas Safe engineers (see *Registration schemes*, above, for more details).

- You must not use any gas appliance or fitting that you know or suspect to be unsafe.
- With the exception of 'room-sealed' appliances, there are restrictions on the installation of gas appliances in sleeping areas fitted after 1 January 1996.
- It is illegal to install instantaneous water heaters that are not room-sealed or fitted with a safety device which automatically turns off the gas supply before a dangerous level of poisonous fumes builds up.

Additional precautions

The Health and Safety Executive highlights additional precautions:

- Whenever draught exclusion, double glazing or a conservatory extension is fitted to a room containing a gas appliance, the appliance should subsequently be checked for safety;
- Never block or obstruct any fixed ventilation grilles or air bricks;
- Never block or cover outside flues.

While there is no legal requirement to install a carbon monoxide detector, their use is a requirement of the VisitEngland National Quality Assessment Scheme, and is considered best practice for properties which have a gas supply.

Your liabilities and those of your agent or landlord

IMPORTANT: if you use an agent to manage your properties (for example self-catering accommodation) or you rent your premises, you should ensure that the management contract or rental agreement specifies who is responsible for the maintenance of gas appliances and for keeping records to indicate when this maintenance has been carried out.

The liability of purely marketing and booking agencies (rather than management agencies) under these regulations is unclear. Some agencies therefore seek to exclude themselves from liability by inserting into their contracts with owners a clause which commits those owners to ensuring that their property complies at all times with the gas safety requirements.

NEW

Gas BBQs and outdoor appliances

Under the regulations, the term 'gas appliance' does not include portable or mobile appliances supplied with gas from a cylinder, or the cylinder, pipes and other fittings used for supplying gas to that appliance. As such, you are not legally required to have appliances such as gas BBQs or outdoor heaters Gas Safe tested.

However, these appliances would need to be included in your health and safety assessment of your premises, and therefore you would need to undertake periodic checks of the connections, pipes and fittings to ensure that they were safe. This does not need to be by someone who is Gas Safe registered, but if you have other gas appliances that needed checking, it would make sense to ask your Gas Safe engineer to also check these appliances while they are on the premises.

Electrical equipment

What do the regulations cover?

The **Electrical Equipment (Safety) Regulations 1994** require, among other things, that all electrical equipment supplied 'in the course of business' is safe. This applies equally to new and second-hand equipment.

Do the regulations apply to me?

The regulations apply to everyone who supplies electrical equipment to customers in the course of their business, regardless of whether or not their business is actually the supply of electrical equipment. The regulations are particularly relevant to self-catering accommodation, as equipment in these premises may not be covered by the Electricity at Work Regulations, which covers fixtures and fitting on the premises (see the *Hazards in the workplace* section for more details).

What does safe mean?

For electrical equipment to be regarded as safe, there should be no risk (or only a minimal risk) that the equipment will in any way cause death or injury to any person or domestic animal, or cause damage to property.

If you are buying any new electrical equipment in the UK, it should be 'safe' as manufacturers and suppliers are bound by the same regulations.

NEW

The Product Safety and Metrology etc. (Amendment) Regulations 2024 have recently been introduced which will allow continued recognition of EU requirements for product safety and allow products with the EU CE safety mark to be sold in the UK. This means that businesses are able to purchase products with either the EU CE mark or the new UKCA mark and know that they both conform to the relevant safety standards.

Do I need to maintain electrical equipment?

Although the **Electrical Equipment (Safety) Regulations 1994** require electrical equipment to be safe, unlike for gas appliances there is no specific requirement for annual maintenance. However, to be sure that the electrical equipment in your business remains safe, you should have it checked and serviced regularly by a registered electrician.

You should also note that you are legally required to undertake a Health and Safety Risk Assessment under the **Management of Health and Safety at Work Regulations 1999**, where you are required to identify hazards that could cause injury to employees or customers and take action to eliminate or minimise the risk. Scheduling regular PAT testing of electrical equipment on your premises would therefore demonstrate that you are fulfilling your legal obligations under both the Electrical Equipment (Safety) Regulations and the Management of Health and Safety at Work Regulations. The frequency of the testing should be based on the age and risk posed by the electrical appliance.

It is important to note that, although the regularity of PAT testing is not defined in legislation, the Home Office's new Fire Safety Order guidance for small accommodation businesses *Making your small paying guest accommodation safe from fire* states that your premises' electrical system should be tested every five years (see the *Fire safety (general)* section).

The Health and Safety Executive (HSE) provides a free guidance publication – *Electrical Safety and You* – which contains useful information about checking electrical equipment.

> **Note:** letting agents and landlords can also be held responsible for the safety of the electrical equipment in premises that they let or rent, depending on the terms of their management or rental agreements. Check your agreement and speak with your agent/landlord to ensure that you both understand who is responsible for the safety of electrical products.

General product safety

The **General Product Safety Regulations 2005** are designed to ensure that all products supplied to customers are safe in their normal or reasonably foreseeable usage.

The regulations cover products that are made available to consumers for their use in the course of a delivery of a service (for example the provision of a hairdryer in a hotel room, a riding helmet provided to someone pony trekking, or a cot for customers who have a baby).

Where a product is already subject to other existing regulations, those regulations will still apply to that product. The General Product Safety Regulations 2005 will also apply wherever they go further than the existing regulations.

Do the regulations apply to me?

Yes: if you are providing equipment for the use of customers.

> **Note:** letting agents can be held responsible for product safety in self-catering accommodation, depending on the terms of their agreement with the property owners.

How do I comply with the regulations?

The essential requirements are to ensure that you supply only safe products to your customers, and take steps (where appropriate) to help ensure that a product remains safe throughout its period of use.

A safe product is defined as: 'any product which under normal or reasonably foreseeable conditions of use presents no risk or only the minimum risk compatible with the product's use and which is consistent with a high level of protection for consumers'.

You are required to provide customers with all relevant information, warnings and instructions for the safe operation and use of products. You are also required to keep yourself informed about possible risks.

General precautions

The regulations require no formal testing of products and, as you can see from the examples below, it is really just a matter of common sense and routine checking:

- If instructions are needed to operate a piece of equipment, ensure that they are provided.
- If a piece of equipment provided is damaged, it should be repaired – for example an ironing board with loose or fragile legs.
- If an item of furniture or equipment can be damaged and made dangerous, ensure your customers know this.

Requirements as a 'distributor' of products

As a 'distributor' of products you are also required, 'within the limits of your activity', to participate in monitoring the safety of products that you supply, and to pass on information about product risks. In practice this means:

- Passing on to customers information provided by producers about a product's risks;

- Passing back to producers' safety complaints, information and experiences on safety-related matters obtained from customers;
- Cooperating with the authorities and others in the supply chain in taking action to avoid or remove those risks.

Note: if you discover that you have provided an unsafe product for your customers to use, you should notify your local authority of the fact and what action you have taken to remove the risks to your customers.

Enforcement

The Trading Standards department of your local authority is responsible for enforcing the regulations mentioned above (except for the **Electrical Equipment (Safety) Regulations 1994**).

Further guidance

Gas safety

Visit the Gas Safe Register website **gassaferegister.co.uk** or call the gas safety advice line on **0800 408 5500**

Checking gas appliances

You can download *Gas Appliances. Get Them Checked, Keep Them Safe* from the HSE website: **hse.gov.uk**

Carbon Monoxide guidance

Guidance on Carbon Monoxide can be found on the Gas Safe website: **gassaferegister.co.uk**

Your duty as a landlord

You can download *Landlords, A Guide to Landlords' Duties: Gas Safety (Installation and Use)* from the HSE website: **hse.gov.uk**

Brief guide to electrical safety

You can download *Electrical safety and you: A brief guide* from the HSE website: **hse.gov.uk**

Contact your local authority

Advice is available from the Trading Standards department of your local authority, which enforces most of the regulations.

General product safety

You can download the Chartered Trading Standards Institute guidance on general product safety in rented accommodation from the Business Companion website: **businesscompanion.info**

Swimming, gym and outdoor safety

KEY FACTS

- There are no specific regulations on swimming pool or gym safety, but you must manage these activities so that they comply with health and safety legislation.
- Anyone who sells adventure activities intended for people aged under 18 must be inspected and licensed under the Adventure Activities Licensing Regulations 2004.

Swimming and gym safety

Drownings in swimming pools in the UK are rare. However, this does not mean that you should not pay particular attention to the safety of guests and staff around pool areas.

General legislation that applies

Currently, there is no specific legislation on swimming pool or gym safety. These are covered by general health and safety regulations. Your main responsibility as a pool or gym operator, in relation to the safety of your guests or clients, is to be found in the **Health and Safety at Work, etc Act 1974** and the **Management of Health and Safety at Work Regulations 1999**.

See the sections on the Health and Safety at Work Act in the *Safety management* section for more information.

Safety in swimming pools is a complex subject, and should be studied closely by those who manage them. A thorough risk assessment should be carried out: among other things, this will determine whether constant supervision is needed. This risk assessment should include topics such as:

- Slipping and tripping;
- Signage;
- Water depth and any changes of level;
- Water clarity;
- The availability of alcohol or likelihood of swimming after drinking;

- Child protection issues;
- Unsupervised children;
- Hazards in changing areas;
- Life-saving equipment;
- Rescue and emergency arrangements.

Guidance on swimming pools

UPDATED

The Health and Safety Executive (HSE) has published a very useful guide, *Managing Health and Safety in Swimming Pools*, which provides detailed guidance on the risks associated with swimming pool operation and the precautions which may be taken to help achieve a safer environment. The 2024 updated guide also covers supervision, signage and the use of inflatable toys.

The guide draws on legislation from the **Health and Safety at Work, etc Act 1974**, the **Management of Health and Safety at Work Regulations 1999**, the **Workplace (Health, Safety and Welfare) Regulations 1992** and the **Provision and Use of Work Equipment Regulations 1998**.

Outdoor activity safety measures

Anyone who sells adventure activities intended for people under 18 must be inspected and licensed under the **Adventure Activities Licensing Regulations 2004.**

Do I need an inspection and licence?

Yes: if you provide, in return for payment, any of the activities listed below to young people under 18 unaccompanied by a parent or guardian.

Activities covered by the inspection and licensing scheme

The scheme covers 26 main activities under the following four specified adventure activity groups:

- **Caving:** underground exploration in natural caves and mines including pot-holing, cave diving and mine exploration.
- **Climbing:** climbing, traversing, abseiling and scrambling activities, except on purpose-designed climbing walls or abseiling towers.
- **Trekking:** walking, running, pony trekking, cycling, off-piste skiing, and related activities, when practised in moorlands or more than 600 metres above sea level in an area which is remote (that is, over 30 minutes' travelling time from the nearest road or refuge).
- **Water sports:** canoeing, rafting, sailing and related activities when done on the sea, tidal waters or inland waters which are more than 100m across or are turbulent.

The scheme does not cover:

- Activities that are offered to young people who are accompanied by their parents or guardians.

- Activities that are not specified in the regulations, such as high ropes courses or zorbing.
- Activities offered by voluntary associations to their members, or by schools to their pupils.

The activity provider's duty under the regulations

The primary duty of the activity provider is to ensure the safety of young people using activity facilities. To be able to comply with this duty, providers must have a safety management system in place that involves a systematic approach to recognising risks and ensuring something is done to control them.

Important factors include:

- The risk assessment process;
- The number of competent instructors;
- The suitability and maintenance of equipment;
- Emergency procedures.

The inspection/licensing process

The HSE currently has responsibility for the AALA, and has enforcement responsibility for the Adventure Activities Licensing Regulations 2004.

All of the inspections, and most of the administration work, that the AALA carried out has been contracted to Adventure Risk Management Services (Adventure RMS).

The role of Adventure RMS is to:

- Examine applicants' health and safety policies and procedures, as well as any other relevant documents;
- Carry out site inspections;
- Make licensing decisions on behalf of the AALA.

Further guidance

Managing Health and Safety in Swimming Pools

You can download *Managing Health and Safety in Swimming Pools* from the HSE website: **hse.gov.uk**

Contact your local authority

Health and safety standards for private pools are enforced by the Environmental Health department of your local authority.

Adventure activities licensing

Information on adventure activities and the change from licensing to Codes of Practice is available on the HSE website: **hse.gov.uk**

Applying for an Adventure Activities Licence

An application for an Adventure Activities Licence can be made on the AALA website: **hse.gov.uk/aala/apply-for-a-licence.htm**

Adventure RMS

The Adventure RMS website provides information on the assessment they will undertake when they receive the application form from AALA: **adventurerms.org.uk**

Fire safety (general)

KEY FACTS

NEW

- The Home Office has published new fire safety guidance for small accommodation businesses that accommodate no more than 10 people and where the accommodation is not above the first floor. This guidance came into effect on 1 October 2023.
- Fire safety legislation applies to virtually all workplaces including attractions, hotels, B&Bs and self-catering properties.
- A 'suitable and sufficient' fire risk assessment must be carried out and recorded.
- There must be a person identified as being responsible for the fire risk assessment and ensuring that fire protection and prevention measures are observed and maintained.
- An emergency plan should be drawn up. It should be displayed in the form of a fire action notice in guest rooms and adjacent to the fire alarm call points in the staff and common areas.

New fire safety guidance for small accommodation businesses

NEW

In spring 2023 the Home Office produced revised fire safety guidance for small accommodation businesses that sleep up to 10 people and where the accommodation is no higher than the first floor of the building. This guidance, *A Guide To Making Your Small Paying-Guest-Accommodation Safe From Fire*, replaces the older *Do You Have Paying Guests?* guidance that was produced in 2008. The new guidance is similar to the old guidance in many ways but provides much more detail on how to undertake a fire risk assessment and contains a large number of recommendations on the steps you should take to ensure that you have fulfilled your responsibilities under the **Fire Safety Order 2005**.

The most important changes in the new guidance are:

1. Recording Fire Risk Assessments

The most important change in the new guidance is that you **MUST** record your Fire Risk Assessment. Previously you only had to record the assessment if you had five or more staff. VisitEngland has always recommended that you record your Fire Risk Assessment in order to prove that you have fulfilled your legal responsibilities but doing this is now mandatory.

2. Undertaking electrical inspections

Previous guidance recommended checking electrical equipment but did not mention the electrical system in your premises. The new guidance states that your electrical system (i.e., the distribution board and wiring of the property) should be subject to inspection and tested at least once every five years. In addition, for self-catering properties, all appliances should be visually checked between lettings and in B&Bs there should be periodic in-house service and testing in accordance with the IET Code of Practice for In-Service Inspection and Testing of Electrical Equipment.

3. Heating system inspections

The new guidance states that heating and hot water systems should be inspected annually by a qualified contractor to ensure they are maintained in good condition. Previously, this requirement applied to just gas systems (your annual Gas Safe inspection), but it is now extended to all heating and hot water systems.

4. Carbon Monoxide detectors

Any property with a gas appliance, fire or wood burner should have a carbon monoxide detector installed. This requirement was missing from the previous guidance.

5. Sweeping chimneys and flues

Any property with a chimney or flue needs to have it swept at least annually. Again, this was missing from the previous guidance.

6. Candles

The new guidance states that operators should not provide candles, tea lights or ethanol burners for use by guests, and there should be a policy in place prohibiting their use. This is important as many operators use candles as decorative features or supply tealights/tealight holders.

7. Inner rooms

Inner rooms (which are rooms where the only escape route is through another room) should not be used for sleeping accommodation unless the rooms are on the ground floor and the rooms have direct access to a door or "escape window" that can be used by the occupants to reach a place of safety clear of the accommodation. Escape windows for rooms on the first floor are not considered a safe means of escape for paying guests.

This will impact many older buildings and cottages where an upstairs bedroom is accessed via another bedroom and operators are advised to contact a fire safety expert to determine what should be done to ensure the safety of people using an inner room.

To help you, the new guidance includes four examples of different accommodation types which demonstrate where fire detectors/alarms should be located. While it is not a legal requirement to follow the exact recommendations in the guidance, due to all properties being unique in nature, it is important to note that the Fire Safety Order states that, in any legal proceedings, a failure to comply with guidance may be relied on as tending to establish that you contravened the legislation.

NEW

In January 2025, the Home Office updated this guidance with a number of clarifications and amendments. The main changes include:

- An update to the definition of a private property to clarify that properties where paying guests stay in a private home with a host are subject to the guidance;
- Adding more detail to the applicability of the guidance to more unusual accommodation types such as yurts, treehouses, bothies, glamping pods, tents and holiday caravans;
- Updated guidance on the provision and maintenance of fire extinguishers;
- Adding new legal requirements introduced through Section 156 of the **Building Safety Act 2022**,
- Clarifying what is meant by the terms "must", "should" and "may" when they are used in the guidance.

Fire safety guidance for larger properties

If you have a property that accommodates more than 10 people, or your premises have sleeping accommodation above the first floor, then this guidance does not apply. Instead, the relevant guidance is *Fire safety risk assessment: sleeping accommodation*.

Fire risk assessment template

The new guidance also includes an updated template that you can use to undertake your fire risk assessment, which can be downloaded from **visitengland.org/fire**.

You can also download supplementary guidance on considering the means of escape for disabled people from **Gov.uk**.

Fire safety

The **Regulatory Reform (Fire Safety) Order 2005** requires the 'responsible person' in virtually all workplaces, including attractions, hotels, B&Bs and self-catering properties, to adopt a self-assessment approach to fire safety in the workplace.

The **Regulatory Reform (Fire Safety) Order 2005** applies to England and Wales, but there is equivalent legislation in Scotland and Northern Ireland.

- In Scotland the **Fire (Scotland) Act 2005** and the **Fire Safety (Scotland) Regulations 2006** apply
- In Northern Ireland the relevant legislation is the **Fire and Rescue Services (Northern Ireland) Order 2006.**

Do the regulations apply to me?

Yes: the regulations apply to all attractions and accommodation premises, including self-catering accommodation.

Houses in multiple occupation

Properties defined as Houses in Multiple Occupation (HMOs) are subject to the **Regulatory Reform (Fire Safety) Order 2005** in that the common areas that may be visited by the landlord or others are subject to a suitable and sufficient Fire Risk Assessment. The individual residential areas are not subject to this requirement. HMOs are still subject to the fire safety requirements imposed by the Housing Act 2004.

How do I comply?

The Regulatory Reform (Fire Safety) Order 2005 requires every business to nominate a person to take responsibility for carrying out a Fire Risk Assessment of the premises and ensure that fire protection and prevention measures are observed and maintained.

It is advisable to identify the nominated responsible person on the assessment document and make that person known to all staff.

> **Note:** New Home Office guidance states that, from 1 October 2023 all Fire Risk Assessments must be recorded. This is a change to previous requirements where Fire Risk Assessments only needed to be recorded if the business had five or more employees.

Note: it is a requirement of VisitEngland's National Quality Assessment Scheme for accommodation that you demonstrate to the assessor that you have carried out your Fire Risk Assessment. In addition, for any business your public liability insurance provider will also require proof that you have undertaken an assessment.

What is a Fire Risk Assessment?

A Fire Risk Assessment is a structured consideration of the fire hazards and management of fire in the premises. It can be undertaken in five steps:

- Identify the fire hazards;
- Identify the people at risk;
- Evaluate, remove, reduce and protect from risk;
- Record, plan, inform, instruct and train;
- Review the assessment periodically.

Remember: you know your premises best, so follow the guidance and assess how your staff and guests would escape from the building quickly if a fire started (<2.5 minutes is the target time). Think about how they would be alerted and how easily they would find their way out. After all, guest safety is the most important thing to consider - and yours too if you live on the premises.

Identify the fire hazards

Potential sources of ignition, e.g:

- Cooking equipment;
- Lighting;
- Electrical apparatus;
- Machinery;
- Display screen equipment, e.g. computer screens.

Combustible materials that may burn, e.g:

- The furnishings and furniture;
- Parts of the building such as panelling and curtains;
- Combustible linings on escape routes;
- Displays.

Flammable liquids and gases e.g:

- Products used for cleaning or maintenance purposes, including those used to clean swimming pools and hot tubs;
- Fuel storage areas.

Identify the people at risk

The people at risk include:

- Customers;
- Staff;
- Contractors;
- Other visitors;
- People outside the property, e.g. neighbours and passers-by.

Particular note should be made of the number of people likely to be on the premises, where they could be on the premises if a fire occurs and any persons - staff or customers - who may require additional assistance in the event of an evacuation e.g. disabled people and children.

Evaluate, remove, reduce and protect from risk

This step involves evaluating the hazards and taking measures to eliminate these where possible. The prohibition of smoking on the premises and the regular removal of rubbish from bins and storage areas are examples of ways to reduce hazards.

Particular care should be taken when selecting curtains and display materials, especially temporary decorations used for specific events or to celebrate public holidays and festivals.

Any simple changes should be made straight away, such as clearing obstacles and removing flammable items from escape routes. If you identify something that would be too expensive or cause too much disruption to rectify straight away, make a note of the work and when you intend to carry it out. Out of season is always a good time to catch-up on such work.

Record, plan, inform and train

As well as recording your fire risk assessment, you should also keep a log book that contains details of maintenance and servicing to fire protection measures including alarms, detectors and fire extinguishers. An emergency plan should be drawn up to indicate the actions that should be taken by staff, as well as customers and others, in case of a fire on the premises. This is particularly important for attractions where the customers are in enclosed spaces and/or in large groups (e.g. escape rooms and theatres).

The plan, in the form of a Fire Action Notice, should be displayed adjacent to the fire alarm call points in the staff and public areas. For accommodation businesses, it should also be displayed in guest bedrooms.

These actions should include the measures that would be taken to identify and assist disabled people to leave the premises safely.

Staff should be trained in the actions that they would be expected to take in an emergency and this should include all staff participating in periodic fire drills at least once, and preferably twice, a year. Where staff do not speak fluent English, special attention should be given to ensuring that instructions are fully understood by the staff concerned.

Where an attraction or hotel is part of a complex of buildings (such as a shopping centre) or parts of the buildings are occupied by franchise holders, then the responsible person should liaise with the appropriate staff in these areas.

Review the assessment periodically

The Fire Risk Assessment for the premises should be reviewed periodically and when:

- Alterations are made to the structure or layout of the premises;
- There are changes in the use of an area of the building;
- There are significant changes to the number or location of the visitors or staff;
- There is a significant change in the mobility level or other factors influencing the response of visitors or staff in an emergency;
- There are changes in the management of the building.

There are no prescribed times for the reviews, but many businesses choose to review their assessment annually.

How do I know what fire precautions I need?

It is up to the nominated person to determine the appropriate fire precautions as a result of their Fire Risk Assessment.

For **accommodation businesses**, the guidance publication *A guide to making your small paying-guest-accommodation safe from fire* is available on the Gov.uk website. It provides advice tailored specifically to small B&Bs, guest houses and self-catering properties located either on the ground floor, or the ground and first floor, providing sleeping accommodation for a maximum of 10 persons, with no more than four bedrooms on the first floor. It is designed to encourage compliance, by giving businesses practical advice on reducing fire risks in their establishments. It explains the risk assessment process, sets out sources of further advice and guidance and contains detailed information on the types of fire safety measures appropriate for different accommodation types.

For **attractions**, the Home Office produces two publications: *Fire safety risk assessment: small and medium places of assembly*, which is targeted at places that accommodate up to 60 people (small) and up to 300 people (medium), and *Fire safety risk assessment: large places of assembly*, for premises that hold over 300 people.

LICENCES & CONSENTS
MARKETING
CUSTOMERS
FOOD & DRINK
ENVIRONMENTAL PROTECTION
HEALTH & SAFETY
STAFF
BUSINESS, MANAGEMENT & TAX
FURTHER INFORMATION

There is also separate guidance for:

- Outdoor attractions and events – *Fire safety risk assessment: open-air events and venues*
- Theatres and music halls – *Fire safety risk assessment: theatres, cinemas and similar premises*
- Zoos and farm parks – *Fire safety risk assessment: animal premises and stables*.

These guidance documents contain detailed information on how to undertake a Fire Risk Assessment related to different business types, as well as templates for the assessment and fire safety maintenance checklists. There are also sections in the guidance documents on how to adapt fire precautions for historic buildings.

The most important factor is fire prevention. Staff should be made aware of fire hazards and safe working practices in order to prevent a fire breaking out. There should be an emergency plan drawn up so that all staff know what actions they should take in the event of a fire. The fire protection provisions will vary according to the particular premises but should include the following:

- **Means of escape:** in all premises it is important that there are adequate means of escape. In all but the smallest guesthouses there should normally be at least two escape routes from all parts of the building and these should be available for use and free of obstructions at all times
- **Fire alarm:** there should be a means of alerting people to a fire, should it break out. See below for more details
- **Emergency lighting:** in order for everyone to find their way out of the building safely there should be automatic emergency escape lighting. In some very small guesthouses there may be sufficient 'borrowed light' from street lights outside but this is not often the case
- **Signs:** these should be prominently displayed to guide guests to the fire exits with which they will not be familiar
- **Fire fighting equipment:** a suitable number of appropriate fire extinguishers should be provided and at least some staff should be instructed in their use.

Which alarm system?

Since the interpretation of the Order may vary with each fire service around the country, it is difficult to advise businesses in a general way on exactly what type of alarm system they should fit.

The types of system required will, however, depend on the level of the risk – a very sophisticated system would not be necessary in small premises. Whatever system is used should take into account disabled people (e.g. those with hearing loss), so that their safety is not compromised.

The Regulatory Reform (Fire Safety) Order 2005 requires that premises are provided with suitable and sufficient means of detecting fire and giving warning in the event of a fire. For small buildings this may be linked mains-powered smoke and heat alarms that both sound in the event of fire.

Guidelines for small premises are that they can install simple systems – LD2 or LD3 – that comprise mains-operated smoke and heat alarms with battery back-up. Current legislation defines a 'small' property as being up to two storeys high (from the ground) with no floor more than 200 square metres in total. This equates to a floor with eight to ten en-suite double rooms.

LD2 properties must have alarms in corridors and all rooms leading off the main escape route, while LD3 properties require them only in the corridor, landing and hallway of the main escape route. These LD3 alarms are the same as those required in all new homes. If the property was built after 1990, it is likely to comply already.

Larger properties may be expected to install more sophisticated detectors and alarms, which are classed as L2 systems.

How do I undertake the assessment?

Guidance on undertaking a Fire Risk Assessment is set out on the *fire safety in the workplace* pages on the Gov.uk website.

Further advice can be gained from a fire safety consultant or your local fire authority.

Fire risk assessment template for small accommodation businesses

VisitEngland provides a free downloadable Fire Risk Assessment template for smaller domestic-type accommodation at **visitengland.org/fire**

How do I record the Fire Risk Assessment?

The legislation does not prescribe a specific format for the assessment but you do have to record the **significant findings** and the **persons especially at risk** from fire. The significant findings are a list of the actions that should be taken to reduce the fire hazards to a minimum.

You should also record any shortcomings that are identified in the management of the general fire precautions. A note should be kept of the remedial actions that are taken to demonstrate to the fire brigade, should they visit, that you are taking steps to address these matters.

Is the assessment a one-off exercise?

No: you are required to keep your assessment under review and update it when necessary. A new assessment should always be undertaken whenever a property is renovated or structurally altered.

Who enforces the legislation?

The **Regulatory Reform (Fire Safety) Order 2005** is enforced by the local fire and rescue service. Fire Safety Officers will make periodic visits to the premises and will ask to see the fire risk assessment to ensure that it is 'suitable and sufficient'.

What do Fire Safety Officers look at?

As well as inspecting the means of escape and other fire precautions, the Fire Safety Officer may ask to see the fire log book containing the records of the servicing and maintenance of the fire protection measures (e.g. the automatic fire detection and alarm system and the emergency lighting).

The officer may also ask to see the record of false fire alarms in the premises so these should also be kept up-to-date

Notices

If your premises does not meet the Order, the Fire Safety Officer will provide practical advice or, if the risk is serious or if the Officer is not satisfied, you may be issued with one of the following.

- **An alterations notice:** this does not require alterations to be made to the premises. It is served when the enforcing authority believes that there will be a serious risk to people in the building if a change is made to any particular part of the premises or their use
- **An enforcement notice:** this requires certain measures to be taken within a specified timeframe
- **A prohibition notice:** this requires the business to cease trading immediately until certain remedial action has been taken.

In all cases, you will have a right of appeal, both informally and formally. An informal appeal can sometimes identify a different way of meeting the Order which satisfies both parties.

The fire authority will work with you to achieve a satisfactory level of fire safety.

Further guidance

Fire safety for accommodation businesses

Download *A guide to making your small paying-guest-accommodation safe from fire*, a guide designed to provide advice on fire safety to small accommodation businesses, from the Gov.uk website

Fire evacuation for disabled guests

Download *Fire Safety Risk Assessment – Means of Escape for Disabled People* from the Gov.uk website

Fire risk assessments: accommodation
Download *Fire Risk Assessment for sleeping accommodation* on the Gov.uk website

Fire risk assessments: attractions (general)
Download general guidance in *Fire Safety in the Workplace* from the Gov.uk website

Fire risk assessment for small attractions
Download *Fire safety risk assessment: small and medium places of assembly* from the Gov.uk website

Fire risk assessment for large attractions
Download *Fire safety risk assessment: large places of assembly* from the Gov.uk website

Fire risk assessment for outdoor attractions
Download *Fire safety risk assessment: open-air events and venues* from the Gov.uk website

Fire risk assessment for theatres/music halls
Download *Fire safety risk assessment: theatres, cinemas and similar premises* from the Gov.uk website

Fire risk assessment for zoos and farm parks
Download *Fire safety risk assessment: animal premises and stables* from the Gov.uk website

The Purple Guide
Guidance from the Events Industry Forum for businesses staging events on their premises, from safety to waste disposal, can be found on The Purple Guide website: **thepurpleguide.co.uk**

Fire safety of furniture and furnishings

KEY FACTS

- If you provide hotel or bed and breakfast accommodation, or operate a pub, restaurant or medium hazard attraction, which includes indoor premises where public entertainment is provided, you need to purchase furniture and furnishings that comply with commercial fire safety standards.
- If you provide self-catering accommodation or have a low hazard attraction, such as a museum or exhibition that contains upholstered furniture, you need to comply with the Furniture and Furnishings (Fire) (Safety) Regulations 1988.
- All furniture (new and second-hand) in self-catering accommodation or low hazard attractions that is covered by the regulations must comply with certain safety tests.
- An agency's liability for the fire safety of the furniture in the properties it handles depends on the terms of its arrangement with the accommodation owner.

The **Regulatory Reform (Fire Safety) Order 2005** requires you to undertake a fire safety assessment of your property, identifying risks and taking practical steps to mitigate these risks. This assessment includes whether the fire safety characteristics of the furniture and furnishings in your property are appropriate to the level of fire risk.

Fire safety of furniture in all premises

The British Standards Institute (BSI) defines four categories of fire risk for all premises – low hazard, medium hazard, high hazard and very high hazard. Residential properties and self-catering properties, along with attractions such as museums and exhibitions, are deemed to be low hazard, while B&Bs, hotels, places of public entertainment, casinos, pubs and restaurants are deemed to be medium hazard because they are generally larger and occupied by more than one party.

For low-hazard properties, you are able to use furniture and furnishings that meet fire safety standards for domestic properties. As such, you are able to use any new products from a reputable supplier because this is the minimum standard for all manufacturers and retailers. However, you are still required to comply with the **Furniture and Furnishings (Fire) (Safety) Regulations 1988**, which cover domestic furniture and furnishings.

For medium-hazard properties, the BSI states that furniture and furnishings should comply with standards BS 7176 (upholstered furniture), BS 7177 (bed bases and mattresses) and BS 5867 (curtains and drapes), which provide greater fire protection than domestic products. This commercial or contract furniture should meet CRIB 5/Ignition Source 5 standards, which means it has been tested for fire safety and is often sold by specialist companies. When ordering furniture for medium hazard premises, it is important to ensure that it complies with these standards. Your local fire safety officer will be able to advise.

The Furniture and Furnishings (Fire) (Safety) Regulations 1988

The Furniture and Furnishings (Fire) (Safety) Regulations 1988 (as amended) set fire resistance standards for upholstered furniture in domestic use (new and second-hand).

Do the Furniture and Furnishings (Fire) (Safety) Regulations apply to me?

Yes: if you are providing self-catering accommodation that contains upholstered furniture or have an attraction that is deemed to be low hazard.

What do the regulations cover?

The regulations apply only to upholstered furniture supplied for domestic use, a type of use that implies a low fire hazard. Most holiday lets are regarded as constituting domestic use and, therefore, are covered by the regulations.

Furniture designed to cope with a greater fire hazard (for example hotel beds and chairs) is available and may be offered to you by some retailers. When re-equipping your self-catering property, it will normally be for you to decide whether or not you require the new furniture to meet these higher fire resistance standards. If in any doubt, check with your local fire authority.

For simplicity's sake in the information that follows, furniture and furnishings is referred to as 'furniture'.

What furniture is affected?

To come within the scope of the regulations, furniture must be upholstered. Such furniture would include:

- Domestic furniture, including children's furniture;
- Beds and divans (including their bases and headboards), mattresses of any size;
- Sofa beds, futons and other convertibles;
- Nursery furniture (for example highchairs, cots and playpens);
- Domestic garden furniture;
- Scatter cushions and seat pads;
- Pillows;
- Furniture in new caravans.

The regulations also apply to loose and stretch covers for furniture.

What furniture is not affected?

The regulations do not apply to:

- Bedclothes (including duvets);
- Loose covers for mattresses;
- Pillowcases;
- Curtains;
- Carpets;
- Sleeping bags;
- Goods made before 1 January 1950 and the materials used to re-upholster them.

Main provisions of the regulations

All furniture (new and second-hand) in self-catering accommodation or low-hazard attractions that are covered by the regulations must comply with certain safety tests. These are very broadly as follows:

- Upholstered furniture must pass a prescribed cigarette resistance test.
- Cover fabric, whether for use in permanent or loose covers, will normally have to pass a match resistance test.
- Filling materials for all furniture must pass ignitability tests as specified in the regulations.
- All new upholstered furniture (except mattresses and bedding) and loose and stretch covers for furniture must carry a permanent label detailing compliance with fire safety requirements. Always look for these labels before buying any upholstered furniture for your property.

If you are having items re-upholstered, make sure that the materials used comply with the regulations. However, remember that the regulations do not apply to materials used to re-upholster furniture made before 1950, unless that furniture is being significantly reworked and upholstered.

Can I use fire-inhibiting sprays to increase the life of my existing furniture?

These sprays are available from a number of companies who will treat the furniture for you. However, the Local Government Association and the Department for Business, Energy and Industrial Strategy (BEIS) advise operators to exercise extreme caution in using them because of issues relating to their durability. The treatment may, for example, be rendered ineffective by laundering.

Before deciding to have your furniture treated, you should:

- Remember that the regulations apply both to covers and to filling materials;
- Make absolutely sure that the spray on offer is appropriate for the covers and filling materials used in your furniture;
- Be sure that the spray will not be affected by previous treatments (for example waterproofing) carried out on the furniture;
- Bear in mind that some sprays are not water-resistant and will wash out, even when fluids, such as tea, are spilled on the treated fabric;
- Ask the company to provide strong evidence and guarantee that the spray does what it is supposed to do.

If the furniture which you have had treated is subsequently found not to meet the fire resistance standards specified in the regulations, it will be you (as the supplier of the furniture), and not the supplier or manufacturer of the spray, who is held responsible under this legislation.

Are letting agencies caught by the regulations?

Possibly. Whether or not an agency is liable for the fire safety of the furniture in the properties it handles will depend on the terms of its arrangement with you, the owner of the accommodation.

It seems that agencies that do no more than market your property and take bookings are unlikely to be liable. However, agencies that also manage and maintain properties on an owner's behalf could possibly be liable.

As this is something of a grey area, some marketing/booking agencies cover themselves by including a clause in their contracts with owners which commits those owners to ensuring that their property complies at all times with these regulations (and others).

Expect any prospective agency to ask about the fire resistance standards of your furniture before it agrees to take your property on to its books.

NEW

Review of the Regulations

In 2023, the Office for Product Safety and Standards and the Department for Trade undertook a consultation on a new approach to the fire safety of domestic upholstered furniture, including the publication of a draft set of new regulations setting out essential safety requirements that all products in scope of the regulations must meet in order to be placed on the market, including the supply of furniture in holiday accommodation. However, following the 2024 election, the development of the new Regulations has been delayed and it is uncertain as to when they will now be introduced. Operators are therefore advised to contact their local trading standards officer when undertaking refurbishments.

Further guidance

Your local authority

For further assistance, contact the Trading Standards department of your local authority.

Further guidance on the regulations

You can download *A Guide to the Furniture and Furnishings (Fire) (Safety) Regulations* from the Government archive: **webarchive.nationalarchives.gov.uk**

Smoking in public places

KEY FACTS

- Smoking is banned in enclosed public spaces and places of work, with some exemptions.
- There is a legal duty for you to display a legible no-smoking sign where it can be seen by customers and staff.
- There is a legal duty for any person who owns or manages smoke-free premises to ensure that guests, visitors and staff do not smoke on the premises.

Smoking ban

There has been a ban on smoking in enclosed public spaces and places of work (with some exemptions) since 1 July 2007, when the **Health Act 2006** came into force.

Does the Act apply to me?

Yes: if you own or manage enclosed or substantially enclosed premises that are open to the public, or are used as a place of work by more than one person, or where members of the public might visit to receive or provide goods or services.

Note: In Wales, the areas of premises to which the ban applies, as well as definitions and exemptions, are the same as they are in England – however, the signage requirement is different.

Definitions

Enclosed places: premises are considered to be enclosed if they have a ceiling or roof and are wholly enclosed (except for doors, windows or passageways), whether on a permanent or temporary basis.

Substantially enclosed areas – the 50% rule: substantially enclosed premises are defined as those that have a ceiling or roof (including retractable roofs such as awnings), but have permanent openings in the walls (excluding doors or windows) which comprise less than half of the total area of the walls. Walls include fixed or retractable structures that serve the purpose of walls and constitute the perimeter of premises (for example windbreaks). Temporary structures such as tents, marquees or similar will be classified as enclosed premises if they fall within the definition.

Exemptions

While smoking is banned from all of the indoor public and communal areas of attractions, hotels and guesthouses, there are a number of exemptions:

- **Self-contained short-term rental accommodation** (holiday cottages/flats/caravans) are not required to be smoke-free, but you retain the right to determine whether to allow smoking in your property.
- The **private areas of bed and breakfasts and guesthouses** are not covered by the ban, provided that the areas are not used by any staff (for example, the laundry may be out of bounds for customers but if a cleaner has to use it, it is covered by the ban).
- **Designated bedrooms** in hotels, guesthouses and bed and breakfasts. To qualify, a designated bedroom must:
  - Be designated in writing by the person in charge of the premises as being a smoking room;
  - Be completely enclosed except for doors and windows;
  - Have a ventilation system that must not discharge into any non-smoking part of the premises;
  - Have doors to smoke-free parts of the premises that shut mechanically after use;
  - Be clearly marked as a room in which smoking is permitted.

It should be noted that there is no legal requirement for an accommodation owner to provide designated smoking bedrooms. Providing such rooms is purely at the discretion of the owner.

Signage

The **Smoke-free (Signs) Regulations 2012** (England only) require you to display at least one legible no-smoking sign. There is no requirement on the location or size of the sign, provided that it is able to be seen by customers and staff.

Enforcement and penalties

Enforcement is the responsibility of local authorities. Environmental health officers have the power to enter all 'no-smoking premises' in order to establish that the smoke-free legislation is being enforced in accordance with the law.

Failure to display appropriate non-smoking signage may result in a fine, and the legislation also places a legal duty on any person who owns or manages smoke-free premises to ensure that guests, visitors and staff do not smoke on the premises.

Owners or managers who are found not to have taken reasonable steps to stop people smoking on their premises will be liable to a fine of up to £2,500 on conviction.

Vaping

The ban on smoking in enclosed public spaces and places of work does not apply to the use of e-cigarettes or vaping. It is therefore up to operators to determine whether vaping is allowed anywhere on the premises, restricted to certain areas, or prohibited in any part of the premises.

Further guidance

Guidance on smoke-free legislation

A checklist and information for employers and businesses can be found on the Smoke Free England website:
smokefreeengland.co.uk

STAFF

Working hours

KEY FACTS

- The Working Time Regulations 1998 as amended) apply to all businesses that have employees.
- You must take reasonable steps to ensure that employees do not work more than an average of 48 hours per week (excluding lunch breaks).
- Employees are entitled to 5.6 weeks of paid leave per year, and rest periods of a specified length in each working day and in each seven-day period.
- You must keep sufficient records to show that you are complying with the regulations.

Working time regulations

Are the regulations relevant to me?

Yes: The **Working Time Regulations 1998** (as amended) apply to any business that has employees, however small the business.

Which employees are covered by the regulations?

The regulations apply to anyone who is working for you – including trainees and young workers (those aged 16 and 17), but excluding the genuinely self-employed.

What are the requirements?

Working time

You are responsible for taking reasonable steps to ensure that employees do not work more than an average of 48 hours per week, excluding lunch breaks. (The number of hours worked each week should be averaged out over 17 weeks.)

- Employees can choose to work longer, but the agreement must be in writing and signed by the worker. This is known as a Working Time Regulations Opt-Out Agreement.
- Young workers may not ordinarily work more than eight hours per day or 40 hours a week. There is no opt-out possible from the young workers' limitations.

Night-time workers

You are also responsible for taking reasonable steps to ensure that any night workers do not work on average more than eight hours in 24. There is no opt-out from the night work limits. Night workers are those who normally work at least three hours between 11pm and 6am.

- You must offer a free health assessment to a night worker before they start working nights, and on a regular basis to ensure they are fit for night work.
- Young workers may not ordinarily work between 10pm and 7am.
- However, they may work between 10pm and midnight and between 4am and 7am in certain special circumstances (for example when working in a hotel, restaurant or pub, in catering and in retail).

NEW

Child employment

There are separate restrictions for employing children under the age of 16. These restrictions mean that children cannot be employed:

- Before 7am or after 7pm;
- During school hours;
- For more than an hour before school;
- In any job harmful to their health or wellbeing;
- For more than four hours without a one-hour break;
- Without having a two-week break from any work during the school holidays in each calendar year.

There are also restrictions on the length of time that children can work during term time and during holiday periods. There may also be local authority restrictions on employing children in your area.

See the *Employing Under 18s* section for more information.

Paid annual leave

Employees, whether full-time or part-time, are entitled to 5.6 weeks of paid leave per year, starting on the first day of employment. One week of leave is the equivalent of the time normally worked in a week. This should be applied pro-rata for part-time employees. For example, if a worker normally works five days per week, 5.6 weeks of paid leave equates to 28 working days per year; for a Saturday worker, it equates to 5.6 days per year.

You must set out an employee's paid holiday entitlement in their 'written statement of employment'. This should enable them to work out their entitlement and pay for any untaken holiday if they leave.

Note: the holiday entitlement can include bank holidays, provided that you pay employees for those days.

Calculating holiday pay for casual and seasonal employees
From 6 April 2024, new rules were introduced to determine the calculation of holiday pay for employees who are employed on either a casual basis (i.e. non-fixed hours) or for only part of the year (i.e. seasonal workers).

Employees who fall into this category have their holiday pay calculated and accrued on the following basis:

- At 12.07% of the hours they work in a pay period;
- On the last day of the pay period (the period when employees are usually paid, such as weekly or monthly).

The 12.07% is based on the statutory minimum holiday entitlement of 5.6 weeks. If an employee's contract gives them more holiday than the statutory minimum, you will need to adjust this percentage.

If an employee's holiday entitlement includes part of an hour, you need to:

- Round this down to the nearest hour if it is less than 30 minutes;
- Round this up to the nearest hour if it is 30 minutes or more.

If a worker gets the statutory minimum holiday entitlement, the most holiday they can accrue in a year is 28 days. Detailed guidance on calculating holiday pay is available on the Gov.uk page *Calculating holiday pay for workers without fixed hours or pay*.

NEW

Rolled-up holiday pay
Rolled-up holiday pay is where businesses pay employees an additional amount on top of their normal wages over the course of the year as holiday pay, instead of paying it as a lump sum when the holiday is taken. ACAS advice is that this practice is **not** legal.

Further information, including a template for a 'written statement of employment', is available on the ACAS website: **acas.org.uk**.

Rest periods
Employees have the right to:

- At least a 20-minute break if they will work longer than six hours. However, organisations often allow longer and/or more frequent breaks;
- Not work on average more than 48 hours per week. Individuals may choose to work longer by 'opting out' (see below);
- 11 consecutive hours of rest in any 24 hour period;
- One day off each week, or two consecutive days off in a fortnight;
- A limit on the normal working hours of an average eight hours in any 24-hour period;
- Young workers are entitled to 12 hours of rest for each working day, and two days of rest for every seven-day period.

Special circumstances

For night workers' rest periods and in-work rest breaks, there are exceptions to the regulations (for example during busy peak periods) but workers must normally be given equivalent rest periods in compensation.

Records

You need to keep sufficient records in each case to show that you are complying with the regulations.

Further guidance

Working Time Regulations

Call the ACAS employer helpline on 0800 470 3521 or visit the ACAS website: acas.org.uk

Zero hours contracts

Guidance on zero hours contracts can be found on Gov.uk.

Working time and health assessments

Guidance on matters regarding weekly and night working time limits and health assessments is available from the Health and Safety Executive website: hse.gov.uk

Further guidance on being an employer

Find key resources to help you recruit and manage employees on a dedicated page in VisitEngland's Business Advice Hub: visitengland.org/businessadvice

National Minimum Wage and tips

KEY FACTS

There are four rates of National Minimum Wage (NMW), as of 1 April 2025:

- For workers 21 and over – the National Living Wage: £12.21 per hour.
- For workers aged 18 to 20: £10.00 per hour.
- For workers under 18: £7.55 per hour.
- For apprentices: £7.55 per hour.

UPDATED

New legislation on tipping came into effect on 1 October 2024 requiring employees to pass on all qualifying tips, gratuities and service charges to employees in a fair and transparent manner.

NEW

Is the National Minimum Wage relevant to me?

The National Minimum Wage (NMW) came into effect on 1 April 1999. It is relevant to all businesses that have employees, regardless of the size of the business. The Government sets the NMW rate for the next financial year in October of the preceding year, following the recommendations of the independent Low Pay Commission LPC. The requirement for businesses to pay their staff these rates is enforceable by HM Revenue and Customs (HMRC).

If HMRC finds that you have underpaid any of your staff, they can issue a Notice of Underpayment requiring you to repay arrears to your staff (paid at the current minimum wage rate) and pay a penalty to the Government. The penalty is 200% of the total underpayment, with a maximum of £20,000 per worker.

Who is entitled to the National Minimum Wage?

Anyone working for you (including part-time and casual staff) is entitled to receive the National Minimum Wage, **except:**

- Anyone 'genuinely self-employed' (for example, someone who controls their own time, what work they do and invoices you rather than receiving wages);
- Voluntary workers;

- Workers who are based permanently outside the UK, such as the Channel Islands or the Isle of Man.

UPDATED

What is the National Minimum Wage?

There are four rates of the National Minimum Wage. Rates as of 1 April 2025 are:

- **£12.21 per hour** for employees aged 21 and over (National Living Wage).
- **£10.00 per hour** for employees aged 18 to 20.
- **£7.55 per hour** for employees aged under 18.
- **£7.55 per hour** for apprentices aged under 19, or those in the first year of their apprenticeship.

Further information on the National Minimum Wage, including current rates, can be found on Gov.uk's *National Minimum Wage and National Living Wage* advice pages.

What counts as part of a wage?

Included: in addition to basic pay, certain other payments may count towards the National Minimum Wage, including:

- Bonuses;
- Incentives;
- Accommodation;
- Money for items such as clothing and shoes, where the worker can decide where to buy the items.

Excluded: other additional payments are excluded, including:

- Premium payments for overtime of shift work;
- Special allowances;
- Expenses;
- Tips, service charges or any other type of gratuity (see *Tips and service charges*, below);
- Expenditure on items such as clothing and tools related to work;
- All benefits in kind, including meals, except accommodation. Benefits in kind do not count towards minimum wage pay, even if they have a monetary value. However, there are special rules if you provide a worker with accommodation.

UPDATED

Accommodation offset

If you provide accommodation to a member of staff, you are entitled to offset an amount for this against the National Minimum Wage. If the accommodation is provided free of charge, the daily accommodation offset rate is £10.66 and the weekly offset rate is £74.62 from 1 April 2025. For more details, see the Government's *National Minimum Wage and Living Wage: Accommodation* pages.

Does the National Minimum Wage apply to rest breaks, sick time and holidays?

There are four main types of work, and each can apply in the tourism sector:

- **Time work**: when you pay the worker according to the number of hours he/she works.
- **Salaried hours work**: when the workers have a contract to work a set number of basic ascertainable hours each year, in return for an annual salary paid in instalments.
- **Output**: paid by the piece – such as the number of things they make, or tasks they complete.
- **Unmeasured**: paid in other ways.

The different types of work give rise to varied ways of determining entitlements. For more information, see the Gov.uk advice on minimum wage for different types of work.

Regardless of the contract type, the determination of work hours does not include rest breaks, sick time or holidays.

What is the National Living Wage and how does it affect me?

UPDATED

The National Living Wage does not replace the National Minimum Wage. Rather, it is a premium to be paid on top of the National Minimum Wage to employees aged 23 and over.

When it was introduced on 1 April 2016, the National Living Wage increased the minimum wage that must be paid to employees aged 25 and over. From April 2025, it applies to employees aged 21 and over at a rate of £12.21 per hour.

As with the National Minimum Wage, the National Living Wage premium is set annually following recommendations from the independent Low Pay Commission. Both rates apply from 1 April each year.

Further information on the National Living Wage is available on the Gov.uk *National Minimum Wage and National Living Wage* pages.

Records

- You are required to keep sufficient records to prove you are paying the National Minimum Wage.
- You must allow workers to see their record within 14 days if they make a request in writing.

LICENCES & CONSENTS MARKETING CUSTOMERS FOOD & DRINK ENVIRONMENTAL PROTECTION HEALTH & SAFETY STAFF BUSINESS, MANAGEMENT & TAX FURTHER INFORMATION

UPDATED

Tips and service charges

The new **Employment (Allocation of Tips) Act 2023** amends the Employment Rights Act 1996 so that employers are now required to:

- Pass on all qualifying tips and service charges to workers without deductions, except in very limited scenarios, such as deduction of income tax. This must be done, at the latest, by the end of the month following the month in which the tips are paid by customers (e.g. a tip received on 14 June must be paid by 31 July);
- Ensure that tips are distributed in a fair and transparent manner when the employer takes control, or exerts significant influence, over their distribution;
- Have regard to the Code of Practice on Fairness and Transparent Distribution of Tips when distributing or influencing the distribution of tips;
- Maintain a written policy on how tips are dealt with at their place of business, and ensure this policy is made available to all their workers;
- Maintain a record of all tips paid at their place of business and their allocation and distribution between each worker, to which workers have the right to request access.

Qualifying tips

The Tipping Act defines "qualifying tips, gratuities and service charges" as monies (or items of fixed value such as vouchers or tokens) that are received by either the employer or staff that are subject to employer control. The means the method by which the tip is received – i.e., as cash, card or electronic payment – is not relevant to whether it is deemed to be qualifying. Nor is whether the tip is added to the bill or paid separately to the bill.

Conversely, tips that staff receive and keep directly from customers are not deemed to be qualifying tips.

It is important to note that that Act requires employers to pass on the full amount of all qualifying tips. This means that all administration costs have to be paid by the employer, including all costs associated with processing the tips, such as the charges applied by credit and debit card companies.

Employer control

Under the legislation, an employer is deemed to have exercised control or significant influence over cash tips if either they tell staff how to distribute tips or if they collect tips and distribute them, for example, at the end of a shift or as part of the regular payroll.

Fair and transparent distribution

Employers must ensure that qualifying tips are allocated fairly between workers (including part-time, seasonal and agency workers) and that they should have regard to the Code of Practice when developing and implementing a system to achieve this. Allocating and distributing tips fairly does not require employers to allocate the same proportion of tips to all workers. Employers can allocate different proportions of the tips to different workers but need to ensure that they give due consideration to all of the workers involved in providing service to customers and use a clear and objective set of factors used to determine the allocation and distribution of tips.

The choice of factors should be fair and reasonable and could include:

- Employee role (for example, different distributions between front of house and backroom workers);
- Basic pay (and how workers are engaged);
- Hours worked during period when tips are received;
- Individual and/or team performance;
- Seniority / level of responsibility;
- Length of time employed;
- Customer intention.

Employers need to take care to ensure that the distribution policy they develop complies with the Equality Act in not discriminating between people with protected characteristics, either directly or indirectly.

To ensure a fair and transparent distribution policy is developed, employers are advised to consult with employees and to regularly review the policy to ensure that it continues to meet the requirements of the Act. The tipping policy must be in writing and include how tips are accepted, how tips are allocated and distributed, and what steps the employer takes to ensure tips are handled fairly and transparently in accordance with the Tipping Act. The policy must also be distributed to all employees.

Distribution of tips

Employers are free to distribute the tips directly to staff, through the payroll system, or to appoint a tronc arrangement (either in-house or through an independent tronc operator). Whichever distribution method is used, the employer remains responsible for the fairness of the distribution and must act if it is found that the distribution is being made in an unfair manner. The employer must also ensure that the distribution is made within the timeframe set out by the legislation (by the end of the month after the month in which the tip was received).

UPDATED

UPDATED

Record keeping

Employers must keep a tipping record which includes details of all qualifying tips received and the amount allocated to each worker. This record must be maintained for a period of three years beginning with the date on which the tip was paid. Employees have the right to make a written request – limited to one request per worker in a three month period – to view their tipping record for a period dating back up to 3 years, provided they worked during the period requested.

Further guidance

National Minimum Wage

The ACAS helpline 0300 123 1100 gives free advice on National Minimum Wage issues. You can also visit Gov.uk for more information.

Calculate your minimum wage

The Department for Business, Energy & Industrial Strategy has published guidance on calculating the minimum wage to help employers: gov.uk/guidance/calculating-the-minimum-wage

Tipping policies

Download *Code of Practice on Fair and Transparent Distribution of Tips* from Gov.uk.

Become a Living Wage employer

The Living Wage Foundation accredits businesses which pay direct employees the 'Real Living Wage': livingwage.org.uk

Further guidance on being an employer

Find key resources to help you recruit and manage employees on a dedicated page in VisitEngland's Business Advice Hub: visitengland.org/businessadvice

LICENCES & CONSENTS
MARKETING
CUSTOMERS
FOOD & DRINK
ENVIRONMENTAL PROTECTION
HEALTH & SAFETY
STAFF
BUSINESS, MANAGEMENT & TAX
FURTHER INFORMATION

Discrimination

KEY FACTS

- Discrimination laws apply to all businesses.
- It is unlawful to discriminate directly against anyone.
- It is unlawful to discriminate indirectly against anyone.
- Employers have a new legal requirement to take pro-active steps to prevent sexual harassment in the workplace.

NEW

The Equality Act 2010

The **Equality Act 2010** consolidated nine pieces of existing anti-discrimination legislation into one single Act. In doing so, it also simplified and strengthened the previous legislation in order to reduce discrimination and inequality.

Under the Act, it is unlawful to discriminate against any employee or customer (that is to treat them less favourably) on the basis of nine protected characteristics:

- Disability;
- Gender reassignment;
- Pregnancy and maternity;
- Marriage and civil partnership;
- Race – this includes ethnic or national origins, skin colour and nationality;
- Religion or belief;
- Sex;
- Sexual orientation;
- Age – this applies to those aged 18 or above.

UPDATED

It should be noted that in 2023, the **Equality Act 2010 (Amendment) Regulations 2023** were introduced to clarify and strengthen various parts of the Equality Act 2010. These are in relation to:

- Direct discrimination related to pregnancy, maternity and breastfeeding;
- Indirect discrimination where a person without a relevant protected characteristic suffers substantively the same

UPDATED

disadvantage as those with that protected characteristic;
- Direct discrimination in the context of access to employment and occupation as regards public statements outside a recruitment process;
- The right to equal pay and employment terms;
- The definition of disability in relation to employment and occupation.

As it applies to employees

You are required to treat all employees and job applicants the same. This covers all areas of employment, including recruitment, terms and conditions, promotion and transfers, training and development and the dismissal process. This requirement applies to all employers regardless of the size of the business.

UPDATED

There are rules against employers asking job applicants protected characteristic-related questions, and you are required to make reasonable adjustments to help people with protected characteristics fulfil the job they are employed to undertake or are applying for. For example, you would not be allowed to reject an applicant who uses a wheelchair for a receptionist position on the grounds that the reception desk was too high or remove an employee from a position because they were pregnant Rather, you are required to make modifications to the work environment or practices to enable people to undertake their roles.

Harassment

You are required to protect your staff from harassment at all times. This means taking steps to protect staff from harassment by other staff members, suppliers and customers. Further, an employee may claim harassment even if they are not the person that is being harassed. This can happen, for example:
- Where witnessing the harassment of another employee results in the creation of an intimidating environment for the witness;
- Where an employer has been informed that an employee has been harassed on two or more occasions by a third party, such as a customer or supplier, and does nothing to prevent further harassment;
- Where unwanted conduct relates to the sex of a person, even if it is not prompted by the complainant's sex.

NEW

The new **Worker Protection (Amendment of Equality Act 2010) Act 2023** came into force on 26 October 2024. This new legislation requires employers to pro-actively address sexual harassment in the workplace by taking "reasonable steps" to safeguard employees.

What this means is that, rather than reacting to complaints regarding sexual harassment, employers have to consider scenarios where their employees could be exposed to sexual harassment and put in place policies and procedures that minimise the risk. This means undertaking a sexual harassment risk assessment in the same way was you would undertake a health and safety or fire risk assessment, and then undertaking mitigating actions based on the findings.

There is no legal requirement for this assessment to be written but, because any legal action will be based on whether the employer took reasonable steps to ensure that their employees were protected, it is important that you have a written record of the assessment you undertook and the mitigation actions that you put in place to show that you fulfilled your legal obligations under this legislation.

It is important to note that this requirement only relates to sexual harassment rather than to harassment related to other protected characteristics such as disability or religious beliefs.

The Equalities and Human Rights Commission has produced detailed guidance on complying with this requirement in Chapter 3 of their *Sexual harassment and harassment at work: technical guidance* publication.

Employers face unlimited fines under the legislation if they are found not to be protecting staff from harassment or treating them in a discriminatory manner. For more details and guidance on discrimination legislation, see the *Equality Act 2010 guidance* on Gov.uk.

As it applies to customers

As with employment, it is illegal to discriminate on the basis of the nine protected characteristics when providing goods and services to customers, unless there is objective justification for doing so. This means that there have to be valid, justifiable reasons why a service cannot be provided to certain groups. For example, there may be medical reasons for not providing certain goods or services.

The Equality Act 2010 makes it easier for customers to require you to make reasonable adjustments in the way that you provide goods or service. For example, making sure that there are suitable options on the menu for people who do not eat certain foods for religious beliefs. The test will be whether the way that you provide goods or services places a person with a protected characteristic at a substantial disadvantage to other customers.

However, the Act does enable businesses to undertake positive action to target their goods, facilities or services to a particular group that is either disadvantaged or currently under-represented in their consumer base, or that has particular needs. For example, discounts could be given to disabled customers or their carers.

NEW

Harassment and victimisation

The Equality Act also protects customers from experiencing harassment or victimisation while on your premises. Harassment includes any behaviour that makes the person feel intimidated, humiliated, or degraded, or that creates a hostile environment. For example, if a barman makes comments or jokes about a person's disability or that fact that they are pregnant. It applies even if these comments are made to a third person.

Victimisation occurs when a customer is treated unfairly as a result of making a complaint about discrimination or their complaint is dismissed without due consideration.

Assistance dogs and support animals

You are legally required to allow assistance dogs (commonly known as guide dogs) onto your premises, even if you do not allow guests to bring pets. A person does not need to provide you with proof that their dog is an assistance dog.

Age discrimination

In 2012 the Government introduced age discrimination legislation. This makes it illegal to provide a different product or service, charge a different price, or to apply different terms and conditions to any customer over 18 years old on the basis of age unless:

- There is an 'objective justification'. Objective justification means that there is a valid objective reason for doing so (for example, charging different premiums for travel insurance could be justified on the basis of different levels of risk).
- The discrimination is beneficial: this means that offering discounts to people that allow them improved access to goods and services would be acceptable (for example, discounts for retired people would be acceptable as it would increase social inclusion).

Further guidance

Equality Act 2010

Further information on discrimination and the Equality Act 2010 is available on the Equality and Human Rights Commission website: equalityhumanrights.com

Be a Disability Confident employer

Find resources to help attract, recruit and retain disabled employees on the Disability Confident website: disabilityconfident.campaign.gov.uk

Further guidance on being an employer

Find key resources to help you recruit and manage employees on a dedicated page in VisitEngland's Business Advice Hub: visitengland.org/businessadvice

Time off for parents and carers

KEY FACTS

- All employers are required to comply with legislation related to family-friendly working.
- Employees' rights in this area include maternity and paternity rights, adoption leave, flexible working and parental leave.
- The Carer's Leave Act 2023 came into effect on 6 April 2024, enabling employees to claim one week's leave to look after a dependent with long-term care requirements.

NEW

Family-friendly working

There are laws that support working parents in combining work with looking after their children. As well as your legal duty to uphold these rights, it is also good practice to support family-friendly working and flexible working arrangements for all types of employees

Maternity rights

Regardless of how long they have worked for you, all pregnant employees (that is, those working under a contract of employment) are entitled to take up to 52 weeks of Statutory Maternity Leave (SML). This comprises:

- 26 weeks of Ordinary Maternity Leave;
- 26 weeks of Additional Maternity Leave.

Additional Maternity Leave starts immediately after Ordinary Maternity Leave.

Statutory Maternity Pay

UPDATED

To qualify for Statutory Maternity Pay (SMP) an employee must have been:

- Employed continuously (some breaks do not interrupt continuous employment) for at least 26 weeks into the 15th week before the due date;
- Earning an average of at least £120 a week (before tax).

UPDATED

SMP is paid for up to 39 weeks, with employees receiving:

- 90% of their average weekly earnings (before tax) for the first six weeks.
- £187.18 in 2025/26 or 90% of their average weekly earnings (whichever is lower) for the next 33 weeks.

SMP is to be paid in the same way as the employee receives their normal wages (for example, monthly or weekly).

Employees can choose when SMP will start, although this will normally coincide with their taking Ordinary Maternity Leave. SMP starts automatically if the employee is off work for a pregnancy-related illness in the four weeks before the week that the baby is due. The earliest SMP can start is 11 weeks before the due date. Employees entitled to SMP are entitled to receive it even if they decide to leave before they start receiving SMP. They do not have to repay it if they decide not to go back to work or leave their job while receiving SMP.

Paternity rights

Paternity leave

UPDATED

Employees who have 26 weeks of service by the 15th week before the Expected Week of Childbirth are entitled to two weeks of paternity leave. From 6 April 2024, paternity leave can be taken in either one two-week block or two one-week blocks at any time within 52 weeks of the birth, provided that 28 days advance notice is given to the employer. Employees may also take paternity leave if:

- They are not the biological father, but are the biological mother's partner;
- They expect to have responsibility for the child's upbringing;
- They have adopted the child or are the partner of the person who has adopted.

Ordinary Paternity Leave is for a period of one or two weeks which must be taken consecutively.

Statutory Paternity Pay

UPDATED

Similar to maternity pay, the statutory weekly rate of Paternity Pay in 2025/26 is £187.18, or 90% of average weekly earnings (whichever is lower).

Note: maternity and paternity leave and pay requirements also apply to same-sex couples.

Shared parental leave and pay

Historically, it has only been an option for a mother to take paid time off work to look after a new-born or adopted child. However, Shared Parental Leave (SPL) allows most couples who are in paid work and bringing up a child together the option of sharing the leave entitlement following the birth or adoption of their child.

An employee may be eligible for SPL and Statutory Shared Parental Pay (ShPP). To quality for SPL, your employee must share responsibility for the child with one of the following:

- Their husband, wife, civil partner or joint adopter;
- The child's other parent;
- Their parent (if they live with them).

Your employee or their partner must be eligible for maternity pay or leave, adoption pay, or leave of Maternity Allowance.

They must also:

- Have worked for you continuously for at least 26 weeks by the end of the 15th week before the due date (or the date that they are matched with their adopted child);
- Still be employed by you while taking SPL;
- Give you the correct notice, including a declaration that their partner meets the employment and income requirements which entitle them to SPL.

They can also receive ShPP if they are a worker and eligible for SMP or SPP.

Under SPL, parents can share up to 50 weeks of leave and up to 37 weeks of pay, and choose to take the leave and pay in a more flexible way (each parent can take up to three blocks of leave, or more if their employer allows, interspersed with periods of work).

Eligible parents can be off work together for up to six months, or alternatively stagger their leave and pay so that one of them is always at home with their baby in the first year.

UPDATED

ShPP is paid at the rate of £187.18 a week or 90% of an employee's average weekly earnings, whichever is lower.

Adoption leave

Employees who are newly matched with a child for adoption, and who have 26 weeks of service when this happens, are entitled to up to 26 weeks of Ordinary Adoption Leave, and up to a further 26 weeks of Additional Adoption Leave.

Employees who adopt individually are entitled to adoption leave and pay. If a couple adopts together, one member of the couple is

LICENCES & CONSENTS
MARKETING
CUSTOMERS
FOOD & DRINK
ENVIRONMENTAL PROTECTION
HEALTH & SAFETY
STAFF
BUSINESS, MANAGEMENT & TAX
FURTHER INFORMATION

entitled to adoption leave and pay; the couple can decide which partner will take adoption leave.

Employees do not qualify for Statutory Adoption Leave or Pay if they:

- Arrange a private adoption;
- Become a special guardian or kinship carer;
- Adopt a stepchild;
- Have a child through surrogacy;
- Adopt a family member.

UPDATED

Statutory adoption pay

Statutory Adoption Pay is 90% of an employee's gross average weekly earnings for the first six weeks, and then £187.18 or 90% of average weekly earnings before tax (whichever is lower) for the next 33 weeks.

Reclaiming Statutory Maternity, Paternity and Adoption Pay

You can usually reclaim 92% of employees' Statutory Maternity, Paternity and Adoption Pay. You can reclaim 103% if your business qualifies for Small Employers' Relief. You receive this if you paid less than £45,000 in Class 1 National Insurance in the last complete tax year before the qualifying or matching week.

Flexible working

Introducing flexible working practices can benefit everyone in your business. Many employers believe flexible working makes good business sense and brings about a range of improvements, including greater cost-efficiencies and better staff morale.

There are many different forms of flexible working. Flexible working can include:

- Part-time working;
- Flexi-time;
- Job-sharing;
- Working from home;
- Term-time working;
- Staggered hours.

As an employer, you have a duty to consider any request for flexible working seriously, and you must have a sound business reason for rejecting a request from an employee.

NEW

Until 6 April 2024, an employee could only request flexible working if they had served 26 weeks of continuous employment. However, this requirement has now been removed and any employee can request to undertake flexible working regardless of their period of employment.

It should be noted that employees can now make two flexible working requests in any 12-month period and that the employer is required to consult with the employee regarding their request before rejecting it.

NEW

Information on making and assessing an application for flexible working is available on the ACAS website: acas.org.uk

Unpaid Parental Leave

Unpaid Parental Leave is a right for parents to take time off work to look after a child or make arrangements for the child's welfare, which may include:

- Spending more time with their children;
- Looking at new schools;
- Settling children into new childcare arrangements;
- Spending more time with family, such as visiting grandparents.

Which staff can claim it?

Employees who have, or expect to have, parental responsibility for a child and have been employed for at least a year.

What are the main provisions?

- Each parent is entitled to 18 weeks of unpaid parental leave for each child, which can be taken up until the child's fifth birthday (or, the end of the fifth year after adoption, or the child's 18th birthday if that is sooner).
- The leave should be taken in blocks of one week, up to a maximum of four weeks per year for each child (greater flexibility is allowed if the employee receives a disability living allowance or personal independence payment for their child).
- At the end of parental leave, the employee is entitled to return to the same job if the leave was for four weeks or less. If it was for longer, the employee is entitled to return to the same job, or if that is not reasonably practicable, a similar job.
- You can reach your own agreement with an employee about the practicalities. If you do not, there are fall-back provisions: for example 21 days' notice; minimum of one week blocks; maximum of four weeks a year for each child. The employer can postpone the leave for up to six months if it would be particularly disruptive to the business, except for leave requested immediately after the child is born or adopted.
- You do not have to keep records, but you can be asked by a subsequent employer about how much leave an employee has taken (you can also ask a previous employer).
- You are entitled to ask to see evidence to confirm that an employee is the parent or the person legally responsible for the child.
- There are additional entitlements for parents of disabled children.

Note: employees also have the right to take a reasonable period off work to deal with an emergency involving a dependent.

NEW

Redundancy protection

Prior to 6 April 2024, redundancy protection for pregnant workers or those on maternity leave was only available during the period where the employee was actually on maternity leave. From 6 April 2024, this protection period was extended to include the time between the employee giving notice of their pregnancy and when maternity leave is taken and until 18 months after the expected week of childbirth or date of birth. In cases of adoption, the 18 months starts from the date of the child's placement or date of entry into Great Britain. This protection also applies for carers on Shared Parental Leave, but only if the employee has taken at least six weeks of continuous shared parental leave.

Carer Leave

New legislation was introduced on 6 April 2024 enabling an employee who has a dependant with a long-term care need to take one week's unpaid leave in any rolling 12 month period, in order to arrange care for that dependant. The dependent can be a close family member or a person who relies on the employee for care, such as an elderly or disabled neighbour.

For part-time employees, the amount of leave that can be claimed is calculated by adding up the hours that they worked over the last 12 months and dividing that by 52. For example, if someone worked 520 hours then they are entitled to take 10 hours unpaid carer's leave.

This leave may be taken in any multiple of individual days or half days over the 12 month rolling period. The required notice period is either twice as many days as the period of leave required, or three days, whichever is the greater. An employer cannot decline a request altogether but may postpone carer's leave where it is reasonably considered that the operation of the business would be unduly disrupted if leave was granted during the requested period.

Further guidance

Your rights and responsibilities

ACAS has a useful range of online guides to maternity, paternity, adoption and flexible working policies, including guidance on the Carer's Leave Act, on its website: acas.org

Further guidance on being an employer

Find key resources to help you recruit and manage employees on a dedicated page in our Business Advice Hub visitbritain.org/business-advice/employ-and-manage-staff

Migrant workers

KEY FACTS

- To be entitled to work in the UK, a foreign national must provide you with the necessary documentation.
- You should check any documentation provided to ensure, to the best of your ability, that it is genuine and that the potential employee is entitled to work in the UK.
- Generally, to employ someone living outside the UK, including the European Union:
  - They must pass a points-based assessment before they are given permission to enter or remain in the UK.
  - You must have a sponsor licence from the Home Office.

Employers' responsibilities

It is important that you are aware of your responsibilities when employing someone. The law on preventing illegal working is set out in the **Immigration, Asylum and Nationality Act 2006**. The act covers all aspects of immigration, from asylum seekers through to permanent migration, including the right to work and study in the UK.

On the basis of this legislation, the Home Office develops and implements the UK's immigration rules, which provide the detail as to how the act is carried out. For more information, see the Gov.uk advice on checking a job applicant's right to work in the UK. These rules are updated on a regular basis, so it is worth checking the site regularly for any changes.

If you employ, or plan to employ someone, including UK nationals, you need to make sure that they have permission to work in the UK before they start.

Note: You do not have to check existing employees from the EU, EEA or Switzerland if they came to the UK before 1 July 2021.

Proof of entitlement to work in the UK

Employers must do one of the following before the employee commences employment, to ensure that they are entitled to work in the UK:

1. A manual right to work check (this can be done for citizens of all nationalities).

2. A right to work check using Identity Document Validation Technology (IDVT) via the services of a certified Identity Service Provider (IDSP) (this can only be done for British or Irish citizens).

3. A Home Office online right to work check (this can only be done for non-British or Irish citizens).

There is a three-stage process for checking whether a person has the right to work in the UK:

Step 1: Obtain

Depending on where the person is from, you need to obtain documents that show that the person has the right to work in the UK. You can check which documents you need to obtain using the Home Office's online check: gov.uk/legal-right-work-uk

Step 2: Check

You must check that the documents you receive are originals, genuine and have not been altered, and that the person presenting them is the rightful holder of the documents. You must also check that:

1. Photographs and dates of birth are consistent across documents and with the person's appearance in order to detect any impersonation.
2. Expiry dates for permission to be in the UK have not passed.
3. Any work restrictions to determine if they are allowed to do the type of work on offer (for students who have limited permission to work during term-times, you must also obtain, copy and retain details of their academic term and vacation times covering the duration of their period of study in the UK for which they will be employed).
4. The reasons for any difference in names across documents can be explained by providing evidence (for example an original marriage certificate, divorce decree absolute, deed poll). These supporting documents must also be photocopied and a copy retained.

Care should be taken over the following aspects of the documentation provided.

- **Photographs:** does the person look like the photographs on their documents?
- **Date of birth:** is the date consistent with the appearance of the candidate?
- **Expiry dates:** are the documents still valid?
- **Stamps and endorsements:** do the passport stamps allow your job applicant to do the type of work you are offering?
- **Name:** is the same name used on all the documents?

The Public Register of Authentic Identification and Travel Documents Online (PRADO) can help you ascertain the authenticity of a document.

Step 3: Copy

You must make a clear copy of each document in a format which cannot manually be altered and retain the copy securely, electronically or in hard copy. You must also retain a secure record of the date on which you made the check. Simply writing a date on the copy document does not, in itself, confirm that this is the actual date when the check was undertaken. If you write a date on the copy document, you must also record that this is the date on which you conducted the check.

You must copy and retain copies of:

1. **Passports:** any page with the document expiry date, the holder's nationality, date of birth, signature, immigration permission, expiry date, biometric details, photograph and any page containing information indicating that the holder has an entitlement to enter or remain in the UK (visa or entry stamp) and undertake the work in question. The front cover no longer has to be copied.
2. **All other documents:** the document in full, including both sides of an Immigration Status Document and an Application Registration Card.

All copies of documents taken should be kept securely for the duration of the worker's employment and for two years afterwards. The copy must then be securely destroyed.

Penalties for non-compliance

Penalties include:

- A civil penalty of up to £45,000 per illegal worker or £60,000 per illegal worker for repeat offenders;
- In serious cases, a criminal conviction carrying a prison sentence of up to five years and an unlimited fine;
- Closure of the business and a compliance order issued by the court;
- Disqualification as a director;
- Not being able to sponsor migrants;

UPDATED

- Seizure of earnings made as a result of illegal working, and;
- Review and possible revocation of a licence in the alcohol and late-night refreshment sector and the private hire vehicle and taxi sector.

Points-based migration system

The Government has introduced a points-based migration system for people living overseas who want to live and work in the UK. Migrants need to pass a points-based assessment before they are given permission to enter or remain in the UK.

Under the points-based scheme, applicants are required to score 70 points.

To achieve the 70 points, the applicants must meet three mandatory requirements which together provide 50 points:

- They have a job offer from a Home Office licensed sponsor;
- The job offer is at the required skill level: RQF 3 or above (A-Level and equivalent);
- They speak English to the required standard.

To gain the additional 20 points, the job offer must meet the applicable minimum salary threshold (£25,600, or the specific salary requirement for their occupation, known as the 'going rate').

Alternatively, the job offer may be as low as £20,480, provided that the applicant can gain 20 points by:

- Filling a job in an occupation where the Migration Advisory Committee has designated a skills shortage;
- Having a PhD in a relevant subject;
- Having a PhD in a STEM subject where they will be able to trade characteristics, such as their qualifications, against a lower salary to get the required number of points.

If the job offer is less than the minimum salary requirement, but no less than £20,480, an applicant may still be eligible if they have:

- A job offer in a specific shortage occupation;
- A PhD relevant to the job;
- A PhD in a relevant STEM subject.

Characteristics	Mandatory/ Tradeable	Points
Offer of job by approved sponsor	Mandatory	20
Job at appropriate skill level	Mandatory	20
Speaks English at required level	Mandatory	10
Salary of £20,480 to £23,039 or at least 80% of the going rate for the profession (whichever is higher)	Tradeable	0
Salary of £23,040 to £25,599 or at least 90% of the going rate for the profession (whichever is higher)	Tradeable	10
Salary of £25,600 or above or at least the going rate for the profession (whichever is higher)	Tradeable	20
Job in a shortage occupation as designated by the Migration Advisory Committee	Tradeable	20
Education qualification: PhD in a subject relevant to the job	Tradeable	10
Education qualification: PhD in a STEM subject relevant to the job	Tradeable	20

Note: There are different salary rules for 'new entrants' at the start of their careers.

Sponsoring overseas workers

If you aim to employ someone from overseas, you must have a sponsorship licence. Applications for a licence can be made online and the licence lasts for four years. The licence fee is £536 for businesses with fewer than 50 employees, and £1,476 for businesses with more than 50 employees. (The fee is per business rather than per employee). For more information, see the *UK visa sponsorship for employers* advice on Gov.uk.

Further guidance

Employer's Guide to Right to Work Checks

The Home Office guidance document *Employer's Guide to Right to Work Checks* can be found on Gov.uk.

Employing foreign nationals

More information on employing foreign nationals can be found on Gov.uk, or call the UK Visa and Immigration helpline: 0300 123 4699.

Further guidance on being an employer

Find key resources to help you recruit and manage employees on a dedicated page in VisitEngland's Business Advice Hub: visitengland.org/businessadvice

Employing under-18s

KEY FACTS

- There are special requirements that you must comply with if you are employing children under the age of 18.
- It is illegal to employ anyone under the age of 13, and children can only undertake full-time employment once they reach school-leaving age.
- Unless the child is a family member, you must undertake a separate Health and Safety assessment of their position that takes into consideration their age and lack of experience.
- Children aged 16 and 17 are able to serve alcohol in a dining room or restaurant without supervision, or behind a bar if each individual sale is approved by a responsible person.

The **Children (Protection at Work) Regulations 2000** were introduced to help ensure that children are protected in the workplace and that employers pay special attention to their safety and wellbeing.

Does this apply to me?

Yes: although there are some exemptions if you are employing a family member on an occasional or short-term basis.

Employing children

It is not uncommon for small businesses to provide part-time or occasional employment to the children of friends and family. However, you need to be aware that it is illegal to employ children under the age of 13 to do any type of work (regardless of whether the work is part-time, full-time, or the payment is monetary or in-kind) and that there are a number of legal requirements and restrictions that govern the employment of children until they become adult workers at the age of 18.

LICENCES & CONSENTS
MARKETING
CUSTOMERS
FOOD & DRINK
ENVIRONMENTAL PROTECTION
HEALTH & SAFETY
STAFF
BUSINESS, MANAGEMENT & TAX
FURTHER INFORMATION

Employing children aged 13-16

Children between the ages of 13 and 16 can only work part-time. There are considerable restrictions on the times at which they can work and the length of time they can work, both during school terms and during school holidays. There are also restrictions on the places where they can work and the type of work they can undertake. In general, it is illegal to employ children in any work that may be harmful to their health, wellbeing or education.

NEW

While some of these restrictions are set nationally, there are also local bylaws that restrict the employment of children. Your local council will have a list the jobs that children cannot do and may also have restrictions on working hours, conditions of work and the type of employment.

Most local councils also require businesses intending to employ school-aged children to apply for a child employment permit, so it is important that you contact your local council to check the rules in your area (a permit is not required if a child is being employed as part of a school run work experience programme).

Employing children aged 16-18

Children can only start full-time work once they have reached the minimum school-leaving age of 16. However, they must be employed as part of an apprenticeship or traineeship scheme.

There are also specific requirements relating to their hours of work. These employees must not work more than eight hours a day (or more than 40 hours a week) and there must be at least 12 hours' rest between each working day and 48 hours' rest per working week. You must also provide a 30-minute rest break when they work longer than 4.5 hours.

See the *Working hours* section for more information.

Minimum pay

There is no minimum pay for children under the age of 16. Children under 16 also do not pay National Insurance, so you only need to include them on your payroll if their total income is over their Personal Allowance.

UPDATED

Children aged 16 and 17 are entitled to at least £6.40 per hour and, if they earn more than £123 per week, you will need to register them as an employee and operate PAYE.

Health and safety

A child under 18 cannot be employed for work that:

- Is beyond the child's physical or psychological capacity;
- Involves harmful exposure to toxic or carcinogenic substances;
- Involves harmful exposure to radiation;
- Involves a risk which cannot be recognised or avoided by young persons because of their lack of attention to safety or lack of experience or training (this is likely to mean that any employment in kitchens involving the use of sharp knives or slicers will be prohibited);
- Involves a risk to health from extreme cold or heat, noise or vibration.

If you are employing someone under 18, you must undertake a separate Health and Safety assessment, paying particular attention to their age and lack of experience. This does not apply if the child is a family member undertaking short-term or occasional work.

If the child is under 16, you must also tell one of their parents the results of the assessment. This must include any risks identified and any measures you are putting in place to protect their health and safety at work.

Serving alcohol

Under-18s can work in restaurants, dining rooms and even pubs, where they can wait on tables, collect glasses, clear tables and take orders from customers.

Children aged 16 or 17 are allowed to sell or serve alcohol in a restaurant without supervision provided that:

- It is sold or supplied to be consumed with a table meal, and;
- It is served in a part of the premises used only for that purpose.

This means that a child aged 16 or 17 can work as a waiter or waitress in a dining room and serve alcohol without supervision.

Children can also work in a bar serving alcohol, as long as each individual sale has been specifically approved by a responsible person. The responsible person is either the holder of the Premises Licence, the Designated Premises Supervisor (DPS), or anyone aged 18 or over who has been authorised by the Premises Licence Holder or the DPS to authorise sales made by under-18s.

Note: you need to check whether your local authority has any by-laws that restrict people aged under 18 from selling alcohol. It is known that some local authorities prevent children under 18 selling alcohol that is not in a sealed container (for example, unopened bottles or cans).

Further guidance

Guidance on the employment of children

Official guidance on child employment can be found on Gov.uk

ACAS guidance on employing younger workers

ACAS has guidance on employing younger workers – including working hours, working at night, and health and safety on their website: acas.org.uk

Further guidance on being an employer

Find key resources to help you recruit and manage employees on a dedicated page in VisitEngland's Business Advice Hub: visitengland.org/businessadvice

Workplace pensions

KEY FACTS

- If you have employees, you must implement a Workplace Pension Scheme.
- You must notify all employees to explain why they either have or have not been included in your Workplace Pension Scheme.
- Those employees not eligible to be included in a scheme must be allowed the opportunity to join the scheme.
- The minimum contributions that both you and your employees have to contribute to the scheme are determined by law.
- Three years after setting up a Workplace Pension Scheme, you must undertake 're-enrolment'.

Background

Under the **Pensions Act 2008**, every employer in the UK must put certain staff into a pension scheme and contribute towards it. The pension is called a 'workplace pension', and the process by which you put eligible staff into the scheme is called 'automatic enrolment'

Do the regulations apply to me?

Yes: if you employ at least one person, either full-time, part-time or on a casual basis, provided that:

- They earn over £10,000 per annum;
- They are aged between 22 and the state pension age.

The usual determinant of whether you have staff is whether you decide the work that the person does, tell them how they are to do it, provide the equipment, pay them for the hours that they undertake the work (rather than a fixed price for the work) and the person is entitled to benefits such as holiday pay or sick pay.

Maybe: if you employ someone outside the criteria above and they ask to join a Workplace Pension Scheme.

No: if you have no staff.

Note: if you have staff who are not eligible, you still have other tasks to carry out in order to meet your legal duties, including writing to these staff to tell them how automatic enrolment applies to them.

Four steps to set up a Workplace Pension Scheme

1. Choose a pension scheme

Your first task is to choose the pension scheme that you will use to provide your workplace pension. If you have an existing pension scheme, you can use this or you can seek advice from a pension advisor. Alternatively, you can use the National Employment Savings Trust (NEST), which is a pension scheme provider that has been set up by the Government and must accept all employers that apply to use it for automatic enrolment.

2. Determine who to include in the pension scheme

You are required to determine who to include in the pension scheme and to supply information on these employees to your pension provider.

NEW

You must include any of your staff who are aged between 22 and the state pension age, earn over £10,000 per year and who are not already enrolled in a company pension scheme. Employees who fall outside this requirement only need to be included if they specifically ask to be included. However, you do not have to contribute to the pension of employees earning less than £520 a month/£120 a week/£480 over 4 weeks.

3. Write to inform your staff

Within six weeks of your workplace pension starting, you must write to all of your staff individually and tell them how the workplace pension applies to them. That means writing to those who have been enrolled to tell them that they are in the pension scheme, and to those who have not been enrolled to explain why, as well as let them know that they can be enrolled if they request to be included.

4. Declaration of compliance

Finally, within five months of setting up your Workplace Pension Scheme, you must complete the online declaration of compliance to confirm that you have met your legal duties.

Note: even if you do not have any employees, you still need to complete the declaration to confirm that your business has complied with the legislation.

Contributions

While there is no maximum level for contributions to a Workplace Pension Scheme, the Government has introduced a minimum contribution level. The minimum employee contribution is 5%, and the minimum employer contribution is 3%, making the total minimum contribution 8%.

Re-enrolment

Every three years, you must put certain staff back into a pension scheme. This is called 're-enrolment'. Your re-enrolment duties must be carried out approximately three years after your automatic enrolment staging date. Your duties will vary depending on whether you identify that you have staff to re-enrol, or whether you have no staff to re-enrol. Either way, you will need to complete another declaration of compliance.

As with setting up a workplace pension, re-enrolment is a four-step process:

1. Choose your re-enrolment date

First, you need to choose your re-enrolment date from within a six-month window, which starts three months before the third anniversary of your automatic enrolment staging date and ends three months after it.

2. Assess your staff

On your chosen re-enrolment date, you'll need to assess certain staff to determine whether you need to put them back into your pension scheme.

3. Write to the staff you have re-enrolled

You then need to write to staff to tell them that you have put them back into a pension scheme.

4. Complete a re-declaration of compliance

You must again complete an online declaration stating that you have complied with the legislation by undertaking re-enrolment.

Re-enrolment tool

The Pensions Regulator has a free re-enrolment tool to help you to meet your re-enrolment date on their website: thepensionsregulator.gov.uk

Ongoing duties

Monitor the ages and earnings of your staff

You must monitor your employees' ages and pay. If any staff reach the criteria of being aged 22 and earning over £10,000 per annum, you must put them into a pension scheme and write to them within six weeks from the day they meet the age or earnings criteria.

Manage requests to join or leave your scheme

If an employee writes to you asking to join your scheme, you must put them into it within a month of receiving their request.

You will have to pay into the pension scheme if they are:

- Aged 16-74 and;
- Earn at least £520 a month or £120 per week.

To find out how much you will need to pay, you should ask your pension scheme provider.

Employees can choose to leave the pension scheme. If they ask to leave within one month of being put into a scheme, this is known as 'opting out'. Many pension providers will manage the opt-out process on your behalf. If an employee opts out, you need to stop taking money out of their pay and arrange a full refund of what has been paid to-date. This must happen within one month of their request.

For more information on your ongoing duties with regards to workplace pensions, visit the Pensions Regulator website: thepensionsregulator.gov.uk

Further guidance

Pensions Regulator

For more detailed information on the process and the rules surrounding it, refer to the Pensions Regulator website: thepensionsregulator.gov.uk

Free auto-enrolment service

The National Employment Savings Trust (NEST) website was specifically set up by the Government to provide a free auto-enrolment service for employers: nestpensions.org.uk

Re-enrolment tool

Use this free re-enrolment tool from the Pensions Regulator to help you meet your re-enrolment date: thepensionsregulator.gov.uk/en/employers/re-enrolment

Further guidance on being an employer

Find key resources to help you recruit and manage employees on a dedicated page in VisitEngland's Business Advice Hub: visitengland.org/businessadvice

BUSINESS MANAGEMENT & TAX

Income tax, VAT and legal form of business

KEY FACTS

- You must establish your income tax position and whether you are claiming all the expenses and capital allowances that you are entitled to.
- There are different tax and legal implications, depending on whether you operate your business as a sole trader, a limited company, a partnership or a charity.
- Tax and VAT are very large and complex areas of legislation that are constantly being revised and amended. For this reason, you should contact your accountant or financial advisor to discuss all related issues.
- **Please note:** the Government has announced that it intends to abolish the Furnished Holiday Letting rules on 5 April 2025. Draft legislation providing details of the proposal and how it will impact self-catering businesses has now been published and is available of the HMRC website. Self-catering operators should contact their accountant to discuss how the tax implications associated with the proposed removal of these rules will impact their business.

NEW

Income tax

It is important that you establish your income tax position and whether you are claiming all the expenses and capital allowances that you are entitled to claim.

You must keep records of your business income and expenses for your tax return if you are self-employed as a:

- Sole trader;
- Partner in a business partnership (if you're the nominated partner in a partnership, you must also keep records for the partnership);
- Charity.

LICENCES & CONSENTS
MARKETING
CUSTOMERS
FOOD & DRINK
ENVIRONMENTAL PROTECTION
HEALTH & SAFETY
STAFF
BUSINESS, MANAGEMENT & TAX
FURTHER INFORMATION

There are different rules on keeping records for limited companies, and you should consult an accountant for advice if your business is structured as a limited company.

Regardless of whether you are a sole trader, a partner in a business partnership or run your business as a limited company, you will need to keep records of your personal income.

Many businesses use traditional accounting, where you record income and expenses by the date that you were invoiced or billed. However, there is an option of using cash accounting if you are a small business.

Cash basis accounting

The 'cash basis' tax scheme is intended for self-employed individuals, or partnerships carrying on the smallest-trading businesses.

You can use cash accounting if:

- You run a small, self-employed business as a sole trader or partnership (you cannot use the scheme if your business is a limited company);
- You have a turnover of £150,000 or less per year.

You can stay in the scheme up to a total business turnover of £300,000 per year. Above that, you will need to use traditional accounting for your next tax return.

VAT Cash Accounting Scheme

In addition to the cash accounting scheme, there is also the VAT Cash Accounting Scheme. Under this scheme, you:

- Pay VAT on your sales when customers pay you;
- Reclaim VAT on your purchases when you have paid your supplier.

To join the scheme, your VAT taxable turnover must be £1.35 million or less.

For further information, see the *Cash basis* page on Gov.uk.

You can speak to an accountant or a financial advisor, or visit the HM Revenue & Customs (HMRC) website (gov.uk/government/organisations/hm-revenue-customs), which has a range of helpful information and contact numbers.

VAT

UPDATED

VAT threshold

You do not have to register for VAT if your turnover for the previous 12 months is less than £90,000. This figure is known as the VAT registration threshold.

You must also register for VAT if:

- You think your VAT taxable turnover may go over the threshold in the next 30 days alone;
- You take over a VAT-registered business as a going concern.

VAT deregistration threshold

The deregistration threshold is £88,000. If your VAT taxable turnover for the year falls below £88,000, or you expect it to fall below £88,000 in the next 12 months, you can ask to be deregistered for VAT.

Flat Rate VAT Scheme

If your taxable turnover is less than £150,000 before VAT is added, you can simplify your VAT accounting by calculating your VAT payments as a percentage of your total VAT-inclusive turnover. The current flat-rate VAT percentage for accommodation businesses is 10.5% and the rate for museums and cultural activities is 9.5% of your VAT-inclusive turnover. Once you join the scheme you can stay in it until your total business income is more than £230,000.

In 2017, the Government introduced changes to the Flat Rate Scheme for businesses with a very low-cost base. These businesses are now called 'limited cost traders'.

A limited cost trader is defined as one that spends less than 2% of its sales on goods (not services) in an accounting period. The amount spent on goods cannot include purchases of:

- Capital goods (such as new equipment used in a business);
- Food and drink (such as lunches for staff);
- Vehicles or parts for vehicles (unless running a vehicle-hiring business).

A firm can also be a limited cost trader if it spends less than £1,000 a year, even if this is more than 2% of the firm's turnover on goods.

Limited cost traders can still use the Flat Rate Scheme, but their percentage is 16.5%.

It is recommended that you talk to your accountant as to whether joining the Flat Rate Scheme would be beneficial for your business.

For more information, see the *VAT Guide* or contact HMRC's Helpline on 0300 200 3700, which is available Monday to Friday, 8am to 6pm.

Setting up a charity

Some businesses, especially historic, cultural or environmental attractions, can be established as a charity. Charities do not pay tax on most types of income as long as they use the money for charitable purposes. Charitable purposes that help the public can include:

- Education;
- Religion;
- Community development;

- The arts;
- The protection of the environment;
- Animal welfare.

However, you may need to pay tax if you have:
- Received income that doesn't qualify for tax relief;
- Spent any of your income on non-charitable purposes.

Charities can also claim back tax that has been deducted, for example on bank interest and donations (see the *Gift Aid* section).

There are six steps to setting up a charity:
1. Find trustees for your charity: you usually need at least three.
2. Ensure the charity has a 'charitable purpose for the public benefit'.
3. Choose a name for your charity.
4. Choose a structure for your charity. There are four different structures that have different responsibilities and obligations.
5. Create a 'governing document'.
6. Register as a charity with the Charity Commission. You need to do this if your annual income is over £5,000, if you set up a charitable incorporated organisation (CIO) and if you want to get tax relief from HMRC.

Detailed information on how to set up a charity is available from The Charity Commission:
gov.uk/government/organisations/charity-commission

Tax and your staff

For information on PAYE and National Insurance, see the Gov.uk guide *Employer Further Guide to PAYE and National Insurance Contributions*.

There is a range of guidance available from HMRC online, as well as the HMRC helpline: 0300 200 3200. You will need your employer reference number or accounts office reference number when you call.

Legal form of the business

There are different tax and legal implications depending on whether you operate your business as a sole trader, a limited company or a partnership. There are advantages and disadvantages for each category. You should seek professional advice from lawyers or independent financial advisors.

Legal advisors

The Law Society (solicitors.lawsociety.org.uk) is able to provide a list of solicitors within your area. Your local destination management organisation or Local Visitor Economy Partnership (LVEP) may also be able to give you details of suitable local firms.

Independent financial advisors

The Unbiased consumer website can help you to find independent financial advisors or accountants in your area: **unbiased.co.uk**

Making Tax Digital

Making Tax Digital is a major HMRC initiative to move all business accounting to a digital format.

The first component of Making Tax Digital is VAT payments. All VAT-registered businesses are now required to keep digital records and file tax returns using software compatible with HMRC's system.

Following the roll-out of Making Tax Digital for businesses, the scheme is to be expanded to include people who are self-employed and/or earn income from property. The scheduled dates for their inclusion in Making Tax Digital are:

- 6 April 2026, for people with an annual income of more than £50,000;
- April 2027 for people with an annual income of more than £30,000.

NEW

Further guidance

HMRC

For further information on income tax, PAYE for employers, VAT and more, visit the HMRC website:
gov.uk/government/organisations/hm-revenue-customs

Making Tax Digital

HMRC provides a wide range of support to help you comply with the Making Tax Digital requirements on the HMRC website:
gov.uk/government/organisations/hm-revenue-customs

Establishing a charity

The Charity Commission provides a wide range of advice and guidance on establishing a charity:
gov.uk/government/organisations/charity-commission

Tax status of accommodation businesses

NEW

Please note: the Government is abolishing the Furnished Holiday Letting rules from April 2025. Draft legislation, which will provide details of the proposal and how it will impact self-catering businesses, has been published which details the proposals. Self-catering operators should contact their accountant to discuss how the tax implications associated with the proposed removal of these rules will impact their business.

KEY FACTS

- In terms of taxation, there is a fundamental difference between the way HM Revenue and Customs (HMRC) treats self-catering accommodation and residential rental properties.
- Having your self-catering property treated as a trade business, rather than a rental property, carries a number of advantages.
- To comply with the HS253 Furnished holiday lettings (2020) guidance, a property must be available for at least 210 days a year, let for at least 105 days and operated in a commercial manner.

Rental and trade businesses

In terms of taxation, there is a fundamental difference between the way HM Revenue and Customs (HMRC) treats holiday accommodation and residential rental properties.

- Residential rental properties are treated as property investment businesses.
- Hotels, guesthouses and bed and breakfasts are treated as trading businesses.
- Self-catering accommodation can be treated as a trading business, provided that the conditions of the HS253 Furnished holiday lettings (2020) rules are met.

Having your self-catering property treated as a trading business carries the following advantages:

- It ensures that income, net of allowable expenses, is treated as earned income. This means that capital allowances can be claimed in respect of all furniture and equipment used in the business. This compares favourably with the treatment of residential rental properties, where losses can only be offset against future income, you cannot claim capital allowances in respect to any new furniture or equipment, and only part of the interest on mortgage payments can be off-set against income;
- Trading businesses are treated as a business asset for the purposes of determining Capital Gains Tax, which grants you far greater allowances than you receive for residential rental properties;
- For Inheritance Tax purposes, the property is also deemed to be a business asset and can be passed on tax-free.

Note: HMRC has successfully challenged the Inheritance Tax exemption of a self-catering property by arguing the level of service provided to guests was not sufficient for it to be deemed a trading business for the purposes of Inheritance Tax. You should therefore seek professional advice as to whether your property is exempt from Inheritance Tax.

Furnished Holiday Letting (FHL) rules

In order for your self-catering property to qualify as a trading business, the following conditions must be met:

1. **Commercial operation:** the business must be carried on commercially, with a view to making a profit.
2. **Pattern of occupation:** total periods of longer-term occupation must not exceed 155 days (approximately five months) during the relevant period. A period of longer-term occupation is a letting to the same person for longer than 31 continuous days.
3. **Availability:** the property must be available for commercial letting as holiday accommodation to the public for at least 210 days (approximately seven months) during the relevant period.
4. **Letting:** the property must be commercially let as holiday accommodation to members of the public for at least 105 days during the relevant period. For the purposes of this condition, a letting for a period of longer-term occupation is not classed as a letting for holiday accommodation.

The reason for these conditions is to prevent people from trying to gain trade business status and the associated benefits, for either their home or their holiday home, when they have no intention of operating them as a commercially viable bed and breakfast or self-catering operation.

Note: if you operate a self-catering property, you are unable to claim sideways loss relief against other income. Also, regardless of complying with the FHL rules, HMRC may deem your self-catering property to be subject to Capital Gains Tax and Inheritance Tax, if it is determined that you do not provide a sufficient level of service to demonstrate that it is a trading business. It is therefore important to gain advice from an accountant who understands the taxation rules for self-catering businesses.

Removal of the FHL rules

The removal of the FHL rules will mean that, in terms of tax treatment, self-catering properties will be taxed in the same way as Buy-To-Let properties (as property investments), rather than as trading businesses. This will result in four main changes to the tax treatment of self-catering properties:

- The finance cost restriction rules will apply so that loan interest will be restricted to basic rate for Income Tax;
- Capital allowances rules for new expenditure and allowing replacement of domestic items relief will be removed;
- Reliefs from taxes on chargeable gains for trading business assets will be removed;
- Income from self-catering properties will no longer be deemed relevant UK earnings when calculating pension relief.

Transition rules

However, in abolishing the FHL rules, the following specific transitional rules will apply:

- Where an existing FHL business has an ongoing capital allowances pool of expenditure, they can continue to claim writing-down allowances on that pool. Any new expenditure incurred on or after the operative date must be considered under the property business rules;
- Under current rules, a loss generated from a FHL property business can only be carried forward and utilised against future profits of that same FHL business. After the changes, any profits or losses will be amalgamated with the profits and losses of any other rental property the owner has;
- Losses generated from a FHL business will be permitted to be carried forward and be available for offset against future years' profits of either the UK or overseas property business as appropriate;
- While roll-over relief, business asset disposal relief, gift relief, relief for loans to traders, and exemptions for disposals by

NEW

NEW

companies with substantial shareholdings will cease, where criteria for relief includes conditions that apply in a future year, these specific rules will not be disturbed where the FHL conditions are satisfied before repeal;

- Where the FHL conditions are satisfied in relation to a business that ceased prior to the commencement date, relief may continue to apply to a disposal that occurs within the normal three-year period following cessation.

Further guidance

Professional legal advice

The changes to the tax rules relating to holiday accommodation following the removal of the FHL rules are complex, so it is best to seek advice from a professional tax consultant.

Business rates

KEY FACTS

- Business rates generally apply to bed and breakfast establishments unless you do not intend to offer short-stay accommodation to more than six people simultaneously and you occupy part of the property as your only or main home and letting out the rooms is subsidiary to the use of the rest of the house as your home.
- Business rates apply to a self-catering establishment unless you offer short-term lets for fewer than 140 days a year.
- Only the part of the property used for business purposes is subject to business rates.
- Business rates apply to visitor attractions. Those that are operated by charities are entitled to a mandatory 80% reduction in business rates.
- Your local authority will calculate the business rates for your property based on its 'rateable value'.

NEW

Note: the Government is abolishing the Furnished Holiday Letting (FHL) Rules from April 2025. In so doing, self-catering properties will be subject to the same tax treatment as Buy-To-Let properties. It is therefore likely that self-catering properties will revert to being charged Council Tax rather than having the current option of paying Business Rates. Self-catering operators are advised to consult with their accountant as to how the removal of the FHL Rules will impact their business.

Do I need to pay business rates?

Yes: if you are a visitor attraction or provide serviced or self-catering accommodation, unless:

- You qualify for Small Business Rate Relief, or;
- For **bed and breakfast**:
  - you do not intend to offer short-stay accommodation to more

than six people simultaneously, and;
- You (the owner) occupy part of the property as your only or main home, and;
- Letting out the rooms is subsidiary to the use of the rest of the house as your home ('subsidiary' is based on factors such as the length of your season, the scale of modifications undertaken for guests, and the proportion of the house you occupy). For example, if you only let two of six bedrooms in your property as a bed and breakfast, business rates are unlikely to apply. However, if you let four of your six bedrooms, you will probably have to pay business rates. Your local authority will be able to advise you.

Note: if you have to pay business rates, but use your property for business and domestic purposes (a composite hereditament), it is only the part you use for business purposes that is subject to business rates. The domestic accommodation is liable to Council Tax. Where parts of a house have a shared use, such as a kitchen or dining room, the Valuation Officer will visit the property and assess the amount to be paid (see below).

- For **self-catering**:
  - You offer short-period lets for fewer than 140 days a year. It is important to note that this is the period of the year when the property is **available** to be let, NOT the period over the year that it is **actually** let.

Small Business Rate Relief

Small Business Rate Relief is available to businesses where the rateable value of the property is less than £15,000. Businesses with a rateable value of up to £12,000 receive 100% relief, while businesses with a rateable value between £12,000 and £15,000 receive tapered relief.

If you have a second property, you will keep getting any existing relief on your main property for 12 months. You can still get Small Business Rate relief on your main property after this, if both of the following apply:

- None of your properties have a rateable value above £2,899;
- The total rateable value of all your properties is less than £20,000 (£28,000 in London).

If your property has a rateable value of more than £15,000 but less than £51,000, your bill will be calculated using the small business multiplier, which is lower than the standard multiplier.

Currently, self-catering properties are only eligible to switch from council tax to business rates if all of the following criteria are met:

a) The property will be available for letting commercially as self-catering accommodation, for short periods totalling at least 140 days in the year after the day in question.

b) During the previous year, it was available for letting commercially, as self-catering accommodation, for short periods totalling at least 140 days.

c) During the previous year, it was actually let commercially, as self-catering accommodation, for short periods totalling at least 70 days.

Note: in Wales, there are new requirements for self-catering properties to be available to let for at least 252 days and actually let for at least 182 days in any 12-month period, in order to be eligible to move from paying council tax to paying business rates.

Mandatory Rate Relief for Charities

Organisations that are recognised as charities, either by being a registered charity or acknowledged by HMRC as being a charity for tax purposes, can claim 80% relief from business rates if:

- The charity (or trustees of the charity) is the ratepayer, and;
- The charity uses the property wholly, or mainly, for charitable purposes.

Any organisation that qualifies for 80% mandatory rate relief may also apply to its local council for discretionary relief for all or part of the remaining 20% of its bill.

How are business rates calculated?

If you need to pay business rates, your property will have a 'rateable value' based on the rental value of your property. These values are set by an independent government agency, the Valuation Office Agency (VOA)

UPDATED

The last revaluation of non-domestic properties in England and Wales took place on 1 April 2021, with the new rates applying from 1 April 2023.

You can obtain details of the rateable value of your property from your local Valuation Office or the Business Rates department of your local authority. The VOA website (gov.uk/government/organisations/valuation-office-agency) allows you to access entries in local rating lists.

Challenging the valuation of a property

The VOA has introduced a three-stage process if you want to challenge the assessed rateable value of your property. The stages are:

1. Check

This is to make a change to your property details. You must provide evidence to support your changes. The VOA may accept your changes and change the rateable value.

2. Challenge

If you still think your rateable value is too high, you may then challenge it, explaining what you think it should be and provide evidence. The VOA may accept your challenge and change the rateable value.

3. Appeal

Finally, you can ask the independent Valuation Tribunal for a review if you do not agree with the VOA's decision on the rateable value.

Guidance on checking, challenging and appealing the ratable value of a property in available online at Gov.uk.

Seeking the advice of commercial valuers

If you feel that the valuation of your business is too high, and you are not satisfied with the advice you have received from the local Valuation Officer, you may wish to consult a private firm of valuers or rating consultants before deciding to lodge an appeal.

Before agreeing to employ any rating consultants, always confirm:

- The terms;
- Their expertise;
- Their professional indemnity insurance cover.

Fees for commercial valuers

The fees paid should depend on the amount of work needed, and on whether the appeal can be resolved by agreement. If a firm is handling a number of appeals from a specific area, it may negotiate a settlement that includes all of them, which will reduce the cost of each individual case.

There have been a number of reports of 'unqualified' firms seeking to obtain rating instructions by offering to represent ratepayers on payment of a fixed fee (payable before any work is done) and 'guaranteeing' a successful outcome to the appeal. Often cold calls are made by telephone or in person to the property, and you should be wary of such organisations; no one, no matter how eminent, skilled or experienced, can guarantee that an appeal will be successful.

It is also important to note that, although rare, it is possible for appeals to lead to an increase in the rateable value of your property (for example, when the records of the Valuation Officer are not up to date on the physical extent of the property or the fact that it is being used for short-stay accommodation). Only reputable firms should be used to help you appeal against your rating assessment. Members of the Royal Institution of Chartered Surveyors (RICS) and the Institute of Revenues Rating and Valuation (IRRV) are regulated to protect the public from misconduct, and are required to hold adequate indemnity insurance.

Further guidance

Valuation Office

For information on the valuation of your property or appeals, contact your local Valuation Office:
gov.uk/government/organisations/valuation-office-agency

Your local authority

For any enquiries about your business rates bill, contact the business rates department of your local authority.

Challenging valuations

Information on how to challenge a VOA valuation is available on the Gov.uk website.

Self-catering letting options

KEY FACTS

- You must consider self-catering letting options if you let a property for holiday purposes.
- Occupiers do not gain any rights to stay on or in your property, as long as it is actually let for a holiday.
- For out-of-season lettings, you may wish to consider an assured tenancy or an assured shorthold tenancy.

NEW

Note: the Furnished Holiday Letting Rules (FHL Rules) on the tax treatment of self-catering properties will be abolished from April 2025 (see the *Tax status of accommodation businesses* section).

Holiday letting

If you let a property for holiday purposes, the law allows you to do this without the occupiers gaining any rights to remain in the property under what is termed a 'licence to occupy'. This is the same form of contract whereby guests stay at hotels. There is no limit to the length of time that someone can stay in a property under a licence to occupy, but their stay must actually be for a holiday. 'Holiday letting' is defined in the **Housing Act 1988** as 'a tenancy the purpose of which is to confer on the tenant the right to occupy the dwelling house for a holiday'.

You are recommended to have a basic agreement with the occupiers (this can be by letter), which includes a statement that you are letting the premises as a holiday let, with the start and end days of the let clearly stated.

If the occupier does not leave at the end of the let, legally you do not have to go to court to recover possession of the property. However, you may still be strongly advised to apply to the Courts for eviction.

Out-of-season letting

If you are thinking of supplementing your income by letting your property for a number of months out of season, you can opt for:

- An assured tenancy;
- An assured shorthold tenancy.

Note: the **Immigration Act 2016** requires you to check the immigration status of guests applying to occupy a property under a residential tenancy agreement. It is an offence to let your property under a residential tenancy agreement to anyone that you suspect is disqualified from occupying a property due to their immigration status. It is also important to note that you cannot only check people who you think are not British citizens. You must not discriminate against anyone because of where they are from.

Assured tenancy

Assured tenancies are designed to give tenants the right to remain in your property until you have reason, or grounds, to seek possession. The relevant grounds, in this case, would be that the property has been let temporarily 'out of season' (such lets are often called 'winter lets', although they occur during any time of the year).

There are two forms of assured tenancy:

- A periodic tenancy: this rolls over on a week-to-week or month-to-month basis.
- A fixed-term tenancy: this is a set period such as 12 or 18 months.

When a fixed-term tenancy expires, it continues as a periodic tenancy unless you sign up for a new fixed term.

Setting up an assured tenancy

You must give the tenant written notice before the start of the tenancy (or include a simple declaration in the tenancy agreement) that says the tenancy is not an assured shorthold tenancy, and that possession might be recovered on the basis of Ground 3 of the Grounds for Possession in the **Housing Act 1988**.

To ensure that you have a mandatory right to repossess a property if a tenant refuses to leave, the let must be for a period not exceeding eight months, and the property must have been used as a holiday let at some point in the preceding 12 months.

Ending an assured tenancy

You have the right to seek possession of the property at the end of the roll-over period or the fixed period of the tenancy.

If you seek possession, you must give written notice of at least:

- 28 days, if the guest pays rent weekly.
- One month, if the guest pays rent monthly.

If the tenant does not leave at the end of the notice, you would have to start court proceedings to recover possession of the property.

Assured shorthold tenancy

The more usual form of assured tenancy that landlords prefer to use is an assured shorthold tenancy. This allows you to seek possession even when there are no specific grounds for you to do so. However, this would mean that the tenant has the right to stay in the property on this basis for a minimum of six months (even if you have agreed a fixed term for less) or the length of the fixed term – whichever is longer.

There are no special procedures for setting up a shorthold tenancy, but you must give two months' written notice to seek repossession. If the notice period expires and the tenant does not leave, you must still recover possession through the Courts. However, for recovering possession on a 'no-ground' assured shorthold basis, you can use the Accelerated Possession Procedure, which can be quicker and cheaper than a full court hearing.

Alternatively, you can set up a fixed-term out-of-season assured shorthold tenancy, by prior notice to the tenant, as for a full assured tenancy.

Note: to maintain the tax status of the property as a Furnished Holiday Let, the total period that a property is let under either an assured tenancy or an assured shorthold tenancy must be less than 155 days in any given year.

Note: remember that planning restrictions may have been imposed on you as a condition of permission being granted for the property's use as a holiday let, which prevent the property from being used as a residential property.

Further guidance

Professional legal advice

You should always take legal advice before you enter into any tenancy agreement.

Tenancy agreements: a guide for landlords

More information on tenancies can be found on Gov.uk.

Houses in Multiple Occupation

KEY FACTS

- In some cases, your local authority may class your accommodation as a House in Multiple Occupation (HMO).
- If you feel that your property is being classed wrongly as an HMO by the local authority, you may appeal to a residential property tribunal.
- HMOs usually need to be licensed by the council and there is a mandatory national licensing scheme for large HMOs.
- Environmental Health Officers are responsible for enforcing HMO legislation locally.

What is an HMO?

An HMO is defined in the **Housing Act 2004** as:

- An entire house or flat that is let to three or more tenants who form two or more households and who share a kitchen, bathroom or toilet facilities;
- A house that has been converted entirely into bedsits or other non-self-contained accommodation, and which is let to three or more tenants who form two or more households and who share kitchen, bathroom or toilet facilities;
- A converted house that contains one or more flats that are not wholly self-contained (that is, the flat does not contain a kitchen, bathroom and toilet) and that is occupied by three or more tenants who form two or more households;
- A building that is converted entirely into self-contained flats if the conversion did not meet the standards of the **Building Regulations 1991** and more than one-third of the flats are let on short-term tenancies.

Tenants

In order to be an HMO, the property must be used as the tenants' only or main residence, and it should be used solely or mainly to house tenants. Properties let to students and migrant workers will be treated as their only or main residence, and the same will apply to properties which are used as domestic refuges.

Therefore, holiday cottages let to families or other groups of people living together as one household for a holiday, who have a main home elsewhere, are **not** HMOs.

Where winter letting to groups of people who are not related is taking place, the premises may well be considered to be an HMO and you should seek advice.

What being an HMO means

Owners who intend anything other than holiday letting should seek advice and talk to their local authority. If the premises are deemed to be an HMO, they will have to meet some strict standards concerning amenities and fire precautions in the building. Usually, they will need to be licensed.

The great majority of holiday homes are not HMOs. Bed and breakfast accommodation may be deemed to be an HMO if it is let to people who don't have another residence.

However, a few local authorities have deemed some guesthouses, bed and breakfasts and holiday flats to be HMOs. When this happens, the implications for a proprietor can be far-reaching.

National licensing of large HMOs

The **Housing Act 2004** introduced mandatory licensing and a new definition for HMOs. This legislation was extended through the **Licensing of Houses in Multiple Occupation (Prescribed Description) (England) Order 2018**, so that a property of five or more people – from two or more separate households – is deemed to be a 'large HMO', and the landlord must be licensed by their local housing authority.

Under the national mandatory licensing scheme, an HMO needs to be licensed if all of the following apply:

- It is occupied by five or more tenants who form more than one household;
- Some or all tenants share toilet, bathroom or kitchen facilities;
- At least one tenant pays rent (or their employer pays it for them).

If your property is deemed to be a large HMO, you must ensure that:

- The house is suitable for the number of occupants (this depends on its size and facilities);
- The manager of the house – you or an agent – is considered to be 'fit and proper', for example they have no criminal record or previous breach of landlord laws or code of practice.

You must also:

- Send the council an updated gas safety certificate every year;
- Install and maintain smoke alarms;

- Provide safety certificates for all electrical appliances when requested.

Where a local authority has a licensing scheme for properties that are smaller than 'large HMOs', the council will grant a licence if it is satisfied that:

- The HMO is reasonably suitable for occupation by the number of people allowed under the licence;
- The proposed licence holder is a 'fit and proper person';
- The proposed licence holder is the most appropriate person to hold the licence;
- The proposed manager, if there is one, is a 'fit and proper person';
- The proposed management arrangements are satisfactory;
- The person involved in the management of the HMO is competent;
- The financial structures for the management are suitable.

Enforcement

Environmental Health Officers, who are responsible for enforcing HMO legislation locally, have the right to enter a property at any reasonable time after giving 24 hours' notice in writing. Also, they may serve legal notices requiring the provision or improvement of amenities.

Standards

Properties of the relevant type must be licensed throughout the UK, while local authorities have discretion to adopt additional licensing schemes in regard to lower-risk properties. Before granting a licence, they will need to be satisfied that a set of standards are met. If they are not met, they will judge the property not to be reasonably suitable and refuse to grant the licence.

The standards come from a Government circular. Most local authorities adopt similar sets of standards, but there are variations. The standards include requirements for fire precautions. See the *Fire safety (general)* section for more information on fire safety.

The **Licensing of Houses in Multiple Occupation (Prescribed Description) (England) Order 2018** also introduces rules that set minimum size requirements for bedrooms in HMOs to prevent overcrowding, and require landlords to adhere to council refuse schemes in order to reduce problems with rubbish.

Appeals

If you feel that your property is being classed wrongly as an HMO by the local authority, you may appeal to a residential property tribunal.

Further guidance

Your local authority

Detailed advice on HMOs is available from your local environmental health officer.

Guidance on private renting and HMOs

Your rights and responsibilities as a landlord can be found on the Gov.uk website.

Guidance on minimum bedroom sizes

You can download *Houses in multiple occupation and residential property licensing reform: guidance for local housing authorities* from Gov.uk.

Applying for a large HMO licence

You can apply for a large HMO licence on the Gov.uk website.

Utilities and waste collection

KEY FACTS

- If the water supplies for your business come from a private supply, the Private Water Supplies (England) Regulations 2016 apply to you.
- Local authorities must take and analyse samples of private water supplies from groundwater sources.
- If you make a specific charge to your customers for gas or electricity, the most you can charge is limited by the 'maximum resale price' rule.
- The maximum resale price is the same price that you have paid to your own supplier.
- If you pay business rates, you must pay for a commercial waste collection service, unless you are exempt under the Controlled Waste (England and Wales) Regulations 2012.

Private water supplies

Private water supplies include water:

- From groundwater sources;
- Drawn from privately owned boreholes or wells;
- Taken from surface water, such as springs and streams.

The **Private Water Supplies Regulations (England) 2016** consolidated and repealed the Private Water Supplies Regulations (England) 2009. Together with the **Water Industry Act 1991**, they apply to all private water supplies that are intended for human consumption, whether this is for drinking, washing or food production. The aim of the regulations is to ensure that all private water sources are safe and free from contaminants.

Do these regulations affect me?

Yes: if any part of the water supply for your business comes from a private supply.

Private water supply tests

The 2016 regulations are very similar to the previous regulations, in that they require local authorities to record the number of private supplies in its area, and for each supply they must record:

- The name of the supply, together with a unique identifier;
- The type of source;
- The geographical location, using a grid reference;
- An estimate of the number of people supplied;
- An estimate of the average daily volume of water supplied in cubic metres;
- The type of premises supplied;
- Detail of any treatment process, together with its location;
- The name of the Health Protection Agency in whose area the supply is located.

After the initial assessment, the regulations require local authorities to monitor the supply on an ongoing basis. The regularity of the sampling will vary depending upon the volume of water used: from once a year for supplies of less than 10 cubic metres per day, to 34 times a year for supplies of up to 10,000 cubic metres per day.

In addition, the local authority must also undertake a thorough risk assessment of each supply at least once every five years.

In addition to the previous requirements, the **Private Water Supplies Regulations (England) 2016** require local authorities to test private water supplies for radioactive substances (this usually means the level of naturally occurring radon in the water) – and undertake a risk assessment of new supplies, and supplies that have been out of use for more than 12 months, as soon as is reasonably practicable. The risk assessments of these suppliers will then be subject to a review every five years, as per the 2009 regulations.

Cost of samples

The local authority will contact the person responsible for the supply (this may be the landowner, a person using the water, or a person representing a group of water users) about sampling. The regulations allow local authorities to charge for testing required under the **Private Water Supplies (England) Regulations 2016**. However, they are only allowed to recover the actual cost incurred in carrying out required testing.

The bill will be sent to the person responsible. If an authority decides to carry out tests over and above those required by the regulations, it has to bear the costs of these tests itself.

If test results show that the water is unwholesome, because it fails to meet the standards or other requirements, the local authority can insist that the water supply is improved. If any private supply of water intended for human consumption constitutes a potential danger to human health, a local authority acting under these regulations will serve a notice to the responsible person. It is an offence to breach this notice. However, the regulations establish an appeal process if you wish to challenge a notice.

The resale of gas and electricity

Maximum resale prices

If you are reselling gas and/or electricity that has already been bought from an authorised supplier, the amount you can charge your customers is limited by the 'maximum resale price rule'. This means that the most you can charge a customer for the supply of gas or electricity is the amount that you yourself have been charged by your gas or electricity supply company. Put another way, you can only sell gas or electricity to your guests on a non-profit basis.

As the provisions relating to the maximum resale prices for electricity and gas are reviewed from time to time, you should also occasionally check the Ofgem website (see *Further guidance*, below) to see whether there have been any changes.

Do maximum resale prices apply to me?

Yes: if you make a specific charge to your customers for gas or electricity, whether or not you use individual meters to record their consumption. The rule typically applies to self-catering accommodation and caravan sites, although it affects all businesses where separate charging occurs. If you overcharge for electricity or gas, your customer can ask for a refund of the excess and can pursue the matter in the Small Claims Courts if necessary.

No: if you do not make a specific charge for electricity and/or gas (for example if customers are charged a single rental figure for fully inclusive accommodation). The rule also does not apply to any gas or electricity that is used in communal facilities, such as for the use of a tumble dryer in a laundry room, or a shower in a washroom block at a caravan park. In other words, there is no maximum limit on what you can charge a guest for using a communal washing machine, provided that this use is billed separately from the charge for general gas and electricity use.

Price of energy units

If you are charged a single unit rate for gas or electricity by your own supplier, you must charge your customers the same rate. If the unit rate varies, for example if you pay on an Economy 7 type tariff or if prices vary on a seasonal basis, you will need to calculate an average price for each unit used.

If you have a meter (either a normal meter or a smart meter) for a property, then you should take readings at the beginning and end of the customer's stay and calculate the cost of use using the price that you are paying your supplier. If you are not using a meter, then you must use your reasonable steps to estimate how much energy the customer has used and be able to justify your calculation if challenged.

Note: the requirement to only charge customers the actual cost of electricity does not extend to the recharging of electric vehicles. This means that if you have a dedicated EV recharging point you can charge customers an additional fee on top of the actual cost of the electricity.

A copy of the explanatory publication, ***The resale of gas and electricity – guidance for resellers*** is available to download from the Ofgem website (ofgem.gov.uk). This gives further information and includes example resale price calculations.

Standing charges

In addition to the charge for units used, many authorised suppliers levy a standing charge to cover the cost of maintaining your connection and billing you for the fuel. You can recover this from your customers: the individual sums need to be calculated according to the number of units of electricity that are used by each consumer. As above, the Ofgem publication gives further guidance.

Waste collection

If you pay business rates, you must also pay for a commercial waste collection service through your council or with a private contractor – unless you qualify for an exemption under the **Controlled Waste (England and Wales) Regulations 2012**. The regulations provide an exemption from waste disposal charges for small businesses that:

- Were operating prior to 6 April 2012 and were eligible for free waste disposal at this date, and;
- Are eligible for Small Business Rate Relief (that is, the property has a rateable value of less than £15,000).

Note: waste collection charges comprise two components: a charge to collect the waste and a charge to dispose of it. Therefore, even if you qualify for the exemption from waste disposal charges, you must still pay for your waste to be collected.

Further guidance

Your local authority

Advice and information on private water supplies and waste collection, including exemptions, is available from your local authority.

Keeping your water supply safe

You can download information on private water supplies from the Drinking Water Inspectorate (DWI) website: dwi.gov.uk/private-water-supplies

Reselling gas and electricity

You can download *The Resale of Gas and Electricity – Guidance for Resellers* from the Ofgem website: ofgem.gov.uk

Gift Aid

KEY FACTS

- Businesses are only eligible to claim Gift Aid if they are registered charities.
- Donations eligible for Gift Aid can only be made by people paying Income Tax and/or Capital Gains Tax in the UK in the year that the donation is made.
- Donations made in exchange for the provision of goods or services are not eligible for Gift Aid, and there are special rules for Gift Aid applying to admission tickets.
- Gift Aid can be a complex area, and it is advisable to contact your accountant or financial advisor to discuss what types of donations you can claim Gift Aid on.

Overview

To qualify for Gift Aid, a business must be a registered charity. For information regarding establishing a charity, see the ***Income tax, VAT and legal form of business*** section.

Charities can use the Gift Aid scheme to claim an extra 25p for every £1 that people donate. All donations must be in a monetary form such as cash payments, electronic payments, cheques or bank transfers – so an eligible donation cannot be the monetary equivalent of a donated item such as food, books, equipment or labour.

A donation qualifies for Gift Aid if it is given to the charity by an individual who has paid, or will pay, UK tax. These restrictions also mean that Gift Aid cannot be claimed for donations which are made by overseas visitors or by businesses.

Eligibility criteria for donations

In addition to being made by an individual who has paid, or will pay, UK tax, donations must also satisfy all of the following conditions:

- The gift is not subject to a condition as to repayment;
- The gift is not a Payroll Giving donation;
- The gift is not deductible from income for tax purposes;
- The gift is not part of an arrangement for the charity to acquire property from the individual or a connected person;
- The gift is not a payment for services, rights or goods.

The fact that a gift is not a payment for goods or services is important, as it means that any payment provided for things such as purchasing a raffle ticket or undertaking some work (for example painting a house or providing staff for an event) are not eligible for Gift Aid.

Special rules

There are special rules if you want to claim Gift Aid on your entrance fees. Generally, entrance fees to visit and view your charity property do not qualify for Gift Aid because they are a payment for a service and not a gift.

However, if as a consequence of a donation, you allow a donor the benefit of a right of admission then, providing one of two conditions is met, the value of that benefit may be disregarded and the donation may qualify for Gift Aid.

These two conditions are:

1. **The annual right of admission rule**: a donation is made and in return you grant a right of admission to the donor (and possibly the donor's family) for at least a year.

Example: a person pays a £20 donation to become a member which entitles them to pay only 25% of the usual entrance fee every time they visit over the next year. In this case, the £20 is a donation on which Gift Aid can be claimed, but the 25% entrance fee they pay each time they visit is not eligible for Gift Aid because it is a payment for entry.

1. **The admission charge plus 10% rule**: a donation is made of at least 10% more than the cost of admission to the general public, and in return you provide the donor (and possibly the donor's family) with admission to the premises on the same basis as the general public.

Example: an admission ticket costs £10 and is not eligible for Gift Aid. However, if a person pays £11 for that ticket then the whole £11 is eligible for Gift Aid as the person has paid 10% more than the ticket's value.

The rules for Gift Aid can be complex and there are also special rules for:

- Funds from sponsored challenges, for example overseas treks or marathons;
- Charity membership fees;
- Charity auctions;
- Charity events;
- Volunteer expenses donated back to your charity or CASC.

It is therefore advisable to consult your accountant or tax advisor on the eligibility of your income-generating activities.

How much can be claimed through Gift Aid

There is no limit to the amount that a person can donate and that a charity can therefore claim Gift Aid on. However, in the financial year that the donation is made, the person donating the money must pay Income Tax or Capital Gains Tax (or both) in the UK, that is at least equal to the Income Tax treated as deducted from the total of all their Gift Aid donations made in the same tax year. If a person has not paid sufficient tax to cover their Gift Aid donation, they are responsible for paying any difference.

Declarations

Because of the donor's potential liability, you must get them to make a Gift Aid declaration that gives you permission to claim Gift Aid against the tax that they have paid.

A Gift Aid declaration must include:

- The donor's full name and home address;
- The name of the charity;
- The amount of the donation;
- Confirmation by the donor that the donation should be treated as a Gift Aid donation.

In addition, the charity must be able to prove that it has given an adequate explanation to the donor of the eligibility criteria and implications associated with making a Gift Aid donation, including the responsibility for paying any difference should the donor not have paid sufficient tax to cover the Gift Aid claim. This explanation can be included on a Gift Aid declaration, but can also be made separately. If the explanation is made separately, this needs to be recorded in a way that it can be linked to the declaration.

It is a legal requirement that you must keep records that enable you to show HMRC:

- An audit trail linking each donation to an identifiable donor who has given a valid Gift Aid declaration;
- That all the other conditions for the tax relief are satisfied, for example provision of benefits.

These records must be kept for six years after the end of the accounting period that they relate to.

NEW

Gift Aid Small Donations Scheme (GASDS)

The GASDS was introduced in 2016 to simplify Gift Aid payments for small donations. Under this scheme you do not need a Gift Aid declaration to claim 25% on:

- Cash donations of £30 or less;
- Contactless card donations of £30 or less collected on or after 6 April 2019.

Using the scheme you can claim up to £2,000 in a tax year.

To be eligible for the GASDS, you must have claimed Gift Aid:

- In the same tax year as you want to claim GASDS;
- Without getting a penalty in the last two tax years;
- In at least two of the last four tax years (without a two-year gap between claims), if you're claiming on donations made before 6 April 2017.

Also, your GASDS claim cannot be more than ten times your Gift Aid claim. For example, you can only claim up to £1,000 worth of donations through GASDS if you have received £100 of Gift Aid donations in the same tax year.

Further information

Gift Aid

More information on Gift Aid can be found on Gov.uk.

WHERE TO FIND FURTHER INFORMATION

For further guidance on a specific area of legislation, contact the following organisations:

Business regulations

Better Business for All

Better Business for All is a BEIS (Department for Business, Energy and Industrial Strategy) initiative that brings together businesses and regulators in local partnerships, to identify the issues facing local businesses and provide support to them. Most local authorities are involved with the programme, preparing and implementing action plans and sharing good practice.
gov.uk/guidance/better-business-for-all

Business Support Helpline

The helpline provides a quick response service if you have simple questions about starting or running a business. It also provides a more in-depth service if you have more complex enquiries.

- Tel: 0800 998 1098 (England – Monday to Friday, 9am to 6pm [except bank holidays]);
- Email: enquiries@businesssupporthelpline.org
- gov.uk/business-support-service

Growth Hubs

The Local Enterprise Partnership (LEP) network has established 38 Growth Hubs throughout England, which are the central repository of information, advice and support for businesses within a defined local area.

The aim of the Growth Hub network is to provide a single point of contact for local businesses that provides all the information, advice or support they require, including compliance with legislation.

lepnetwork.net/local-growth-hub-contacts

Legal advisors

The Law Society

The Law Society is able to provide you with a list of solicitors within your area. Your local Destination Management Organisation or Local Visitor Economy Partnership (LVEP) may also be able to supply names of suitable local firms.
solicitors.lawsociety.org.uk

Independent financial advisors
Use the IFA consumer website, Unbiased, to find independent financial advisors, accountants or solicitors in your area.
unbiased.co.uk

Utilities/facilities

These include the following:

Gas Safe Register
- Tel: 0800 408 5500
- register@gassaferegister.co.uk
- gassaferegister.co.uk

OFGEM (Office of Gas and Electricity Markets)
- Tel: 0207 901 7295
- ofgem.gov.uk

OFCOM (Office of Communications)
- Tel: 0300 123 3333
- ofcom.org.uk

OFWAT
The economic regulator of the water sector in England and Wales.
- ofwat.gov.uk

WRAP (Waste and Resources Action Programme)
- Tel: 01295 819 900 (England); 02920 100 100 (Wales); 01295 819 900 (Northern Ireland)
- wrap.org.uk

For any matters regarding collection of rubbish or recycling, contact your local authority.

Trade associations
These include the following:

ALVA (Association of Leading Visitor Attractions)
- Email: email@alva.org.uk
- alva.org.uk

Bed and Breakfast Association
- Tel: 01749 814 908
- bandbassociation.org

BACTA (trade association for the amusement and gaming machine industry)
- Tel: 0207 730 6444
- Email: info@bacta.org.uk
- bacta.org.uk

BALPPA (British Association of Leisure Parks Piers and Attractions)

- Tel: 0207 403 4455
- Email: information@balppa.org
- balppa.org

BAPA (British Activity Providers Association)

BAPA monitors safety standards and quality within the activity sector throughout the British Isles. It also provides a detailed consumer guide which is available on request.

- Tel: 07407 161 273
- Email: info@thebapa.org.uk
- thebapa.org.uk

British Holiday and Home Parks Association (BHHPA)

The BHHPA is the representative body of the parks industry, including caravans, chalets, tents and all types of self-catering park accommodation.

- Tel: 01452 526 911
- Email: enquiries@bhhpa.org.uk
- bhhpa.org.uk

British Destinations

British Destinations represents the interests of resorts and destinations throughout the UK.

- Tel: 01519 342 285 / 07714 341 379
- Email: cathgibson@btconnect.com / peter.hampson@btconnect.com

Farm Stay UK Ltd

Farm Stay UK Ltd is a consortium of farmers throughout the UK who provide serviced and self-catering accommodation on working farms.

- Tel: 02476 696 909
- Email: info@farmstay.co.uk
- farmstay.co.uk

Holiday Home Association (HHA)

The HHA is a trade association for self-catering operators, from individual owners through to agencies and associations.

- Tel: 07585 948 572
- Email: ce@holidayhomeassociation.org.uk
- holidayhomeassociation.org.uk

Tourism for All

Tourism for All, a national charity, is the UK's central source of travel and holiday information for disabled people, older people and carers.

- Email: info@tourismforall.org.uk
- tourismforall.org.uk

PASC UK (Professional Association of Self-Caterers)

PASC UK lobbies on behalf of the professional self-catering sector throughout the UK.

- Tel: 07771 678 028
- Email: chair@pascuk.co.uk
- pascuk.co.uk

People 1st International

People 1st International is an employer-led skills and quality assurance group for the hospitality and tourism sector. It is the lead agency on all issues relating to education, training and qualification within the sector.

- Tel: 0203 074 1222
- Email: info@people1st.co.uk
- people1st.co.uk

The NCC (National Caravan Council)

The NCC is the representative trade body for the UK caravan industry, and is involved in setting standards and promoting quality. The NCC operates the Product Approval Scheme for new caravans to ensure compliance with minimum health and safety standards.

- Tel: 01252 318 251
- Email: info@thencc.org.uk
- thencc.org.uk

UKHospitality

UKHospitality represents accommodation providers, restaurants, catering establishments and leisure companies.

- Tel: 0207 404 7744
- Email: info@ukhospitality.org.uk
- ukhospitality.org.uk

Publications

The publications mentioned within individual legislation sections are available from the following organisations:

ACAS (Advisory, Conciliation and Arbitration Services)

- Tel: 0207 492 2222
- acas.org.uk

Advertising Standards Authority (ASA)

- Tel: 0300 123 1100
- asa.org.uk

Equality and Human Rights Commission (EHRC)

- Tel: 0808 800 0082
- equalityhumanrights.com

Food Standards Agency (FSA)
- Tel: 0330 332 7149
- Email: helpline@food.gov.uk
- food.gov.uk

Health and Safety Executive (HSE)
- Tel: 0300 003 1647
- hse.gov.uk

HM Revenue and Customs (HMRC)
- VAT Helpline: 0300 200 3700
- Employer Helpline: 0300 200 3200
- gov.uk/government/organisations/hm-revenue-customs

Home Office
- Tel: 0207 035 4848
- Email: public.enquiries@homeoffice.gov.uk
- gov.uk/government/organisations/home-office

Information Commissioner's Office (ICO)
- Tel: 0303 123 1113
- ico.org.uk

TSO (formerly The Stationery Office)
- Tel: 0333 202 5070
- Email: esupport@tso.co.uk
- tsoshop.co.uk

Chartered Trading Standards Institute (CTSI)
- tradingstandards.uk

Valuation Office Agency
The VOA is an agency of HMRC.
- Tel: 0300 050 1501
- gov.uk/government/organisations/valuation-office-agency

Index

Note: Legislation is in bold. Page numbers in **bold** refer to major discussions. Regulations or Guides beginning 'A', or 'The' are alphabetized under the following word.

A

D

E

I

Q

R

U

V

W

Y

Z